THE LADY AND THE TIGER

A memoir of Taiwan, the Republic of China

by

PATRICIA LINDER

authorHOUSE

1663 LIBERTY DRIVE, SUITE 200
BLOOMINGTON, INDIANA 47403
(800) 839-8640
www.authorhouse.com

First published by AuthorHouse 09/23/04

ISBN: 1-4184-5605-5 (e)
ISBN: 1-4184-3774-3 (sc)

Library of Congress Control Number:2004094095

Printed in the United States of America
Bloomington, Indiana

This book is printed on acid-free paper.

According to the Chinese calendar, the Year of the Tiger is one of the most revered birth signs. Associated with power, courage and pure will, Tigers are rebels with cause. They are colorful and unpredictable with boundless energy and a love of life, which stimulates them and affects all those they come in contact with.

This is a book of perceptions. Because I was not in an official position, I had no "need to know". My opinions were formed by the events as they occurred and as I observed them. Ensuing years have softened the bad memories and heightened the good ones. I have chosen to change some names in order not to offend those people whose perceptions may differ from mine.

The Author

Dedication

The Lady and the Tiger is dedicated to the people of Taiwan,

the Republic of China,

for their determined pursuit of democracy and freedom.

Acknowledgement

My thanks to Rear Admiral Paul Engel for his unwavering interest in the writing of this book. The resulting research he provided made possible *The Lady and the Tiger.*.

To Carna Miller and Norman Weis for guiding me through the forest of editing.

And to my husband, Jim for his official memories of Taiwan.

PREFACE

June 1998

I clicked on CNN in time to see President Bill Clinton address the Chinese people on Beijing television. It was a news clip and as I idly watched and listened to words that have become a trademark for any political speech on any given subject in this country, I wondered if those words sounded as naïve to anyone else as they did to me. I came to know the Chinese in the Republic of China on the island of Taiwan for two very educational years and learned to appreciate them for the cultural sophisticates they are.

My attention sharpened at the word "Taiwan" and I listened closely to what President Clinton said. His words of denial of this country struggling to become a democracy compelled me to find paper and pen and begin to write the story of Taiwan, as I knew it.

It was time.

PROLOGUE

Norfolk, Virginia

June, 1977

As a Navy wife for twenty-eight years, I knew a good tour of duty when I saw one. China. My mind supplied the pictures I grew up with from Pearl Buck's books, and her descriptions of vast, rolling plains, jagged, misty mountains and its people, poor in tangibles but rich in heritage and family. As a child, I explored her books, lived the stories and dreamed of someday, going to China.

Reality was a different matter. It was even a different country. My husband's orders read: Rear Admiral James B. Linder is to report to CINCPAC (Commander-in-Chief, Pacific) for duty as Commander, U.S. Taiwan Defense Command, July 1977.

So much for Pearl Buck.

Library books and maps provided the answers to where it was located. The name had changed from Formosa to Taiwan. Formosa meant "beautiful island" and from the description, Taiwan was a microcosm of

China proper. There were mountains much like those found on the mainland, with plains where crops were grown. But the burgeoning population since 1949 had changed the face of the island and from the one small picture of Taipei I could find, the city looked like piles of concrete shaped into office buildings. The name was changed to Taiwan in the 1950's and the tiny island was positioned in the Far Western Pacific, only ninety miles from the eastern coast of Mainland China. Looking quite small and defenseless, tucked under the bulging eastern coastline of that country – not unlike David and Goliath, its vulnerability was obvious. Taiwan's history read like a good novel, giving me the clues I needed to understand our presence there.

Because of Taiwan's position in the China Seas, it had over the centuries been overrun, invaded and occupied by nearly every country with Asian trade ties. The Taiwanese suffered Portuguese, Dutch, German, Japanese and Chinese invaders and the results were a meld of those cultures both in its people and its customs. In 1949, the official designation became the Republic of China.

I ignored this particular moment in history. My soon-to-be husband graduated with the class of '49 from the Naval Academy and we were married after an engagement that had lasted five long years. Chinese politics somehow escaped my attention.

When the controversial Generalissimo Chiang Kai-shek came to Taiwan in that same year, he brought with him two million people – refugees, the remnants of his Nationalist government, and its army that had been beaten back to the eastern coastline of China. They came in order to escape the communist rule of the People's Republic of China on the mainland, ninety miles away. They hoped to establish a military base from which they could build and train that army to return to the land of their ancestors and free it from the tyranny of communism.

Because of subsequent raids by the communist forces, determined to secure Taiwan, the U.S. Government sent naval forces to defend it against a takeover. As a result, in 1954, the Mutual Defense Treaty was drawn up between the Republic of China on Taiwan (Chiang Kai-shek's Nationalist government) and the United States. This alliance carried the promise of Nationalist Chinese military support if and when the United States needed it. In turn, the U.S. Government would protect the tiny island from invasion by the Chinese communists.

In 1979, the Carter administration refused to renew the treaty that had become the linchpin of Taiwan's security for a generation.

In the Navy, there is a saying, "It happened on our watch". This is the story of how it all came to an end.

CHAPTER ONE

THE FIRST RIOT

Quarters A.

Taipei, Taiwan Republic of China

November 1978

*F*ists *pounded on the great red lacquered doors of Quarters A. The gabble of Chinese threats nearly drowned out the insanely repetitive strains of Aulde Lang Syne, played at top volume from a sound truck parked on the other side of our front stone wall. "Should old acquaintance be forgot?"— an angry choice and one that clearly stated the mob's opinion of the Carter administration's foreign policy. I had heard its message for twenty-two hours without pause and knew the meaning of*

Chinese water torture. Crouched with The Girls, our two dogs, Suzie and Boom Boom on the sitting room floor, our heads below the windowsills, I heard the crack of rock against rock as the hysterical mob stoned Quarters A. The phones rang incessantly with no one on the other end.

We were alone – the three of us. Earlier in the morning, I sent the house staff home for their own safety and at the U.S. Embassy, far down into the heart of Taipei, my husband Jim was under siege by an angry mob of University students. The Girls and I were locked in with curtains drawn shut so I could no longer see the Chinese house guards with their guns trained on us.

The world was upside down.

On December fifteenth, President Carter had failed to renew the Mutual Taiwan Defense Treaty, a treaty that had lasted for thirty years between the United States and the Republic of China. When the announcement was made the people of Taiwan realized the United States had pulled the rug out from under them.

They had been sold out.

Our presence was no longer viable. In just a few days, on January first, 1979 a State Department team would arrive in Taiwan to abrogate the treaty and offer a cultural and trade agreement. Upon their arrival, a signal was apparently given to riot against U.S. official personnel.

Within the next few months, one after another, the U.S. installations throughout the Island would close down, twenty-one American flags lowered *and taken away and the military presence of men and their families sent back to the United States.*

My husband's Command would end, the Island swept clean of all U.S. defense systems, leaving its inhabitants, Taiwanese, Chinese, Americans, and Europeans unprotected and vulnerable to a threatened invasion by communist China to the west. We had been their umbrella of protection for thirty years, but trade considerations now pushed the United States to align with the Peoples Republic of China on the Mainland. Diplomatic relations would then begin with that communist giant as they were ending in Taiwan, the free and democratic Republic of China. I feared for this small country and its people, I was furious at the injustice of the whole thing.

The noise increased. The Chinese guards on the iron gates of our driveway had opened them to the Cultural College students and they poured in, angry and armed.

Automatically, I ducked as something hit the window. Suzie's growl was low and deep in her throat. Boom Boom, curled up in my lap snored and slept on. The thought occurred to me that I should consider leaving the Quarters. I had no way of defending myself and as the noise level grew louder, the thought took shape. Moving Boom Boom out of my lap, I crawled to my desk, pulled the phone onto the floor and laid the receiver on the carpet. The caller would get a busy signal and hopefully, hang up. In time, it worked. Quickly, I dialed my husband's aide at his home a mile away where Jim had sent him to protect his family. Their house was a scant two blocks from the Cultural College and with the students on the prowl, we all needed protection.

"Skip, it's Pat. Are you all right up there?"

"We are for the time being, but are you? I've tried to call your number, but all I get is a busy signal."

I could hear the concern in his voice. "The phone has been ringing constantly for hours now. They just keep dialing, but no one ever speaks. The staff left this morning and I have Suzie and Boom Boom with me." The little clown was on my lap again. "The gate guards let the students through and at the moment they're throwing rocks at the house. I'm not sure how long I should hold out here." My hand felt damp on the phone. " I don't think they will damage the house since it belongs to the Chinese, but we may lose the windows. Any suggestions?"

"I'm coming down right now to pick you up. Be ready, and bring anything you think you should, but plan on running from the front door to the car door as quickly as you can."

"I'll only have The Girls with me. Hopefully, the mob won't break in after I've left. Have you had any word from Jim?"

"No. I know he's holed up at the Embassy and can't get out. He has a walkie- talkie and so do I, so we may be able to contact him after you come here." His steady voice calmed me and I began to plan my escape "I'll see you in a few minutes."

"Girls, we're going for a little adventure. Boom Boom, you will have to wake up. I need your cooperation." She opened sleepy eyes, yawned and staggered to her feet. Suzie, watching the windows, was tense from her head to the end of her tail.

I found my purse, checked its contents and, satisfied I could do no more for the Quarters, grabbed my coat then dropped to my knees and crawled down the long hall, keeping below the window level toward the front doors with The Girls following along behind.

The next person I saw was my husband's Master Chief, Mike Tatosian. He knew of the danger, and came up the mountain from the TDC (Taiwan Defense Command) Headquarters, using his key on the kitchen door on the floor below.

"I thought you might need some help, Mrs. Linder."

"Oh, Mike. I've never been so glad to see anybody. Skip's on his way to pick me up. We'll try to call the Admiral at the Embassy from Skip's house .You must come with us. It's definitely not safe here."

Grinning, he said. "Thanks, but I'll stay here and make sure nobody gets in." He grabbed a poker and fireplace shovel and stood in the middle of the cavernous living room. A former Navy Seal, he looked right at home. And enjoying the challenge. I only wished his weapons carried more clout.

At that moment, there was a lull in the shouting. Skip, in his station wagon had roared through the front gate, horn blowing and shouting at the rioters as he moved into position in front of the doors. Skip stood six feet four inches tall and even sitting behind the wheel of a car he was impressive. The rioters were confused and for a moment, grew silent as the long station wagon with a big man in the front seat, pulled up to the doors. Using that time, I turned to Mike.

"Take care of yourself, Mike. I owe you one."

"Just part of my job, ma'am." We both knew it was more than that. "Now, get going. I'll take care of things here."

I ran. Although it was only a short four steps to the car, the crowd was still mesmerized by its size and the sight of a woman with a white dog under each arm, bolting out of the Quarters. We raced out of the circular driveway through the crowd and sped up Yangmingshan Mountain to Skip's home.

The rest of that evening was spent bent over the walkie- talkie, trying to reach Jim. Skip's two little children played with The Girls while his wife Shannon manned the kitchen. I felt safe and cared about, but worried for Mike at the Quarters. The sight of him with poker and shovel left a permanent imprint on my mind.

At last, the walkie- talkie produced. Between sputters, we heard Jim's voice as he repeated his name, then clicked over to Skip. "This is the Admiral. Is anyone where they can hear me? Over."

"Boss, we're here. Pat's with us and wants to talk to you."

"Jim? Are you all right? It's been a ratty day up here. I sent the staff home and Mike is at the Quarters now, guarding it with a fireplace poker and shovel against the mob. Over."

His voice was firm when he answered. "I'm going to make a run for it from the Embassy in a few minutes if my driver doesn't take off first. Over."

Sputters, static, then more static. The contact was gone.

My mind's-eye picture of Jim leaving the Embassy fit the man. Tall, lean, intense, totally concentrated on the problem at hand, his dark amber eyes narrowed and knowledgeable of the danger he was deliberately putting himself into. It had always been this way. Through three wars, he sought out the most dangerous situation and beat it. A bit hard on the old girl at home, but borrowing the words from the Marine Corps, he reminded me from time to time that he had not promised me a rose garden. I would have settled for a petunia patch if he was anywhere in the vicinity to help me tend it.

Mike called. " They're gone, Mrs. Linder. I think when they saw you jump into Commander Wright's car, they figured out there was nobody here to harass."

"Did you have to use the poker and shovel, Mike?"

He chuckled. "No. I guess I looked too dangerous to mess with."

"You're a good man, Mike. Your boss will hear about this when he makes it up the mountain."

The walkie talkie sputtered again and I heard Jim's voice. "I'm out and headed home. Over." Brief, to the point and only lacking in "no big deal."

"So am I. Mike called and it's safe at the Quarters now. See you there. Over."

The children and The Girls had become an entity and none of them wanted to part company. We pried them loose, and Skip returned me to Quarters A.

Rocks littered the grounds around the house, but the windows were still intact. Because it was dark by this time, the student mob had gone, taking their sound truck with them and leaving behind an eerie silence.

Jim's arrival found me below in the kitchens, putting together something for him to eat. I checked the lock on the kitchen door again, making sure the guards couldn't get in. In friendlier times, they stacked their guns near the door and sat at the table while Mama San fed them their lunch of Chinese stew. Now, they were a definite threat, armed or not, and I wanted them nowhere near us.

The line of my husband's shoulders was no longer straight. He was tired, frustrated and angry. "They came over the Embassy walls like ants on a mission, surrounded the Embassy, tore down the American flag and threatened the Marine guards at the entrance. By the way, thanks to an order by the Defense Department, there were no bullets in the Marine guards' guns. It is no longer lawful for them to be able to defend themselves or those inside the Embassy. I wish someone could tell me what in the hell is going on in Washington."

An answer to that would be a miracle. I was fresh out.

CHAPTER TWO
THE PHONE CALL

Summer, 1977

Naval Air Station, Norfolk, Virginia

The floor-shaking roar of an Air Force C-5 transport plane as it took off over our Naval Air Station Quarters broke into my conscious thought. We were in the flight pattern for any kind of plane that flew in or out of that Base. Only a few weeks before, as the Blue Angels in their supersonic fighter planes practiced their dress rehearsal for Norfolk's annual Azalea Festival, they just cleared our chimney, causing a chocolate cake to fall in the oven and reminding me once again, I was the wife of a Naval Aviator.

Freshly -ironed linens were laid out on the bed, ready to go into the empty cardboard cartons on the floor. The packing of our household effects was nearing its end and soon we would cross a continent and an ocean to our next tour of duty.

Our destination was China. It sounded exciting, mysterious, immensely challenging and, to a veteran Navy wife of more than thirty moves in twenty-eight years, one more chance to build another nest – a Chinese nest. The thought amused me. During the last six years of living throughout the Mediterranean area, I hung pictures, fluffed pillows, and put down whatever kind of rug they sold in the local market to make a home out of a hotel room or an apartment furnished with only the barest of essentials.

My husband was a Rear Admiral in the U.S. Navy, under orders to report to Taiwan, the Republic of China, to be in charge of the U.S. Taiwan Defense Command – TDC. At the time, we had no idea why he had been chosen for this particular type of duty after six years of commands in the Mediterranean area. The answer to that would come later – much later.

Taiwan. I knew it as Formosa -- and not very well at that. The island, shaped like a tobacco leaf, was near China, just north of the South China Seas. I pulled down an encyclopedia and looked it up. What I found were only sketchy descriptions.

The Taiwan Straits with some tiny islands called the P'eng hu's in between, separated Taiwan from Mainland China. Because of mountains that plowed down its center from far north to far south, only one third of the island was habitable. Since Taiwan was in the middle of a busy shipping route, they had endured invasions by many cultures over the centuries. What caught my attention was the population count. Eighteen million people lived on one third of a piece of ground 250 miles long and 90 miles wide, which was surrounded by water.

I also knew I spoke not a word of their language and the State Department made no attempt to see that we were knowledgeable of anything connected with the Chinese. Jim received military briefings, but I received no instructions. It puzzled me, for many of our friends with orders to foreign countries as attaches, received a year's training in language and the customs of the country to which they were reporting. We had lived on another continent for the past few years and there was a certain incongruity that occurred to us both, but in the Navy, when orders come, you go.

With briefings, the wife is usually the last to know. However, a few days before, Jim returned from Washington, D.C., after one of these meetings, grim-jawed and somewhat pale. As he set his briefcase on the kitchen table, he made a statement. "I have to buy another new car, and that means I now have to figure out a way of getting rid of our own new car in a matter of days and find the money to buy a Cadillac Seville before we leave for the West Coast."

Only two months before, he had purchased a new car. Now the "suggestion" was, because of is position in Taiwan, he would need a more prestigious automobile, specifically, a Cadillac Seville, brand new.

The chicken that was browning in the pan sputtered and a drop of hot grease caught me on the hand. The word I said reflected both my pain and disgust at Navy rules. "Damn! Just another one of our 'fringe benefits'?"

No response to my bit of sarcasm. " The car will be shipped with our household goods. I called Taiwan today to ask about buying one there but they said the cost would be double, so we're stuck with the situation." He looked and sounded resigned.

There were a lot of those "situations" along the way and I learned that the world was not a fair one. But the deed was accomplished and we looked forward to having our new silver Seville, however long it took.

The shrill ring of the phone startled me out of my reverie, and I turned from the packing box of linens to answer it.

"Hello?"

"Is this Mrs. James Linder?"

11

"Yes, it is."

"Mrs. Linder, I am calling from the China Section of the State Department."

It seemed late to be scheduling a briefing for me which meant a trip to Washington from Norfolk, where we were living. I responded uncertainly, "Oh…yes?"

The disembodied voice spoke hurriedly. "I imagine from your schedule that you're in the middle of packing for your trip to Taiwan."

"Yes, I am." How did he know?

"Mrs. Linder, don't go any further with your packing. I can't say any more than that, but I'm just trying to help you."

I was speechless. Never, in the past twenty-eight years had I received a phone call like this. Once my husband was given a set of orders, the die was cast, no questions asked, I knew my job and did it. No one had ever told me not to.

As the line went dead, I was left staring at the phone. Jim was aboard his Flagship the aircraft carrier America, tied up at Pier twelve on the Norfolk Naval Base. Although our Quarters were a scant mile away, there was no way to communicate with him. I sat down on the side of the bed, laid my hand on a freshly- ironed sheet and wondered what we were getting into.

Outside the bedroom window the Virginia landscape looked lush and peaceful. The magnolia tree in the side yard was in bloom, and the station gardeners had planted summer flowers along the garage wall. I liked this house that came with the job and was my first set of Quarters. As a large, square, red -brick two-story with big rooms and high ceilings, it was a house of the Deep South, gracious and welcoming. There were many bedrooms and bathrooms, a formal dining room with an adjoining pantry, a long glassed in porch and servants' quarters, but no servants. Domestic help in the Quarters was phased out long before I moved in and my responsibility was to maintain the house as best I could. I turned the steward's bedroom off the blindinly all-white kitchen into my television/sitting room. To cut the operating room sterility of the fluorescent ceiling lights, I painted the pantry door a high gloss emerald green and felt quite snug there on cold, winter nights.

Soon after Jim sailed off for a Mediterranean deployment, I found myself rattling around alone in this big house. That, and the knowledge it would take me an entire week to vacuum the whole place and another week to do the dusting, motivated me to pull down the suitcases, pack up and head for Europe to find my husband. But there were nice memories of living in this house that sat at the end of the Naval Station runway. Today was quiet and squirrels played in the sunlight that lay on the closely clipped grass.

Ahead were our goodbyes with our children, leaving them for three years, for that was the designated time on Jim's orders. Our daughter Jamey was married with two little girls of her own. I knew we would lose three years of their growing up. Our son Jeff was in college and there would be no home for the holidays and summers with the family for him. I tried not to think about that.

Our children were products of a difficult life and their flexibility never ceased to amaze me. We lived in California in the sixties. With Jim in Viet Nam, it was a lonely, discouraging time. In the newly emerging drug culture, the enlightenment of those days condemned anyone having to do with "that dirty war" and too often, the children paid the highest price. They were encouraged to "kick the Establishment, let it all hang out and do your own thing." It was the decade of sexual revolution, a foolproof recipe for disaster. Because of the divisiveness of the war, anyone participating in it was treated like a pariah and high-school age children had the edge on cruelty. We all carried our own private scars from those nightmare days.

Now, time was running out for us. Ahead were our last few days together, promises of trips back to the United States if possible, swift hugs and quick turn-aways to swallow the tears. It was a way of life.

Norfolk

When Jim came home from his office aboard ship, we sat at the kitchen table with our drinks and chatted idly about his day. Trying to use up the food in the freezer before we moved, our meals bordered on the bizarre. Tonight was chili and cornbread, although the temperature outside was a humid ninety-two.

"Is everything ready for the Change of Command?" It was imminent, and I knew of the many details that demanded attention. The farewell parties were over. "The wives were great yesterday at the luncheon and I'm sorry I haven't been with them more."

Because of my travels during this tour of duty, I didn't know them as I always had in the past. Navy wives are a strong, closely-knit group of women who early on, learn the importance of supporting and being supported. Their strengths are unique to the profession and there were times in the past, I needed those strengths of a particular friend or the group, as our husbands pursued their dangerous work. The Squadron wives of men engaged in carrier flight operations, catapult takeoffs and night landings, must possess the certainty that when he leaves in the morning, he will come back through the door that night. When he does not, the family of women is there; bringing individual strengths to the one who needs it. I turned down the heat under the chili.

Jim's Flagship, the aircraft carrier America, would host the final event, his Change of Command. "I had my last briefings with my replacement today and I think we're ready."

The phone call slipped back into my thoughts. I decided to mention it and let him make his own assessment of crank call or the real thing.

"The linens are packed. And while I was in the middle of that, I had a very odd telephone call."

"Oh?"

I took the other chair at the kitchen table. "Some man called, said he was from the China Section of the State Department, but I don't remember him giving his name."

There was a pause as Jim shifted his attention from the evening paper to the words, State Department.

There was a faint look of concern on his face "What was the call about?"

"Actually, he asked if I was packing to go to Taiwan and when I said 'yes', he told me not to go any further with it."

I had Jim's full attention, now.

" Then he said he couldn't say any more than that and the call ended when he told me he was only trying to help me. I couldn't reach you on the ship and it slipped my mind until just now." I peeked into the oven. The cornbread was coming along nicely.

"You're sure he didn't give his name?"

"If he did, I didn't hear it."

Jim mentioned the names of people he knew in the China Section, but none of them sounded even vaguely familiar.

"Well, I don't think it's anything to be concerned about. May have been some staffie who got tired of shuffling papers." He gave a short laugh and said, "Anyway, can you imagine me telling the Defense Department my wife had a strange call from the State Department, telling us to unpack? They'd laugh me out of the office first, then tell me to get the hell out to Taiwan by the date assigned."

The movers came the following morning and for the next four days, everything we owned was packed and loaded into a truck to be driven to the West Coast and there, transferred onto a ship for the journey to the South China Seas. I looked lovingly at a few of my favorite pieces of furniture as if to say a final goodbye. We had lost many things in past moves and becoming attached to those that were replaceable was foolish; still, they were important to our family history and I wondered if I would ever see them again.

The Change of Command, although very familiar to me, was still a thrilling ceremony to attend. The men were in white dress uniforms, shoes polished to a high shine, hats squared, a direct contrast to the massive gray steel structure of the ship. The formations of men were precise, even their walk was formal, their backs straight. NATO and semaphore flags hung from the high steel beams of the Carrier's hangar bay that was nearly as long as a football field, where close to one hundred planes were kept until the huge elevator smoothly raised them to the flight deck above for takeoff. Today, the elevator was level with the hanger bay deck. The view was of a long line of ships, berthed and anchored alongside. The sky bristled with antennas, guns and bridges, where the men who sailed them stood their watches and manned their ships.

On the America, long dress ropes with large tassels cordoned off the walkways from the quarterdeck ladder to the seats placed on either side of the steel deck, an aisle running down the center. Steel doors, two feet thick and 25 feet high served to partition off one half of the bay. The platform in front of them would hold the outgoing and incoming commanding officers and the dignitaries who had flown down from Washington, D.C. to attend, give speeches and preside over the actual exchange. The shrill notes of the Bosun Mate piping the guests aboard, rose over the music the band played for the ceremony. The women were in their prettiest clothes.

This was the culmination of an officer's two -year tour of duty as, in Jim's case, command of a Battle Group – many ships of all kinds, for which he was responsible. Personnel numbers averaged close to 14,000, sometimes more, sometimes less, as ships were assigned to his group for certain types of maneuvers. The command was demanding, rewarding and one he hoped for throughout his naval career.

As for the wife of the outgoing, every eye is upon her as a white-gloved, always handsome, young officer, offers her his arm and escorts her past the many rows of guests to the first chair of the first row. There is a certain interest in how (and if) she has survived these difficult two years. In summer, she worries about the trickle of perspiration that is slowly tracking down the back of her neck. In the winter, she hopes her feet, numb from the cold, steel deck, will hold her steady when she rises for the National Anthem. But when the Navy band plays The Star Spangled Banner and the first familiar words, "Oh, say can you see" roll out across the adjoining piers, the chills and trickles are completely forgotten in the adrenaline rush of simple patriotism.

Yet, despite the sights and sounds of a successful day, in the back of my mind was the phone call – still anonymous and somewhat foreboding. I wondered if it was an omen.

CHAPTER THREE
TRANSITIONS

Son Jeff flew to San Diego from Austin to see his departing parents off to the Orient. He had completed his third year at the University of Texas and it was a bittersweet time. Our children had outgrown me. These were adults, living adult lives and I felt proud but desolate that I would miss out on so many of the things that were important to them.

We held our reunion at Jamey's house, complete with our two granddaughters, a cat and a dog. I tucked my arm around his lean waist. "Jeff, send me the date for your graduation in the spring, so I can make travel arrangements. I plan to be there." Years of experience had taught me to keep my pronouns singular. Too often, Jim was gone or going and plans changed according to his schedule.

Both of our children were accustomed to our absences and had made lives of their own, but the bonds were strong between us. We spent many years together – just the three of us.

Jeff looked like a typical college student of the 70s. He was tall, thin, slightly bearded, and always somewhat reticent with his father. A few more years and his own accomplishments would give him the confidence to be a friend as well as a son to a man of so many achievements. Often, my heart went out to him when he seemed unsure of his occasional father. But as he grew up in years, he also grew in understanding of the life and responsibilities that his father had taken on. I hoped that in time, these two would become close to each other.

His voice was low as he draped his arm around my shoulder "I'll take care of myself if you'll do the same. Just don't worry about me." I cherished the moment, knowing I would worry, anyway. He needed feeding and new socks and I was just the person to take care of that. Reality was a different matter.

Jamey, our first child, was a beautiful woman with children of her own. Her teenage years had been tempestuous. Being close to her father, she missed his presence more than either of us would have imagined. Tucking her in one night during the nightmare years of Viet Nam, I found my fourteen- year old asleep, her cheek wet with tears on one of his sweaters. There is nothing easy or palatable about war, but the silent damage it does to children is the most difficult to bear. Yet, here she was with the husband she cherished and their two little girls, living a happy, normal life. My motherly instincts told me she would be fine. They would be fine.

I hoisted five-year-old Ashli and looked into her elfin-like face. Instead of tears, her mouth turned down at the corners, but her eyes were always full of mischief.

Jamey said, "Mom, I have a surprise for you. I've rooted some of my houseplants, put them in little plastic bags and I want you to take them. Plant them in pots and think of me when you water them."

Looking at the tiny bits of green life, I said a prayer they would make it to Taiwan. As I held our little granddaughters, the impish Ashli, and dark-haired Anna with her luminous eyes, I closed mine to seal the sight of them in my memory. They would be older and changed when we returned, but I knew with certainty, we would still be a part of their lives.

It was time to board the plane. For no reason, the phone call slipped into my mind. "Don't go any further with your packing, Mrs. Linder." As we held each other and said our final goodbyes, I wanted to stay in the shelter of their arms.

Seated in the first class section (Chinese arrangements) with a China doll to grant my every wish, I concentrated on the few words I would say at the welcoming ceremony in Taipei. With no thanks to the State Department, a friend who spoke the language carefully tutored me in saying the right words with the right inflections. Intent on not creating an international incident, I paid attention and with the long flight ahead of us, would hopefully, sound like a native when we arrived.

A Lieutenant Commander was waiting for us as we made our way into the Tokyo terminal. He was six feet four inches tall with the build of a football player. His face was friendly and there was a warm way about him. His uniform was crisp and fresh, we were somewhat wilted, but there was an understanding smile on his face. Ahead, was a time when he would protect my life, and although I didn't know that now, I already felt safer with him nearby.

"Admiral Linder, I'm your aide, Skip Wright."

They shook hands and I was next in line. I liked him. He was enthusiastic and friendly. This man would be in my camp when I needed him to help me over the rough spots.

"Mrs. Linder, do you mind holding the briefcases while I take the Admiral through customs? They're expecting us, and it won't take but a few minutes."

I nodded.

" If you'll just wait here, we'll be right back."

I nodded again. "Oh Skip, would you clear these through customs? Our daughter, Jamey handed them to me as we were leaving and I'm to plant them in pots in Taipei." I fished Jamey's bedraggled little cuttings out of my tote bag and held them out to him. The look on his face was one of complete disbelief. This great, tall man studied me and in a moment of wisdom, promised to do his best.

With the three briefcases at my feet, I felt rooted to the floor in the middle of a chaotic, oriental mass of moving humanity. "If you'll just wait here…." Easy for him to say. He and my husband both towered over everybody there, but my height was Japanese height and the rushing mob promptly swallowed me. I could feel panic hovering. There was such an impersonal quality to that crowd, due I imagine, to the impassive expressions on the faces that sped by me. They jostled me in their anxiety to meet a schedule or get to the next plane and I realized my "space" was gone. As an American, that twelve- inch airspace we wrap around ourselves that separates us from each other was being violated and my defenses were down. The briefcases helped. With one in each hand and my right foot on the other, I used them as an anchor and prayed the men would show up before I disappeared under that teeming mass of humanity. They returned after my right arm with briefcase attached, went straight up, telling them where I was.

"Your plants, Mrs. Linder. I hope they make it the rest of the way." There was laughter in his eyes and I thanked him as we were ushered into an official car, which immediately sped down a one-way street the wrong way.

Clutching my husband's arm, I said, "My God, Jim. This is madness. We're all going to die on a one-way street in Japan. Who is this driver? A kamikaze?" He obviously had a death wish.

From the front seat, Skip grinned. "Don't worry, Mrs. Linder. He has the Admiral's flags on the front of the car and the other drivers will get out of his way."

I was not convinced "They lost the war, too and there *is* such a thing as revenge."

Jim patted my hand and I subsided, closed my eyes and prayed to God that I would live to see our children again.

Our car careened its way to another airport, and stopped next to a helicopter waiting to take us to Atsugi, the U.S. naval installation southwest of Tokyo. By now, it was raining – the kind that comes straight down and soaks you to the skin. This meant a futile attempt to dry our clothes before packing them the next morning for the continuing leg of our trip, Okinawa. I was frazzled and out of my element.

"Admiral, I've checked with the weather people and there's a typhoon down near Taiwan. I don't think it will affect us, but we can get a better picture of it in Okinawa." Skip looked hopeful, but I could see he was concerned.

I had to ask. "Skip, is the welcoming ceremony in Taipei inside or out?"

"It's outside, Mrs. Linder. When your plane puts down, there will be troops and military dignitaries and their wives waiting to greet you."

I silently added, in the middle of a typhoon with high winds and a driving rain. So much for the hairdo.

Okinawa was very hot and very humid. We poured over the weather maps in the military terminal, calls were made and the men's faces looked serious and worried. The typhoon was gearing up to give Taiwan a good swipe. Remaining overnight in Guest Quarters, our sleep was uneasy and the next morning dawned dim, foreboding and still raining.

There were more calls and the decision was made to go. The ceremony was laid on for that afternoon and our presence was a necessity. The night before, I had unearthed a turban that matched my dress and with it clutched in my hand, boarded an Air Force T-39 jet for the final flight. As the pilot climbed to the altitude he needed to be above the storm, Skip explained about the oxygen masks.

"Mrs. Linder…."

" Skip, please call me Pat. Every time you say Mrs. Linder, I age ten years."

A quick grin and a nod. "Pat, if the mask drops down, put the harness over your head and fit the mask to your face." He was dead serious now and I paid attention.

I sincerely hoped this would not be necessary. It was. The mask dropped, Jim grabbed and pulled it over my face. Then the pilot spoke, the mask was removed and I was left with surging adrenaline and hair I should have left at home. This drill occurred three more times during the flight, due to a malfunction in the oxygen apparatus and as we lurched onto the Taipei runway, buffeted by high winds and lashing rain, I gratefully pulled on the turban and made ready to meet the crowd.

As promised, on the runway, the Chinese Admirals, Generals, high ranking government officials and their wives waited for our arrival. They each stood in a small circle chalked on the tarmac with nothing to shield them from the rain and wind. I was appalled until I realized that this wife would be doing the same during the entire ceremony. My few Chinese words, so carefully memorized, were swept away by the howling winds. Standing in an open Jeep, Jim and the head of the Joint Chiefs of Staff slowly moved to review the troops at the edge of the runway. The troops, at attention for God knows how long, looked drowned.

Standing in my little chalked circle, I stole a sideways glance at the line of ladies to my right. They were stoic, eyes front, nothing moving, and the phrase, "the inscrutable Chinese" describing them perfectly. But I had to add one more word – gracious, for in the brief moments I had with them before I stepped into my circle, their eyes told me they were glad we had come to their island.

It was over. The weather cleared for a moment and pictures were taken. Then we broke for the terminal and ran for the official car waiting to take us up the mountain to our quarters. The trip was long, slow and hair-raising. Rocks were tumbling down the mountainside onto the road and Sergeant Fan, our driver, had to dodge and skid his way around them as we climbed. The wind threatened to push us over the edge and after what had seemed an eternity, we finally turned into the almost vertical little gravel road that led to our quarters. It was simply too much. I shut my eyes and instantly fell asleep. When the car slowed to a crawl and stopped, I opened my eyes.

We faced a guardhouse with two armed Chinese soldiers.

Jim and I looked at each other with the same thought. What are we doing here that we need armed guards? The gates opened and we stopped in front of the Quarters, obscured by the pouring rain. Once out of the car, we ran for the tall, red lacquered doors.

Inside the doors, my eyes adjusted to the gloom. There was no electricity, the storm was growing in intensity and we were high enough on the mountain to be in the middle of it. Trees were being pulled out of the ground by the twisting force of the gale and I realized the grinding noises I heard were those trees as their roots left the soil that had held them for decades.

A man was spreadeagle on the outside of the glass windows of the long porch that faced down the mountainside. Though not tall, with his arms outspread, he looked formidable. Hanging on to a small outside ledge of the porch, he tried to put up metal shutters to protect us from flying glass. He was the first thing I saw as we entered our new home and I knew with certainty, if the rest of the people in my husband's command were anything like this man, we had little to worry about. But as fast as he put the metal sheets into place, the wind sucked them out and they cartwheeled down the mountainside.

Skip beckoned him in and introduced us to Mike Tatosian, a former Navy Seal who would be one of the members of Jim's staff and, among his other duties, the man designated to help me when help was needed. The four of us, sodden and cold from the rain, shared our experiences of the day and a friendship was forged that would serve me well in the months to come.

Meeting us at the doors when we stumbled into the house, was the houseboy, Hogo and a Welsh Corgi dog named Baron that belonged to Jim's predecessor. He was awaiting shipment back to the United States and would remain in the Quarters with us for a week or two.

I had my first lesson in the uniqueness of the Chinese. When nervous, they giggle. Hogo was giggling nonstop and in the face of a raging typhoon, falling trees and a somewhat menacing-looking dog, I failed to see the humor in the situation, although we all looked like refugees who had swum ashore.

We had no luggage, only Jim's briefcases which Hogo placed, along with the umbrella, in the guestroom, just past the library. Our suitcases would come up in another car in the morning. The winds were getting stronger every minute and the mountain road was too dangerous to drive. As we sat in the empty living room with two candles for light, we heard the sound of breaking glass. The men reacted first: I followed with Baron behind me. Clay roof tiles from the house across the road crashed against the windows, shattering the glass and a waterfall of rain was pouring in. Only one of the briefcases was on the bed. The other two were under water and as I reached the door, three things happened; the door began to slam shut on my hand, the umbrella slid in between the door and the opening and Baron fastened his very strong and panic-stricken jaws on the back of my right heel.

I reacted.

Jim's comment as he stood ankle deep in water was, "I don't know why you get so clutched."

The terrified dog was still hanging onto my heel. Phrases like I didn't sign on for this and how do I get out of this chicken outfit? flitted through my mind, but training prevailed and I gently pried Baron's jaws apart and vowed to keep at least twenty feet between that animal and my heels from that moment on.

My first night in Taiwan, I was cold, wet, dogbitten and hungry. I had faced armed guards, falling rocks and trees, an empty house and no lights But somewhere in the back of my mind was a tiny spark that told me to hang in there, lady - there's a lot more to come and it will never be dull.

CHAPTER FOUR
THE IVORY TOWER

The typhoon lingered for two more days. Because of the lack of electricity and the black clouds that surrounded it, the house loomed large and dark. Hogo the houseboy was downstairs in the kitchen and since there was no one to talk to except Baron the dog, who looked like he was ready to drop down dead asleep at any time, I prowled. As always, I felt the excitement about seeing our next home for the first time.

As I roamed, I could visualize the placement of our furniture that would be lost in these cavernous rooms. A dining room table with twenty chairs and porch furniture stayed with the quarters, although the tenants changed. But the living room alone would accommodate two full sets of couches, chairs and all that goes along with them. I made mental notes as I studied each room. Taiwan was a shopper's paradise and I had heard that the furniture makers could do anything from a picture, so my dreams of Asian travel faded and were replaced by the necessity of having enough things to sit on.

Running almost the length of the back of the house, was a glassed-in porch. Because of the high winds and falling trees, I had timidly stayed in back of the tall French doors that led onto this room, but curiosity got the better of me and I ventured out to see if there was a vestige of the view I knew must be there. The clouds were pressed against the windows; dense, angry and filled with rain. But as I turned to find the quiet of the living room, my eyes caught a movement in one of the nearby bushes. Partially behind it was a man in the same uniform as the guards at our gate. He carried a gun and was hastily climbing into a slicker type of poncho. Apparently, he had just come on duty without time to get under cover before taking his place, wherever that was. The same disquiet that niggled at the back of my mind since arriving, returned. Uneasily, I wondered if there were more guards and if so, why?

There was little to be done until the storm lifted. The official car had arrived with our luggage and then taken Jim to his office at the foot of Yangmingshan, this mountain we lived on.

"Do you really have to go in today?" The storm was still hanging on and since the ride down would be as dangerous as the ride up, I was worried about him. Besides, he looked tired from too little sleep.

"I'm afraid so. There are briefings scheduled with Admiral Snyder and he's due to leave the island in a few days." He was checking the papers in his briefcase.

"I hope we see them before they leave. I have a ton of questions to ask Mrs. Snyder. I'm really apprehensive, Jim about what I don't know and should."

"Don't sweat the small stuff. Between Skip and my Chinese aide, we'll find the answers for you." The briefcase closed with a snap, I received a hasty kiss and he was on his way before I could answer. That was the pattern of our life together. Gone, before I knew it. Sometimes it worked, sometimes it didn't. But this time, there was more at stake. We were unknowns in a tricky diplomatic position and I did not want to be the one to make some colossal mistake. Ignorance was not bliss.

The noise was unnerving. The trees groaned as the wind pulled at them and the bushes whipped and slammed against the house. Hogo prepared what food there was in the kitchens below and I ate another cold meal, grateful for whatever could be provided. The Snyder's cook left when they did and ours had not yet arrived. I hoped someone would provide Jim with a decent meal at Headquarters. Mine came out of a can.

"Hogo, let's get the guest room cleaned up. The standing water will ruin the carpet."

I didn't know if he understood me, but he giggled and working together, we mopped up the water, cleared the beds of their soaked sheets and blankets and stood the mattresses on their sides to dry out. The windows were hung with old sheets that came with the Quarters to keep the rain from coming in but the carpet was too wet to walk on with shoes, so we padded around in our bare feet, sopping up water and washing down walls. For all the pomp and circumstance that accompanies this kind of command, the realities are something quite different.

At last, we finished as the typhoon wore itself out and the electricity came on. When the clouds drifted away, I could see the devastation. Branches littered everything. The trees that survived had raw places in the bark and some had been torn from the ground, twisted around and still stood on the tortured tangle of their roots. Nature is very forgiving in the tropics and sub-tropics but it was hard to believe that in a few short weeks, the damage would be unnoticeable. The guards however were more visible than ever. As I watched, three more soldiers with guns took their assigned places behind beaten-down bushes and scarred trees and once again, I felt the prickle of fear and uncertainty. It was no longer in the back of my mind.

A small team of Chinese workers appeared out of nowhere and the guest room windows were repaired. With the telephones reinstated, Jim called. "How's everything on the mountaintop?" I liked the faint sound of concern in his voice.

"You made it down all right. I was worried. It's about the same up here, but Hogo and I have the guestroom under control. Oh, and I almost forgot. There are armed guards all over the place. This is no Club Med."

He chuckled. "I didn't promise you a rose garden." Oh yes, I knew that one. " Don't worry about it. We'll sort it out when I get home."

I heard a clicking sound as we talked, but chalked it up to a different phone system than we were used to.

The following day, as the staff returned, I met each one; Mama San who spoke no English was a round lady with a sweet smile. She tended the laundry end of life on the mountain and fed the guards at noon. Papa San, rail thin and slightly stooped, picked up his big, long stick and worked the garden each day, always mindful of the snakes. On the back of every bedroom door was a poster, showing each type of snake with descriptions in Chinese and English and the antidote, if there was one. When the Japanese ceased their occupation of Taiwan at the end of World War II, they turned loose poisonous snakes on the island. The poster said they had multiplied over the years, so long walks were difficult, if not impossible.

My driver was Sergeant Hsiu. He was not a tall man, but carried himself proudly and his smile was warm and friendly. He seemed shy, but his eyes told me I would always be safe in his keeping. As an Army man, he had been trained in the martial arts that teaches killing with bare hands. His respectful attitude never wavered, yet we were friends immediately and from him I learned many things I needed to know about this country and its people. His job was to drive me wherever I needed to go. There would be official functions day and night, occasional shopping trips when time and finances allowed and as I grew more accustomed to the culture, side trips to feed my curiosity to learn more about as many aspects as possible of life in the Republic of China. Sergeant Hsiu knew his job and would undoubtedly enjoy the new car. I would undoubtedly enjoy being chauffeured about through some of the worst traffic in the world.

After the introductions, I once again wandered onto the long porch and for the first time, looked past the devastation. Slightly to my left was a mountain range - the spine of Taiwan and it traveled the length of the island, separating east from west. Some ancient earthquake had thrown up this dragon's back of high peaks, leaving them sharp and jagged. Typhoon clouds scudded just below the peaks and I wondered if I would ever see a more breathtaking sight. In the valley below, was the little town of Tien Mou, nestled at the base of our mountain, Yangmingshan. In the distance, a muddy river meandered through the flat, flooded rice paddies. In front and to the right were more mountains, but lower and softer and as I studied their profile, something familiar slipped into my mind, but without pursuing it, I turned my eyes to the right and drew in my breath. Above me, a building with gilded, tilt-tipped edges sat perched on the edge of a cliff. Because of the clouds swirling around its base, it looked suspended instead of sitting on solid ground. This was the Cultural College where young Chinese learned about the history and culture of their homeland - China. I had always imagined the Palace in Beijing to look like this but for these first moments of discovery, I could think of nothing to compare it with.

Directly below me in our backyard, was an Olympic-sized swimming pool, thoughtfully provided by our host country. Too bad I didn't swim. There had been no place but the quarry and the Skunk River near my little Iowa town, and my mother insisted I keep a far distance from both. Jim was the swimmer in our family and I liked knowing he would have a place to work off his frustrations. To the left of the pool was a small shed with a lock on the door. As I glanced at it, I had no idea that I, alone, would one day, defend that tiny building from a group of Chinese bent on breaking the lock. But that was yet to come.

So this was to be my home for the next three years. A picture of a serene ivory tower removed from reality slipped into my mind. I would be lonely here, even with the demanding schedule that came with the job. But for now, I could almost feel complacent. Yet, behind the bushes and at the gates were the armed guards. The price for this serenity would be steep.

Day four brought brilliant sunshine and a country washed clean. The landscape sparkled with the residue of water from the typhoon. The river far below us was swollen and as I looked down the mountainside, I wondered where those metal shutters had landed. Later, as I came to understand the Chinese work ethic, I knew that wherever they were, they were being put to good use.

Skip came up the mountain to help me make out a food list for our immediate needs. The cook was still absent, so we would make do. The TDC Compound included a commissary for the military personnel and their families, but until the cook arrived, someone would take care of picking up the necessaries and I would figure out what to do once it came into the Quarters. The kitchens were on the lower level down a steep flight of stairs and more or less off limits for me. Mama San cooked the food for the guards – all fifteen of them. The count kept going up and we supplied their food. Staggering their watch times, the guards with their guns were in the kitchen at any given hour.

Because of the typhoon and the cook's late arrival, I laid siege to the kitchens and became acquainted with the equipment and utensils that had remained with the quarters.

With cooperation, we could probably put a pretty good meal on the table but there was to be a long way between what I planned in my mind and what would appear in front of us in the way of food. However, at the moment, supplies were on their way up Yangmingshan Mountain, so I turned my attention to the house. My first impression had been correct. It was cavernous. But lovely. Perched where we were on the mountainside, I felt like a bird about to fly. The house had a solid feel and no wonder—the architect, who became a friend of ours as time passed, had designed it to withstand earthquakes and the house was anchored to giant steel beams driven straight into the side of the mountain.

It was on one level, with the exception of the kitchens, and from habit, I walked to the great red lacquered double doors, placed my fingers on them to see if they were sticky – everything else was—then turned and surveyed my home. This was a ritual with me. I had moved so many times, and putting a home together required continuity so the rituals served their purpose. Directly in front of me in the foyer, was a flagstone floor with a stone pond and golden carp, swimming languidly about. Serving as a backdrop was a glass brick wall that soared to the ceiling. It was dark when we entered for the first time and remained so during the typhoon, and I paid no attention to this part of the house. On impulse, I turned, opened one of the red doors with the great brass handles and walked outside. Then I turned and started back into the house. I wanted to be a stranger and see it for the first time. Out of the corner of my eye, I saw the gate guards watching me closely. This was a crazy lady who walks out the front door, turns around and walks back inside. Hopefully, they would get used to me. I did not think I would get used to them.

The little trip was worth it. Was I really going to live in this aerie palace? Skip mentioned the Chinese government planned to allocate an amount of money to redecorate and a fix-up was overdue. For me, being given money by someone else and carte blanche to do the Quarters, was nothing short of a miracle.

I unearthed my notebook and pencil and beginning at one end of the house, worked my way through the many rooms, making notes. The feeling of being on a cloud must be preserved, so I chose carefully. And when all was finally finished, we had our cloud.

I noticed the carpet in the hallway was old and stained, moldy from the constant moisture of a tropical climate. On impulse, I pulled up a corner of the rug and found beneath it, solid teak, inlaid squares, dull and green with mildew. I had found the mother lode. After an excited call to Skip to see if the Chinese would go along with my idea, and was told they would, I called in my list and was assured the work would begin the next day. That in itself, was startling, after waiting weeks in the U.S. for a workman to appear. A trip to the long porch to put my feet up, celebrate my new world and marvel at the ease of accomplishment, gave me such a feeling of security I could ignore the bushes, bristling with guards.

Skip called with further information about the mechanics of the painters, floor finishers, drapery measurers and always, the strange clicking in the background. I made a mental note to ask him about the sound, but the excitement of the moment, pushed it from my mind. He also mentioned that Admiral and Mrs. Snyder were to leave Taipei the following day. Jim had invited them to the quarters for late afternoon. I was to meet my predecessor in about an hour. I was curious, pleased and had many questions in my mind about what was ahead. This was Navy wife talking to Navy wife, so I knew my questions would be answered.

The kitchen was very bare, but Hogo promised to find something to serve. Baron the Corgi seemed to know they were coming. He actually woke up and began to pant. They were nice people who had enjoyed their three years in Taiwan and were sorry to be leaving. Indeed, it was nearly impossible to get the Admiral on the plane the following day, for all of the goodbyes that were said.

We sat on the porch on the only furniture in the house and shared the view. Baron was as hysterical as a Corgi can get to see them and after his very wet hello, he fell down on the floor and returned to his three-day sleep. The men spoke of inconsequential things and so did we.

"Nancy, could you tell me something about the kind of food the Chinese like so I'll have some idea of what to serve?" I considered this a fairly innocuous question, devoid of any political overtones.

She looked up at the ceiling fan and placed her finger on her closed lips. I was totally mystified. Was the subject of food considered seditious and what did it have to do with an overhead fan?

Nancy replied, "I think Skip can answer that question and probably a lot more you'll have. Tell me about your children." Another look at the ceiling fan.

What a shift of subject, and although like any mother, I enjoyed talking about our progeny, this was not what I wanted to hear. There was so little time and because I knew nothing of what to expect, I hoped for direction. Then it dawned. There was a recording device in the fan. Someone was listening - deliberately. First lesson, with many more to follow. I backed off immediately, smiled, nodded and launched into a glowing account of our final visits with daughter and son. By the time they left, we all knew the children's names, where they lived and anything else of a non-political nature. Nancy placed her hand on my arm as we stood by the front doors Her eyes swept around the house, glancing at every room she could see and nodded. Every room was bugged. I wondered about the bathrooms and our bedroom. Wouldn't that be dandy? We promised to be at the airport to see them off the following day.

Realizing the restrictions of being bugged, I led the way down the porch steps to the lawn chairs by the swimming pool.

"Am I crazy, or did Nancy tell me the entire house is bugged?"

"As far as we know," We were speaking softly and the bushes near us were without moving figures in camouflage, so we were safe to talk, if only for now." I only found out today."

"Does this mean we have to talk over everything beside the pool? And if so, what do we do if it rains?" The conversation took on a James Bond flavor,

"Until I figure out an alternative, we will do our talking by the pool. And if it rains, we'll postpone our talks."

I couldn't resist. "How long is the rainy season?"

"About six months."

"Oh wonderful. If, in the next six months, you forget who I am, you can contact me through the ceiling fan."

He laughed and the tension eased. Neither of us knew how innovative we would become just to have a conversation.

The next day, we said goodbye to the Snyders. Nancy and I grinned at each other in that silent language of women that says, "Thanks. You've helped a lot." I imagined that they too, had spent many an evening by the pool. Arrangements were made for Baron's departure in two week's time. We had made peace, that low-slung, heel - biting dog and I, and watching the plane on the runway, I felt a sadness that his trip home would be so arduous.

Then, looking past the plane, I saw something that put Baron completely out of my mind and caused a shiver to run down my spine.

On both sides of the runway, fifty yards apart from each other, stood men in combat dress, each holding a gun – with bayonet fixed. This was martial law -- the law imposed by the military that supercedes civil law and is put into effect in perilous times. Because of the driving rain the day we arrived, they were invisible to me. I was beginning to wonder if we were in the right place. No one prepared me for this and I vowed to find out from Jim what the real story of Taiwan was and why we were here.

During World War II, there was a saying, "Loose lips sink ships." That little bromide bit my husband because he seldom if ever, confided in me. Almost from the moment we began our married life in the early Fifties, he was off to war and security was always tight. Many times, he shielded me from the more frightful aspects of his job and although I appreciated that in the long run, in the short run it was downright maddening. That, coupled with "No Need to Know" (and I was not on the list of needing to know), put me at a distinct disadvantage. This would change. If I had to live with the potentially threatening armed guards twenty-four hours a day, I wanted to know why, if it meant going underwater in the pool to find out.

When we returned to the Quarters later that afternoon, the new cook had arrived and with the groceries in place in the kitchen, we looked forward to something besides snacks for dinner The meal was less than mediocre – canned soup with a side dish of something dubious. We gave him the benefit of the doubt, since it was his first day on the job. I wish it had been that easy. He didn't know how to cook. What he did know how to do and why he ended up with us, remains a mystery to this day. I was facing mandatory dinner parties of thirty to forty people on a fairly regular basis and this young man could hardly put a sandwich together.

Jim pushed the indistinguishable lump of food around his plate. "What is this stuff?"

"I haven't the foggiest. I'm afraid to ask him. We might not get breakfast."

"Well, I'm not going to put this in my mouth. It doesn't even smell like food. Maybe you ought to consider giving him a lesson or two on how to cook."

Assuming he had lunched in some exotic restaurant downtown, I said, "So eat the soup. I have a better suggestion. Get another cook." I was staring at disaster.

Jim had never fired anyone in his entire career and he visibly winced at my words. "Teaching him to cook wouldn't be too hard, would it? You packed some of your cookbooks. Maybe if you just spent a couple of hours with him."

A couple of hours? It would take up to a couple of years to teach him the difference between a boiled egg and a fried one. What he would do with a leg of lamb caused me to close my eyes in pain.

"Get another cook, dear, a.s.a.p."

Another cook it was. Someone found him in the hospital kitchen doing what, I'm not sure. He ambled up the mountain with a book of recipes and a big smile on his face. He was amiable enough but what he did best was sleep – off and on the job. From what came up the stairs and on to the table, I sometimes wondered if he cooked in his sleep.

We were stuck with each other and the nightmare of a formal dinner party was mine to live with.

CHAPTER FIVE
THE LADY AND THE LICHI NUT

No furniture yet. They said another two weeks, but that worked well for the work to be done on the house. Arrangements were made for us to move our clothes to a guesthouse a mile or two up the mountain. It was described as a very exclusive and lovely place and we were to stay there for the length of time it took to finish the Quarters. After the typhoon, the guards and the cook debacle, I was looking forward to the next two weeks.

The guesthouse was attractive from the outside. But when we walked through the door, I held onto the nearest things at hand to keep from running back to the official car. No one mentioned that Yangmingshan Mountain was peppered with sulfur mines and the guesthouse had tapped directly into one of them. The smell reminded this Iowa native of a chicken house full of rotten eggs. As we gingerly moved through the rooms, the bathroom came into view. A tiled, sunken tub big enough to hold ten people was filled with steaming water and coming from the water was the smell. We had our very own sulfur bath. We have taken the waters in Baden Baden, Germany, seen people sitting in hot mud in New Zealand, strolled across the bubbling crust of a live volcano in Naples, Italy, but this was different. The obnoxious odor was six feet away from our beds and the windows wouldn't open.

We survived the night and Jim left early the next morning for a golf game with three Chinese officials. Although our car was with the furniture on the high seas, official cars were not provided for the Admiral's wife.

I was trapped with the tub.

But the view was wondrous. High mountains rose straight up before me and as I watched, a flock of white birds, pigeons perhaps, winged their way together across the face of the nearest mountain. It was a Chinese painting in motion. It completely charmed me.

The door opened and a very tall Chinese man entered the room, ducking his head to make it through the door. No mention had been made about a servant, but he motioned to the table and chairs, spread a cloth, napkin and flatware then fixed me with an impassive look and waited. He was going to serve breakfast.

"Can you tell me what you're serving for breakfast today?" I asked and he simply looked at me, his face motionless. He did not understand English so I took a chance and said, "Toast and coffee will be fine," and turned back to the window.

A plate with six pieces of dry toast was brought to the table and coffee was poured. I ate one piece, drank the coffee and was just pushing the chair back, when the door opened and he came in again with another plate of six pieces of toast. I laughed, shook my head and said thank you in his language (one of the ten words I knew). He placed the toast beside the other five pieces and left. A few moments later, he appeared with another plate of toast and I began to panic. How do you turn off a six-foot two-inch man with a toast fixation? I offered another and final thank you and returned to my room with the tub, closed the door, put a chair under the knob and waited for Jim to return.

Then it rained. At first, there was a soft, thrumming sound on the roof. Hearing it I wondered if they used tin roofs in this country as they had in the United States in earlier times. As the rain increased to a roar, I looked at the past week's adventures. Was I being paranoid about this new life? Surely, the presence of so many guards, listening devices in our home and martial law—I stopped on martial law. Wasn't this country in danger from Mainland China? Martial law was what any government turns to for protection. They call up the troops What about the year I lived in Greece during a military coup which produced a change in government and I found myself face to face with a tank gun as I rounded the corner on my way to market? That was martial law and aside from a rapid jump in adrenaline and a quick decision to choose another way to buy apples, I took it in stride. I tried to tick off in my mind the many countries I either traveled or lived in while following Jim around the Mediterranean, that could very well have been under martial law. There were several. Politics change so rapidly and those years in the early seventies found many countries experiencing turbulent times. This included my own country. That was the year of Watergate and as I listened to the Armed Forces radio station for coverage of the hearings, I concluded a little martial law might have helped that situation.

The "bugs" in the Quarters had to be dealt with. Feeling very American, I was indignant that my privacy was being invaded. But this is China, not the United States and too often, we Americans tend to take our privileges with us. "When in Rome, do as the Romans do." became my personal philosophy as I moved from country to country.

Typical of a woman, I switched my thoughts to the work being done at the Quarters and tried to imagine the final results. It would be right; right for us and right for the house. I had a mental picture of the teak inlaid floor in the long hall connecting the front foyer with our bedroom suite of rooms and remembered my conversation with the worker assigned to that job.

He looked like he understood English, but I don't think he did. I tried to explain satin finish varnish to him,

"Use brush, put on varnish. No shine like mirror. Dry – flat – no shine." All of this with generous facial and hand gestures which he enjoyed, but obviously hadn't the faintest idea what I was trying to get across and I wondered what the finished product would look like. A friend of mine had taught me the saying, "Never mind and not to worry." It sounded like a good idea to me. Little did I know Confucius had invented it.

The front door slammed and I heard my husband's voice as he spoke to Toast Man in the living room. I removed the chair from the doorknob, feeling quite silly that I put it there in the first place. He came through the door, hair plastered to his head, clothes clinging to his tall frame, wringing wet from head to toe. His shoes sloshed as he walked.

"We had to cut the game short, but not in time to miss the storm." He took his wallet out of his pocket and laid the sodden money on the bed. He was too wet to tease, so I commiserated, instead.

"I'm sorry your game ended early. The mountains are so high here, I didn't notice storm clouds."

" Neither did we. It came up fast and we were pretty far from any shelters, so I'm soaked. Get along all right here?"

"Why don't you take a hot bath? We certainly have the tub for it." My Toast Man story could wait.

He had already planned to. As I moved into the living room, T. M. prepared the massive tub with fresh, hot, steaming sulfur water. I opened the front door and hung my head outside to breathe.

When Jim finally appeared, dry and wrinkle-free, I posed the question formulated during my long afternoon with the smelly tub and the chair under the doorknob. "Jim, will there eventually be a car and driver available to me up here?"

"I doubt it. Nothing was said about it when they moved us to the Guest House."

"Then I have a problem. Toast Man brought me eighteen pieces of toast this morning for breakfast and I spent the afternoon with the sulfur tub and a chair under the doorknob. I'm not sure I can do that for two more weeks."

"A chair under the doorknob?" He looked dumbstruck.

"Yes. He's bigger than I am and I don't know how to argue in Chinese."

"Do we have an alternative?"

"Somebody said something about the Hilton Hotel downtown. I would be very happy there. I can have something besides toast for breakfast and I'm sure it smells better."

Point made. We moved to the Hilton.

The manager of the hotel was a charming Scotsman who made us feel like royalty, and the vagaries of the past week slipped into oblivion.

In the lobby were exotic shops to explore and although I was cautioned to remain inside the building, I didn't mind. Strolling through these shops was like a miniature tour through China. Examining the merchandise displayed, I marveled at the skill necessary to produce such treasures. But we had only just arrived and there was time ahead to shop. Besides, there were letters to write and invitations to answer or at least, consider. I knew the answers came from Jim's office, but it was fun feeling rather queenly, even if only for a week or two. It beat sloshing around in the Quarters A guestroom in my bare feet.

The hotel was a delight, the service supreme and I was finally introduced to some of the finest cooking I experienced while in Taiwan. Jim returned that evening with an envelope of invitations and we sat down together to see what lay ahead. There was a luncheon at the Officers' Club, my introduction to the wives of the men in Jim's command. It was his first Joint Command, a term that defines it as having nearly every branch of the military represented; Navy, Marine, Army and Air Force. The Coast Guard was left out of this one. Wrong coast.

But the one that caused me to take a deep breath was the creamy card that began; "President and Mrs. Yen Chia-Kan request the honor of your presence at dinner....." We were to dine with the President of Taiwan and his wife.

"Any idea who will be there besides us?" I asked. I've never liked surprises so I kept my tone casual.

Jim's attention was on a separate piece of paper from his briefcase, "I imagine the Ambassador and some of the higher-ranking Chinese military officers and their wives. "

"Any chance of seeing a guest list so I'll have their names in my mind?" I knew enough to remind him or it would stay in his brief case.

He produced the list and I studied what looked like impossible names to pronounce, let alone remember. With so much to learn, I shook a mental fist at the State Department for not giving me some kind of direction. Oh well, Jim's previous commands, in fact, his whole career had placed me in similar positions from time to time and I had managed not to create any international incidents. This could be a first.

The luncheon was the next day. I appeared on time at the Club, to be met by Shannon, Skip's wife, a tall serene girl from Montana with thick, dark hair, eyes that danced and a smile that told me I had just met a friend. She introduced me around and as I looked at each woman, I realized what a diverse group we were. All military and Embassy wives, yes – but each branch of the U.S. Military operates separately from the other and our life patterns are totally different. It would take a bit of doing to know these women, but that was a big part of my job.

They were curious about me. To some, I was obviously just another senior officer's wife they would have little contact with because of our social obligations with the Chinese. To others, I was from the wrong branch of the military and therefore, to be avoided. I caught the hint of interest and an occasional offer of friendship from a few and I was grateful for that. This was not shaping up to be an easy tour of duty.

Shannon told me of their two small children, a boy and a girl. With our grandchildren always in the back of my mind, I was happy to be reminded of them, if only by descriptions of other children. They lived a scant two blocks from the Cultural College, the ethereal palace with the tilt-tipped roofs that drew my eyes every time I stepped onto our porch. Shannon told me what she knew about it and I stored it away for future reference.

The college had close to two thousand students studying their mother country's heritage and customs. I wondered how the classes were conducted and how far back in time they went to present the fascinating story of their ancestors' history.

Our stay at the Hilton provided us with a chance to talk. I assumed the guesthouse had the same listening devices as our quarters, so I bided my time. Jim knew I was disturbed about many things. Doing his homework, he came prepared with answers.

"I checked into the guard situation and here are the correct numbers and the reason why they're there." As long as I have known this man he has, from time to time, sounded like a Navy memo.

"Are there really as many as I think there are?" I asked.

Patiently, he explained the reasons why we were so overcome with armed guards. We weren't the only people in jeopardy on the mountain. Our neighbor was the Ambassador from South Africa, Chiang Kai-shek's palace was just up the road and other government officials lived in places scattered over Yangmingshan. Our guards numbered fifteen, but were on a rotating basis – three or four at a time. I could live with that.

He continued, "…and with the College there and all those students, it's a pretty good idea to have a strong guard group."

I said a silent "Amen".

I had no idea how this would impact on our very lives later on.

Jim continued, " The guards' barracks are at the foot of our road and they come up to the Quarters for Mama San's cooking."

"And stack their guns in the kitchen. No wonder it looks like an arsenal down there." Before we moved into the Hilton, I had made a run through the kitchen areas below and departed hastily when I saw the weapons lined up against the wall.

I felt truly stupid until I remembered that we were paying the bill for their groceries. But I was relieved there was not one behind every bush. However, and I did not say this to my husband, I intended to keep count on the ones I saw on a daily basis.

" I've cooled down on martial law," I said, "by remembering my stay in Greece. But I did hear something about an act of terrorism just before we came out here. One of the wives mentioned it at the luncheon."

" I heard the same thing. I believe it was a letter bomb that took a Chinese official's hand off."

"Much of that going on out here?" I knew the question was academic. If there was, he wouldn't or couldn't tell me. No need to get the little lady upset. But in time, I would know. Wives are good at that.

I had come to Taiwan with eye problems. Five years previously, an exotic, incurable disease was discovered in the backs of both eyes. Its effect was degenerative and already, cataracts were forming from the steroids and the disease itself. A good ophthalmologist was a must and I wondered where that road would take me.

Jim pulled another piece of paper from his briefcase and handed it to me. "Skip did some research on doctors in Taipei and we've decided you're to go to a Doctor Lin. He's the Premier's doctor."

My! Things were moving fast. I didn't get this kind of service in the U.S., but I was more impressed that Jim had taken care of the problem without prompting from me.

"Is he nearby?"

I didn't know what else to ask. Is he young, American trained, knowledgeable in my particular problem? I was at a loss and felt slightly cornered. If it turned out he was not up on the latest treatments, how would I be able to change doctors? After all, he was the Premier's eye doctor and it would cause a furor were I to request someone else.

I was borrowing trouble. Wait and see. Twenty-eight years of military medicine had conditioned me to flexibility. I seldom saw the same doctor twice, no matter what the problem was and with almost yearly moves, I was always starting over again in an unfamiliar hospital with an unfamiliar doctor. Still, I wondered if there would be a language problem and my puny "hello, thank you, how are you and goodbye" would not get me far.

"He's across town, so you'll have a car and driver."

"When do I see him?" Obviously, I would have to work out the kinks myself, but at least, I was plugged into the system.

"Tomorrow morning – ten o'clock. How's that for service?"

I was impressed and told him so. He looked pleased.

"Jim, may I take Chinese language lessons while we're here?" He didn't blink an eye.

"That will take a little time to set up. And don't forget, there's the move-in that comes next…."

I could hardly wait.

"…and once we accept these invitations, we have to schedule our own parties."

Oh God, the cook.

But I agreed with him and asked about the furniture shipment.

"So far, that's on schedule."

"So, the doctor is tomorrow morning and the President's dinner party on Friday. When will I be able to see the house?" The thought of creamy walls, billowing sheer curtains and teak floors left me limp with anticipation.

"Probably on Saturday. We'll go up together and you can do your prowling then." He knew he was pleasing me.

"Oh, you dear man. Bring on the dinner parties and old doctors. I can handle it all."

The doctor's offices were in the Veteran's hospital and Sergeant Hsiu escorted me to the elevator.

"Sergeant, you don't need to wait for me. I can find my way to the eighth floor."

He nodded and waited. The doors opened and what looked like fifty people got out. Fifty also got on and I was one of them. It was an Otis elevator and the sign clearly stated that the capacity was twenty-one people. The only problem was the sign was in English. It was obvious there was the same space problem here that I had in the Tokyo airport, but this was ridiculous. I could only hope everyone would depart on the floors below the eighth, otherwise, I was in there for life. We were jammed together and my real fear was the elevator falling with so much extra weight. It was a very long ride. If I made it to my floor alive, I would walk down – and up, from now on.

Dr. Lin was a pleasant, older man. He spoke very little English and as I handed him my record, I wondered if he could understand any of it. I didn't and I knew what the doctors had written. That first visit was perfunctory; I sat in the chair, he looked through machines at my eyes and nothing was said. How familiar it all was. If this didn't work, maybe something else would. I had no idea what was in store for me, but luckily, I listened carefully as the doctors discussed my eyes during the past five years and realized I was pretty knowledgeable about the disease and the treatments.

"Is good to meet you, Linder Tai Tai. I hope we help you while you visit in our country. We try." His face was expressionless, but his eyes showed kindness, intelligence and curiosity. I knew this was the way it would be for the time he was my doctor.

"Thank you, Dr. Lin. I will see you then, in two months." All very formal.

We shook hands solemnly, bowed slightly and another appointment was made at the main desk of the clinic. Every two months – maintenance case.

54

The walk down the eight flights of stairs cleared my eyes of the drops and gave the backs of my legs a wake-up call. Faithful Sergeant Hsiu was waiting for me at the foot of the steps. He had seen the panic in my face when I turned around in the elevator. This man would be my anchor in many situations.

Dr. Lin became a good friend and as time went by, we developed our own method of communication. I told him what I learned by listening to the other doctors and he tried many of the same tests and experiments .I trusted him, although I sometimes wished for a younger American- trained doctor. However, my choice was to stay with him. It occurred to me that I was beginning to think like the Chinese. Venerable means older and wiser and that culture had been curing people for many centuries. The new technology hadn't done much for my problem, so what did I have to lose? I tried not to think.

Friday came and I faced my first dinner party as a guest. I worked on a secondary list, but the only saving grace was that nearly everyone had American first names; Helen, Linda, Chris, and David. Where were their Chinese names? As the months passed and I learned more about these people who had come from Mainland China in 1949, I realized their American names were for our convenience. It was easier for us to say them. That was troublesome for me. They changed their identity to accommodate us – we, who were the guests in their country. I knew they were gracious, but this was more than that.

The official car picked us up at the Hilton and we began a dizzying ride through streets packed with people. I tried to see as much as possible,

55

but it all went by too fast. Jim and I quizzed each other on couples' names, memorizing who went with whom. When at last, we parked in front of a building, I forgot to look at it, I was so intent on our list and hoping I could get through the evening without a mishap. We were greeted at the door and guided into a room adjoining the dining room. It was exactly seven o'clock PM.

We met the other guests and I found myself relaxing. They were friendly, warm, and I thought to myself, this is a good party. President Yen and his wife were like old friends, their eyes told me they understood my hesitancy and were there to help me over the bumps, should any occur. And of course, they did.

We sipped orange juice, then at seven fifteen, were ushered into the dining room and seated at a round table, spouses across from each other. The American Ambassador, Len Unger, sat to my right and I felt immediately at ease. He was an impressive man and his wife Anne across the table had a lovely, warm smile that brought an answering one from me. I was trying to take it one couple at a time, assessing them as they in turn, made their assessments.

"Tell us about your family. You have children?" his from the President on my left.

"We do indeed and I miss them already. Our son is in Texas at the University and will graduate in May and our daughter and her family live in California. We have two lovely, little granddaughters."

He seemed delighted that our family was the size I described. The months ahead would teach me how important children are to the Chinese.

I would also learn that questions about our children were often the only questions asked of me.

Chopsticks lay beside my plate. Several years ago, with no knowledge in anyone's mind that we would be living in China, we were guests at a dinner party given in a tiny restaurant near Washington, D C. Closing it down to the public for that one evening, the Chinese family who owned it cooked the many courses that flowed out of its kitchen as their four children, ranging in age from two to seven, peeped around the door and softly giggled. The guest of honor was S.K. Chow, Taiwan's Ambassador to the United Nations, and his wife, Lily. We were a small group and I sat to his left. Peking duck had been ordered and as the chopsticks began to click, I realized I was out of my element – way out. S.K noticed, then patiently and quietly, taught me on the spot how to use those sticks.

"Pat, lay the chopsticks along your hand like this."

He showed me his hand with the sticks resting happily where they had rested for all of his life.

"Find your comfortable way with them and try."

I did and it worked. I was a quick learner and by the end of the meal, using only my chopsticks, I could fill the little pancake with Peking duck, roll it, tucking in the ends and guiding it to my mouth without any of it ending up in my lap. I blessed the lesson and the man who taught me as I picked up the sticks and clicked through the President's dinner.

All went well until dessert. A small bowl that contained three round blonde things in syrup was placed in front of me. Not noticing that everyone had switched to ceramic spoons, I picked up the chopsticks and clamped onto one of the slick, round things. At chin level, it dropped from my grip and found its way down the V neckline of my dress to lodge where Mother always tucked the house key. The blonde things were lichi nuts in syrup and the one resting between my skin and my slip was cold and wet. Conversation at the table ceased and the Ambassador, sensing something was wrong, but not knowing what, turned to me and asked, "May I help you?"

What could I do? Go red in the face and flee the party?

"Mr. Ambassador, I thank you for your offer, but this is one problem you cannot do anything about." I did not look across the table at Jim.

We all dissolved in laughter and when he realized what had happened, he laughed the loudest. The lichi nut was not going anywhere, so we finished the meal.

An after dinner drink was offered and I was sure they said Galliano. I liked the taste of that golden Italian liquid. I nodded my head and a small glass of what looked like water was placed in front of me. Noticing it lacked the color I remembered, I assumed there was more than one kind of Galliano. As the conversation picked up speed, I lifted my glass to my lips and took a sip. It was gasoline – high octane, and there was nothing in my mouth but fumes. The expression on my face brought the party to another high and it was some time before I could intelligently listen to the explanation of why I was served gasoline.

"This is Kaolien, Mrs. Linder. It's our brandy. We were all surprised you wished to have some. It is very strong."

I managed to croak, " I thought they said Galliano."

Further explanation would have to wait until my voice returned and by then, it would be too late.

Because I was able to laugh at myself, the other guests began to look at me as a person instead of an icon and the Kaolien caper would follow me to future dinner parties. At least, it always provided a chuckle. I felt accepted and liked and if it took being the town clown, it was worth it.

The President and his lady were more than gracious when we said goodnight. Their dinner party had been anything but stuffy, but I couldn't help thinking – this will be a tough act to follow, unless the coming parties serve lichi nuts for dessert.

CHAPTER SIX
THE BROWN SACK

Trepidation was the key word on Saturday morning when we opened the door to our new home, Quarters A on Yangmingshan Mountain. Jim planned for us to go in the afternoon, but over a remarkable breakfast of Scottish delights, I needled my husband into leaving as soon as we finished.

The day was sunny and hot. Summer in Taipei is moist like anywhere in the tropics. But the official car was air-conditioned and I was able to concentrate on the sights as they sped by; people – many, many people, all moving, all busy doing something. If they stood at an intersection, waiting for the light to change, they were reading or their hands were occupied. All of the children wore glasses. No one loitered or "hung around". Their walking pace was swift, their bodies bent forward. Their faces were impassive, but determined. The darting bicycles reminded me of a disturbed anthill.

As we began the climb up the mountain, I saw the Grand Hotel, a scaled down replica of the Imperial Palace of the Forbidden City in Beijing. It was positioned at the base of Yangmingshan and at the head of Chung San Road North, which was like a royal highway, cutting through and running the length of Taipei. The road split at the base of the hill leading up to the hotel, creating the effect of a crossroads or the keystone of the beautiful mountain it was built on.

The official car kept a steady pace as motorbikes whizzed around us, busses belched black diesel smoke and women in shapeless peasant dress with coolie hats on their heads and some with towels around the lower part of their faces, swept the mountain road with rush brooms. Everyone worked. With so many people crammed onto such a small island, it was imperative that they earn a living. Work was their salvation and as survivors, they understood the importance of a job. That put the rice in the bowl, here as on the Mainland. In time, I would learn to recognize the person by the province they came from. Whoever coined the phrase, "they all look alike" had never stopped at a red light and studied their faces. It made me anxious to learn the language and history of these people who had fled their homes almost thirty years ago in order to be free.

An ancestor of Ghengis Khan waited for the light to change and our eyes met, his with veiled curiosity, mine with interest as I realized what he reminded me of. We drove on and although the moment ended, it was not lost. For just that brief bit of time, I could imagine the steppes of Mongolia.

Quarters A

The trees that had escaped the typhoon shadowed the narrow vertical road that turned off Yangmingshan and led to the Quarters. Already the ferns and foliage along the road were thickening with new growth. The guards knew we were coming and were at attention with the iron gates open for the car. I waved. They waved back and smiled. If you can't lick 'em, join 'em. For some obscure reason, I wanted them to be friendly and I knew the first gesture would have to be mine.

Hogo opened the great, lacquered red doors and we walked into the front hall. Things were looking very good from where we stood. The walls were clean and fresh, as was the carpet. All seemed ready to receive the furniture and family that would live there. I turned my head to the right to look down the long hall with the inlaid teak floor to the bedroom wing and caught my breath. The floor was a mirror, reflecting the high windows on the wall above. I could have ice -skated on the surface. As suspected, satin finish had not translated into Chinese. This was high gloss varnish and meant, if not a broken leg, at least a mincing walk. There was nothing to do but laugh. We inspected the glassy hallway and realized we had a conversation piece. Throw rugs would be disastrous. Rubber soled shoes were the only answer and I could see in my mind's eye, two pairs of Nikes lined up beside those elegant red doors.

Examining every room was more exciting than I had anticipated. The workmanship was professional and with furniture, pictures and memorabilia, this would be a good home for us. It had a solid feel; no cut corners here as we experienced with so many of the houses we had lived in. This house would stand.

The paint had a peculiar smell. In my years as a Navy wife, I painted many rooms and this did not smell like the paint I was used to. Later, we discovered that mushrooms thrived on it. During the rainy season, the damp wall in the dining room sprouted with little tan toadstools and once a day, Hogo harvested them. Whether they were served to the guards for lunch, I never knew, but I checked our plates carefully when they came up the stairs from the kitchens.

Renaldo, the new cook, ambled in, a big happy smile on his face and I asked if he could fix us something to eat. The smile slipped a little, he looked up at the ceiling for inspiration and murmured something neutral before sliding back down the stairs to the kitchens below. A dinner party for forty looked like a nightmare to me, but I kept quiet. You can't keep firing cooks because they don't know how to boil an egg.

It was such a lovely day. "Jim, let's take a walk. There's a little road in front of the Quarters and I want to see the view from there."

We finished our inspection and I knew 'Naldo needed time to use his inspiration for lunch. Besides, there was nothing to sit on but straight-backed chairs. We told Hogo where we were going and when he could expect us back. He giggled nervously, another thing I would have to adjust to.

The driveway was a circular one, beginning at the guard gates, passing the house and ending at another pair of iron gates. On the house side of the outer road and running along the entire length of the house, was a stone wall, eight feet high. Although there was a feeling of safety, I knew it would be like living in a fortress. On the other hand, the back of the house was wide open to the view and once inside the red doors, it was a different world.

We passed through the guard gate, smiling and nodding. Jim returned the guards' salutes and they seemed to like that. We turned right to pass along in front of the stone wall, then continued on the road that climbed the mountain. On my left was a stately white home with perfectly groomed grounds. Jim told me it was the residence of the Ambassador from South Africa. They were to become our very good friends, despite the fact our government had no diplomatic relations with that country due to apartheid.

But today, they were still strangers to us and my mind was on the beauty of this green land.

Turning to my husband to point out a view, I caught sight of a man in khaki shirt and pants several yards behind us. He was carrying a brown paper sack and he stopped when we stopped and walked when we walked. I watched him for a while.

"Jim, have you noticed the man behind us? He's all in khaki and has a small brown paper bag in his hand."

" I've noticed him."

"I suppose that's his lunch in the bag and since his forward motion seems to depend on ours, maybe we should stop so he can eat."

He was silent for a few moments, obviously weighing his next words.

"It's not his lunch. It's a gun. He's our personal bodyguard when we leave the house and grounds."

Oh grand. "Is it really that dangerous here? Are we going to be escorted and watched everywhere we go?"

Despair was about to set in; first the "bugs" in the house, armed guards at the gate and in the bushes, martial law all over the place and now, we were walking down a road with a gun-toting man behind us.

"It's necessary." End of conversation.

Renaldo's search for inspiration had taken him first to the refrigerator and then to the pantry shelf and we looked silently down on a tuna fish sandwich and canned peaches. But there was one saving grace – the napkins were folded into the shape of toy ships. At that particular moment, I would have preferred to strangle him with one where he stood by the kitchen stairs, but instead I looked him in the eye and asked,

"Renaldo, did you bring any cook books with you when you came to us?" Big smile.

"Yes, mum. The Navy gave me one when I worked in the hospital kitchen."

That meant hospital issue food – bland, basic and steamed. "Mum" was the name he always used for me.

Mum said, "Then Renaldo, I want you to start on page one and read everything the book has to say."

When 'Naldo's smile slipped, it was like his whole face fell down.

"Then I want you to choose a menu for our first dinner here after we move back into the Quarters." He was rather heavy-set, but at that moment, he looked light as a feather and ready for take-off.

"We'll be anxious to see what a good cook you must be and that first night in our new home will be a special one."

Blank disbelief.

" I really liked your napkins. Be sure and do that again. And Renaldo, I will work with you on the rest of the menus, but for this first one, surprise us."

Take-off was accomplished before I thought of anything else. I could sense Jim was quivering, but I didn't know if it was from laughter or the desire to hold school on the poor soul. 'Naldo shuffled down the stairs, brow furrowed. I looked at the mountains and wondered what terrible sin I had committed to earn this punishment. And I knew if Jim mentioned the word challenge one more time, I would give him chapter and verse on what it's like to live with a cook who can't cook. The mountains sat serene and permanent. I did not feel like the mountains looked.

We walked down the porch steps to the pool after lunch. The guards slid around tree trunks or over the terrace hill and for a few moments, we felt alone. Now that we were away from the "bugs", I didn't know what to say. It should be something important, something we couldn't talk about in the house, but like Renaldo, I was blank. I settled on further reconnaissance of our Quarters.

We were on the kitchen level and I noticed the garage area was next to the kitchen door. The outer wall of the carport looked like it might contain a small room. We found this was Hogo's room, level with the back yard. Not important now, but later on, I would spend a very bad day because of the location of that room. This same area was where Sergeant Hsiu would care for the Seville when it finally arrived, washing and waxing it in the driveway every day it wasn't being used. The guards would gather there for their meals while Mama San hung clothing on the small lines near the kitchen's high windows. Papa San's garden tools waited for him – the big stick on top of them all. I pictured in my mind the activity that kitchen generated and realized we had a village on this lower level, busy with people doing their various jobs, laughing and talking in the patois of dialects that was a combination of Taiwanese and Chinese.

Hogo and Sergeant Hsiu were from Mainland China, but the guards were too young to have made the trip over with the army in 1949, so they would be from Taiwan. Mama San and Papa San were Taiwanese and not related. They simply bore the title of their jobs and were called that by everyone. Renaldo was from the Philippine Islands and I imagined there was a common language they all shared and understood.

The pool looked green. Making conversation, I mentioned the color and added, "I'm not sure I want to wade around in that. There's enough algae floating for water lilies."

"Nobody will be swimming in it for a while. I checked the medicine cabinets in the bathrooms and they are full of fungus medicines for just about every part of the body."

"What a shame. That great big pool and nobody can use it." I was genuinely sorry because I knew how Jim liked to swim.

" I'm going to get Mike Tatosian out here this next week to tell me what needs to be done. By the way, did you know there are dressing rooms under the pool? "

Wonders upon wonders - another new discovery We walked down the first terrace hill, nodded to the guards behind the bushes, opened the door and stepped into a gray concrete bunker with showers and dressing rooms. Stretched out on a board were some bats, dead and drying. Steady. I ignored the bats and inspected the place. It was the size of a house, and full of spiders. It would take weeks of work before any swimming parties could be held and with the pool the color it was, I checked that off my list of things that must be done very soon.

This man of few words who sat next to me in the official car as we drove down the mountain remained somewhat of an enigma. He was a man of few words, but half of our twenty-eight years of marriage had been spent apart so I grew accustomed to solitude where words were not necessary. Although we had known each other since high school days, he was still a stranger to me in many ways. His years with the Navy had been good ones for him with all the opportunities to enjoy the jobs he hoped for. Because of the wars he had flown in, some called him a warrior and to be operational was the goal of every Navy pilot. Following our wedding, he fulfilled the rigorous training requirements and immediately went to Korea – twice. Our children were born during those years and we began the cycle of continuous moves and separations as his career followed the Naval Aviator pattern. When he returned after an absence of many months, I didn't bother him with the children's problems, or my own and he kept his fears and anxieties to himself. We spared each other.

When the United States entered into the "containment" of Viet Nam, once again he executed orders, this time in positions of command. He was highly decorated for his two tours of duty in that theatre of war, earning the coveted Navy Cross. Twice during that time, I was told he was shot down during air strikes over Hanoi. Mistakes in communications are commonplace in wartime and fortunately, both reportings were wrong.

To forget is therapeutic but it also dismisses the many acts of heroism among the women as well as the men. Husbands were lost in air strikes almost every day over North Viet Nam and there were scars on our souls with each new loss. One woman's sadness was every woman's sadness, for the life we lived made us as close as a family. In time, these scars softened and became our earned medals.

I turned to look at him as we sped down the mountain. His jaw was set his eyes thoughtful. I knew his mind was on the coming week when many of his duties began with briefings with the Embassy Directors, the Minister of Foreign Affairs, heads of the military establishment, and the Joint Chiefs of Staff. He would be briefed on the American civilian presence in Taiwan because of the commercial industries that were scattered throughout the island.

China loomed large and foreboding to the west, and the threat of invasion was veiled but constant. Under the treaty that existed between Taiwan and our country, the stakes were too great for China to do anything but flex its muscles. But patience was a characteristic of its people and China's history had proven its willingness to wait centuries to achieve its goals. In the case of Taiwan the buck stopped at my husband's desk.

Both of us had so much to learn. I knew he would be distracted and aloof as he sifted through the new information. Coming from a highly operational command of a Battle Group in the Mediterranean made this seem tame in comparison.

He was schooled, trained and prepared for this life and now he faced a different kind of challenge – one of waiting out the enemy to the west and at the same time, maintaining the peace of Taiwan. And if that peace was to be violated, he had the expertise to defend it. That's why we were here.

In the silence of the car, my fears and frustrations of the past few weeks took on a lesser importance, but I had found in the past that the mundane aspects of our lives provided a balance to the intensity of his career. The subtlety was to know when to intrude. Today, he spent a few hours away from the immediate problems and tomorrow, his perspective would be different. That's the way we worked it.

A few days later, the phone rang in our rooms at the Hilton. It was Skip with the news I had been waiting to hear.

"Mrs. Linder, the ship's in and the trucks will be arriving at Quarters A as soon as the loading is finished."

Hallelujah, I have a home again.

CHAPTER SEVEN
HANDWRITING ON THE WALL

Navy life and moving nearly every year had taught me my home was my continuity. I might not see my husband for months or years on end, but the place that sheltered us would be there until the next set of orders moved us on.

Waiting for the truck to come, I joined Papa San who was patiently beating the bushes for snakes, found a weapon and joined him to fill up the time. With our floppy hats and long sticks, we flailed away, taking care not to damage the flowers he had planted. The neighboring house had geese to protect them from the snakes and they sounded like rusty gate hinges. I straightened my back, looked at the mountains, and realizing where I was and what I was doing, laughed aloud. Papa San seemed to understand the humor of the moment and his weathered face produced just the vestige of a smile.

The truck holding our furniture arrived with Mike Tatosian there to help. He was a jaunty, compact man who had held every dangerous job the Navy offered. As we came to know each other, he shared his experiences with me.

The familiarity of our possessions wrapped around me like a warm blanket on a cold night and I knew I was back in my proper element. They unloaded the damaged pieces last. There is a designation made by the packers that indicates the state of your furniture. M.S. & G. means "marred, scratched and gouged". Because of our many moves, that designation appeared often on the inventory sheet. This time, my cherry-wood kneehole writing desk with the leather top was in three pieces. There was no designation to cover that.

"Don't panic Mrs. Linder – I'm sure it can be repaired and you'll never know it was ever damaged." Mike could see the shock on my face as I gazed at the wreckage. "I know some good people in downtown Taipei who can do miracles with wood."

The pecan wood dining room table had a deep groove down the middle and one of its hand-carved chairs looked as though someone had taken an axe to the back of it.

Mama San laid out clothing to air. It had been over a month with three of the weeks spent on the high seas and there was mildew, but she was talented in the care of cloth, performing her miracles on the sloping back lawn where the sunshine lay.

The progress was faster than the other thirty moves. There had never been so many hands to help. In the middle of it, Sergeant Hsiu drove majestically into the driveway in the new silver Seville. He looked like he was in some particular heaven and so was I. Freedom. At last I could climb into the car and begin to know this alien place.

Renaldo, after reading Chapter Two of his recipe book, fixed sandwiches for those of us upstairs. There was the ubiquitous tuna fish, ham and cheese and something that tasted like chicken, but looked like something else. It all came with olives, pickles, lettuce and chips and one of 'Naldo's big smiles. I smiled back.

Mama San had a great pot of stew simmering on the back of the stove since dawn for the guards. The movers quit as one at lunchtime, took out their little buckets of rice and chopsticks and ate every grain. Their strength belied their slender frames. They were all sinew. They were also barefoot, their answer to the slick hallway. I smiled at the thought of Hogo erasing all the footprints that marched up and down that floor.

The day finally ended. Papa San had some new tools, Mama San a new iron and there was silverware in the kitchen drawers for the staff and the guards, in case somebody forgot their chopsticks. Hogo was given the small kitchen appliances, which he would ignore in the pursuit of his chores in Quarters A. Everyone seemed to approve of our accomplishments on this difficult day and I felt satisfaction that we had worked together so well. This was no Missy who sat and directed traffic, this was a hands-on lady who knew what to do and how to do it.

Jim arrived, looked at the jumble, asked about damage and Mike said, "Admiral, I assured Mrs. Linder that it will all be taken care of. When the woodworkers in Taipei find out who they're working for, you'll have nothing to worry about."

There were times that I was truly glad of Jim's rank. Along with the bad stuff, it did provide some good stuff – but I certainly couldn't say that out loud.

The library was paneled in a dark wood with bookcases and a handsome stone fireplace set in the middle of the long wall. I tried to keep that room clear, so we could have one place to sit without clutter. We surveyed our untidy world that looked wonderful to me. Order would come in due time.

Renaldo served his first dinner and as long as our parties featured Filipino stew and something called lumpia, we were in business, but with this easily distracted sleeper, my work was cut out for me. I would be holding school with my cookbooks, once they came out of their box.

This day of extreme highs and lows ended as I collapsed into my own bed with my own sheets in this unique house. Nightbirds sang from the bushes outside the bedroom. Sometime I would listen to them, but not tonight.

I had heard the phrase several times and each time, I grew uneasier. Someone owed me an explanation and soon. Jim came up the mountain at five thirty for an evening at home. We were settled now and had fallen into the routine that was our life here. We attended official dinner parties many nights a week and it was rare to have one to ourselves – and the bug in the fan. Wanting enlightenment, I hoped this would be a late afternoon by the pool where we could talk.

I checked with 'Naldo and the dinner menu for the evening. He seldom had to cook at night; we were gone so often. The cookbooks had helped and after many sessions of explaining and coaxing, he was beginning to turn out some palatable food. I considered having him checked for a sleep disorder, for he did have a tendency to drop off in the middle of a recipe. However, he was trying and, with time, would be a passable if not inspired, cook. We didn't discuss the chef category.

Dinner looked interesting. He had thumbed through the book, picked three things at random and clattered around the kitchen. My fingers were crossed. With the continual round of official dinners, our turn was coming up and my nightmares had not gone away. Tonight, Hogo had set a pretty table with flowers from Papa San's garden, and with the sunset, the mountains looked majestic.

The evening seemed strange. Summer still lingered, the sky was fairly clear, but when I turned to look at the Cultural College, farther up on the mountain, there were clouds drifting across the face of the building, giving it a detached look. The high mountains in front of me held a haze around their bases and a tiny breeze fingered the leaves of the fragile plum tree on the lip of the first terrace. The world seemed to be holding its breath. Perhaps that added to the unease I felt so strongly.

Changing out of his uniform, Jim joined me on the porch. Hogo appeared instantly with the drink he liked and I was handed my glass of wine. The two men chatted for a few minutes with Hogo giggling. He had served the Taiwan Defense Commanders in this house for twenty-three years, as long as there had been TDC Commanders and I often wondered if he made comparisons. If he did, we were never aware of them. The friendly smile seemed reserved just for us. I liked this small, wiry man who kept the Quarters humming along smoothly. That the time would come to be afraid of him never occurred to me.

I gave Hogo the hour for dinner to be served and suggested to Jim we sit by the pool to share the unusual evening. I looked at the fan as I spoke. Carrying our drinks, we walked down the steps to the grass below. The pool still looked green and I made a mental note to find out why.

The guards were out of sight. By now, I could look at a tree or a bush and tell if there was a body behind it. We were becoming used to each other and they responded hesitantly to my overtures of wave and nod. Hogo quickly placed a bowl of potato chips and napkins on the low table between the chairs and we settled in with comments on the view, the haze on the mountains and the clouds above us at the Cultural College. When the time for interruptions was past, I asked my question.

"Jim, I've heard the term *handwriting on the wall* several times since we've come here and it usually is in discussions about the future of Taiwan. I don't understand and I think I should."

Jim looked startled. This was not what he had expected when I signaled we needed to talk.

"That's a pretty sensitive subject and I'm not sure I should discuss it."

"Let me put it another way. I am politically uninformed and that could be a problem for us both. I'm not asking you to breach security, I'm asking for information from you rather than someone else."

"Okay. I had planned to tell you this, but only when you asked. I just didn't expect it this soon."

Somewhat reluctantly, he continued. "We signed the Mutual Defense Treaty with the Republic of China in 1954."

I could tell he was uncomfortable with this, but I stayed quiet, not letting him off the hook.

He studied his glass. " The people I've talked to feel pretty sure it will hold, but the *handwriting on the wall* means a gearing down of the American defense posture out here and since Nixon went to China and toasted everybody back to Confucius, there have been some uneasy moments for this government."

Most of this I knew or had guessed about. But what he said next came as a complete surprise.

"The man I replaced, Admiral Snyder, was a three-star Admiral and I'm a two star. That carries its own message. The Chinese are very sensitive about things like that. Actually, in discussion with my Chinese counterparts and government officials, I find them more knowledgeable about our situation here than we seem to be in the U.S. Why not? After all it's their country."

"What happens if the Treaty goes away?"

"Taiwan will be vulnerable to a communist Chinese invasion. The ROC's army is well trained, but the fact that the U.S. has forces here and more available if needed, has kept the bad guys at bay. The U.S. is getting very chummy with communist China and it's an uneasy tine for Taiwan."

My thoughts swirled. The anonymous phone call from the State Department before we left: "Unpack, Mrs. Linder."

And now I knew why Jim had been pulled from the European theatre to come here. Not only did he know how to defend a country, he could conduct a war should one occur.

The placid, peaceful beauty stretching out before us took on a different look. I didn't need a vivid imagination to know what would happen to this lovely island or the gentle, gracious people we had met if the communists invaded. Much of the population of Taiwan had come here to escape communism and their names would without doubt, be on a list. I felt despair. The feeling of fear would come later.

Hogo announced dinner and I realized I had lost touch with reality. To lighten things a bit, I asked about the pool.

Jim looked relieved at the change of subject. "Mike says the whole thing could use a good cleaning. I don't think anyone has done much in the way of maintenance since it was put in several years ago. The staff tells me that Baron the Corgi swam in it, too. Mike's to come up on Monday and begin the job."

I looked at all that water and wondered how they would accomplish that.

Dinner was a surprise. 'Naldo had done very well and I asked Hogo to have him come up the stairs after we finished. Maybe this nightmare was about to end. We made small talk and I asked Jim if he knew of any bookstores in Taipei with English text. I wanted books that could tell me what had, and was about to happen to the Republic of China and the people who lived here. I'm not a stupid woman. I had listened and learned, but past a certain point I was met with a reluctance to explain and I needed explanations.

Naldo climbed the stairs, smiling happily – he knew he had done well and we congratulated him on his delicious dinner. To keep him motivated, I suggested he think about a menu for a small dinner party of ten or twelve sometime in the near future and hurriedly added as his smile faded, I would help him make the decisions. Hogo giggled.

By now, the sun had vanished as the haze deepened on the mountains. There was a yellowish look to the sky and if I were at home in Iowa on a night like this, I would have scanned the horizon for a long, black roll cloud that spelled tornado. But surely not here. This climate was different, this was a different part of the world and I idly wondered if they called a tornado a tornado out here. Yet tonight the conditions were the same. The air was hot and heavy; the kind of night you can hear the corn grow in the Iowa fields. The breeze freshened and the plum tree bowed in acknowledgement.

In the middle of the night there was a sound like the end of the world or a freight train approaching head on, but it was a primordial grinding noise and later I realized the earth was moving into a new position.

Earthquake.

Our bed lifted off the floor, then danced and bounced. We could do nothing but hang on and hope the ceiling didn't fall on us. Then stillness – just a shrug, but we had no way of knowing if there was more to come. The rain began – a deluge with no let up. I thought of the "forty days and forty nights" rain and from the sound, we were not far behind. We still had electricity. Hogo was the only one of the Staff who remained overnight at the Quarters, and his inspection revealed little or no damage but we couldn't be sure until daylight. Perhaps the pool had cracked and emptied. At least that would solve one problem among the many that seemed insolvable. We returned to an uneasy sleep.

The rain continued through the night and dawn looked more like dusk. Jim left early for the office. The TDC duty officer called to say the building was still standing, which was a relief, but I knew he was anxious about damage there and to the people who worked for him.

We were lucky. The steel beams that were the ribs of our house had held it firmly against the mountainside and the pool was still intact. All we could do now was wait for the rain to stop.

The phone in the library rang and when I answered I heard the usual clicking sound, then a whirring began. I waited for silence before saying, "Hello?"

"Pat, is everything all right at the Quarters? This is Sandra Cummings – we met at the Wives' Luncheon last month and I'm in charge of the next one and needed to talk to you."

"Sandra. Yes, I remember you. We came through the earthquake very well and if this rain will ever stop, we'll be back to normal. How about you?"

"We're okay. We live on the mountain above the American School and the water is running down pretty strong, but if it quits soon, we'll get by without any damage. There are some cracks from the earthquake, but I haven't heard of anybody up here in trouble."

"Good, Do me a favor and keep me posted if anyone needs help. And Sandra, before we talk about the luncheon, did you hear a whirring sound on the phone, before I said hello?"

She laughed. "Oh that's just the tape being rewound. Actually, we should wait for them to get it ready to record before we talk, but with the storm and all, we're both too busy to wait around for that."

Once again, I was left staring at the phone in my hand.

My first impulse was to drop the thing or quickly hang up. Instead, I shrugged, gave a laugh of my own and said I would have to be more careful about that in the future. We finished our conversation and I slowly sat down on the couch. Had I not talked with Jim the night before, I would be very angry, or as my Mother used to say, "mad as a wet hen". But I was seeing things in a different light now and found myself rationalizing this latest indignity. Wouldn't a government under threat of invasion and annihilation, do anything to protect itself? And isn't the country that has promised to protect them fair game for information? And if that country might possibly withdraw support, wouldn't they be justified to take any steps to know that? If there are still heroes in this decade, they might very well be these people, determined to live in a free, democratic society and willing to do anything to keep what they have. I was learning fast.

The rain lasted another two days. We would all be little green people if this kept up much longer. Mama San and Hogo used mildew spray on all the bathrooms and our clothing was brought out of the dark closets and hung in the guestrooms. Our bedroom area consisted of a very large sitting room – more like a living room than just a place to sit, a good-sized bedroom with French doors and steps leading to the sloping back lawn that ended at the pool. A bathroom connected the two rooms.

I was helping Mama San with the clothing and passed through the bathroom to lay some of the things on our bed. With air conditioners in all three rooms, today they were turned on to help dry out the carpets and bedding. As I stopped to check the setting on the bathroom air conditioner, something moved on the floor near the metal drain cover. A snake had come through the slits and was heading my way. I remembered thinking the drains must be filling up before I backed into the sitting room and called Hogo on the intercom. The panic in my voice brought him on a dead run and he knew exactly what to do. I didn't stay around to watch.

When the phone rang, I carefully headed down the long, shiny hallway to take it in the library. It was Sandra.

"Pat, people are having trouble up here on the mountain. The water is coming down so fast, it's breaking through back doors and washing away furniture. So far, everyone's okay, but Nancy Sloane's mother-in-law washed out the front door with the couch and chair. She's all right – just shaken and scared to death. I think she wants to go home."

Who wouldn't? And when she gets home, what a story she'll have to tell.

"Sandra, I'll contact Jim's office right away, in case they don't know, and thanks so much for telling me. If anything more happens, I'll be here. We'll do all we can."

Rescue efforts were made, but the baby daughter of a TDC couple died when she was swept away and found drowned at the bottom of the mountain a day later. It was a sad community that surveyed their damage and mourned their losses. Many lived just above the American School and the flood had turned the building and grounds into a disaster area.

The Ambassador called, asking us to join them in helping clean up the school so the children could return as soon as possible. After the rains slowed, we joined the families, were handed rubber gloves, buckets of bleach, cloths and sponges and began the job. The Ambassador and his wife Ann worked with us as we found our rooms. The biology classroom was our assignment and the chairs and desks were tumbled upside down like tossed matchsticks. Everything had a coating of slick mud on it and the stench of spilled chemicals mixed with the ever-present smell of sulfur. We worked silently, trying not to miss any of the slime. In this climate and with mud from who knows where, disease is always a danger. More families turned out to help, putting the school before their own devastated homes.

Since the ground was saturated, cleaning the pool was put off until the soil on the mountain dried out and could absorb the runoff. Mike Tatosian was Jim's senior Master at Arms and he gave the Quarters a thorough inspection that proved we had come through in good shape. I joined him on the back lawn by the little shed to the left of the pool. The padlock was still in place.

"Mike, what's in that shed? The door's been locked since we came and I've often wondered why."

"A generator for emergencies. If you had lost electricity last night, Hogo would have started it up. It's pretty valuable. There are only a few on the island."

"Why didn't we use the generator when we arrived here during the typhoon? Remember the candles and the cold supper?"

"The previous cook had stashed the key to the padlock somewhere and no one knew where. Mama San found it a couple of weeks ago behind a can of lard."

"Lard? Did you say lard? Do they use that when they cook?"

Mike grinned. "I don't think they would know how to cook without it. That and MSG."

"You're serious? We're eating food loaded with lard and MSG?" I was appalled. Things were going to change below the stairs whether I was allowed down there or not.

Jim returned from his office that night with a look of wonder on his face. "You will never guess what I saw when I left the office an hour ago. Remember the stream that runs by the TDC compound? We started across the bridge and there were hundreds of people in the water and on the banks, picking up – eels."

"Eels?" I did not like the thought of a stream squirming with eels.

" Apparently, the rains washed out the eel ponds up in the mountains and they all swam down the river."

"They have ponds full of eels?"

"The Chinese export them to the Japanese and other countries, but they consume a lot of them here. It was quite a sight, seeing people lunging into the water and coming up with a handful of squirming eels. They're expensive in the restaurants and this must have seemed like a bonanza."

"You said in the restaurants. Will we be eating eels?"

"Probably."

Probably not, I thought. I'm not into rubbery things. Then I remembered something. In Spain, we discovered Chinquitas – baby eels dipped in batter, deep -fried and when served in a heap on a plate, looking like shoestring potatoes--were beyond comparison, and the Calamari in Greece – thin deep-fried rings of squid that looked like French -fried onion rings. That and a glass of ouzo almost convinced me I should linger in Greece longer than the year I did. But chunks of eel held little interest for me.

Would there ever be just an ordinary day on this island? My two months in Taiwan felt like a lifetime. Impending disaster was always just around the corner and I longed for one simple, boring day. It was not to be.

CHAPTER EIGHT
A PAIR OF SHOES

Following the storm, everyone on the mountain needed help. Many had lost everything and would have to replace it all. I loaned copies of Architectural Digest and my big Colonial Williamsburg catalogue of furniture replicas to the wives. Since the furniture makers in Taipei were renowned for their way with woods and with the exotics so available – teak and rosewood, the ladies chose to have the pieces made. The thick book and magazines were passed around and Chinese woodworkers saw what Americans sat on in the early days. Weeks later, at one of the luncheons, I talked with the girl who had first borrowed the book, then made sure that the other wives had their turn.

"Diane, how's the furniture project coming along? Did the book help?"

A look of embarrassment crossed her face and she all but scuffed her toe when she answered, "Pat, a very strange thing has happened about that. The first wife who saw the Williamsburg book met with the man she had chosen to do the work and he started right away. By the time we passed the book around and made our decisions, she had one finished chair back."

"Was it all right? Did it turn out like she expected?"

"Not exactly. He made it just like the picture and all the curves were on the front but the backs were flat. It wasn't dimensional. The chair looked like a photograph."

I was stunned. Talk about a literal translation. The poor man had obeyed orders when told to make it just like the picture. I started to laugh and so did Diane. "Did you catch it in time, before any more came back flat?"

"Yes we did, and he said he would make another for her at no cost."

What a remarkable place with such remarkable people. There was a childlike quality to their anxiety to please. As a Navy wife, I had often tangled with merchants and tradesmen and in the early days, came away with anger and bruised feelings. But as time passed, and I was a woman in a man's world, I learned to play the game as a man would.

I'm sure it was the same here, but not for us. We were the guests and should be treated in a special way, but because I lived in my ivory tower on the mountain, I was unaware of many of the frustrations the wives felt every day, being in a foreign country with the added barrier of such a difficult language.

Today, I was just trying to keep my cool. My own furniture that had been so damaged from the move had gone down the mountain on the back and the bicycle of Johnnie Wong. As I wrung my hands, this thin, wiry young man loaded and lashed my desk, and slipped his arms through the harness attached to a framework of scaffolding.

"Johnny, I'll call TDC and have a truck sent up to take the pieces down the mountain. You can't possibly make it down the mountain with that much weight on your back."

"Ah no, Linder tai tai. My back just fine. Do many times. Everything OK. You see." And he wobbled off.

The desk in three pieces went first. Because of its weight, I could never move it without help and now the jumble of wood and leather disappeared down the vertical road as Johnny and his bicycle picked up speed.

Two weeks later, Johnny pedaled the repaired and refinished desk back up the mountain. It was like new. Even the leather was clean and supple. He looked a little out of breath. The dining room table, three leaves and one chair all went down the same way and two weeks later, appeared on the back of the bicycle at our front doors. The workmanship was masterful. His uncle had hand carved a new back for the dining room chair and Johnny told me his whole family had helped. The cost was under $150. My conscience made me give him $200 and I told him there would be more work in the future than he and his family could probably handle and assured him I would pass his name along to the other wives. To see him start off down the driveway with furniture towering over his head was a brilliant lesson in the cultural differences between their country and ours. We would have used a truck. Johnny used his back and his bicycle.

I had the day off. There was no luncheon, 'Naldo was given his early morning briefing and was probably asleep by now. Someday I must ask him how he spends his nights to be so tired in the daytime – maybe not. Sergeant Hsiu stood ready at the Seville, awaiting my exit through the great red doors, there was money in my pocket and the house needed "things". It was a perfect day for such a mission and I intended to enjoy every minute.

I chose to go alone. With my precarious eyesight dimming out faster than I anticipated, it took me longer to look at objects, figure out what they were and check the price.

Sergeant Hsiu drove smoothly, carefully, and I'm sure, enjoyed having the other cars make way for us. The license plate read *001* and I felt very grand and a little foolish as, parting the traffic, we proceeded down the mountain. The sweeper women in their gray, shapeless clothes and coolie hats were brushing the gutters with their rush brooms. They moved in a continuous motion, stopping at intervals to collect the refuse and stuff it into a bag hung around their necks. They looked like part of the landscape, as they worked with infinite patience. Because their stance and clothing were the same, they could have been in a rice paddy in some remote province of China. The cars on Yangmingshan seemed to weave an intricate pattern as they sped in and out, just avoiding collision and gaining a second or two of time before the traffic light stopped them. I could smell the acrid exhaust fumes even with the air conditioner on and thought again about the sweeper women, vulnerable to it all.

I saw it before I realized what had happened. Coming toward us was a city bus, belching diesel fumes and threading its way through the mass of bicycles and cars. In the next instant, a blur of black pants and white shirt was cartwheeling through the air, arcing over our lane and landing with such force that it resembled nothing more than a pile of castoff clothes. The motorbike went in the other direction and people scattered to miss its impact. As I was trying to understand what had happened, we were past the accident. Sergeant Hsiu immediately speeded up, using the horn to clear the way. Looking back, I could see a knot of bystanders, staring at what remained of a man in the black pants and white shirt.

"Sergeant Hsiu, we must stop. That man is badly injured, if not dead. We should see if we can help."

Shaking his head to reinforce his answer, he said, "No, Missy. We keep going. No stop."

It was obvious there was more here than I knew about, so I subsided and waited until the good sergeant drove the car into the TDC Command Compound at the foot of the mountain. He switched the engine off, turned slightly, and meeting my eyes in the rear-view mirror, said, "Missy, I protect you. That is first job. Second job to drive you where you go. Today, you need protect. When you are in car, people know. Not safe. I protect you."

And what do you say to that? I felt safe As long as I was with this quiet man, nothing would happen to me. Only yesterday, Mike had mentioned the sergeant did not carry a weapon - just his bare hands and with his years of training in the martial arts and all forms of combat, I was safe in his keeping.

I closed my eyes, said a silent prayer for the young man lying on the curbstone, adding, "Lord, let me understand these people and let them be patient with me as I learn."

Leaning forward, I laid my hand on his shoulder to tell him I understood and was grateful, then sat back in the seat. He nodded and we slipped into traffic. I had hoped to take in the street scenes and the people milling about, but my thoughts were filled with the young man whose life had ended so suddenly. Another time.

Shopping seemed frivolous and meaningless after the ride down the mountain, but the sergeant knew where to take me and as we stopped in front of a shop, he waited patiently while the car at the curb hurriedly left to make room for us. He parked quickly, was out and opening my door before I realized we were there.

Motioning to the shop door, he walked me to the entrance, looked inside, found the owner, and delivered me into his hands for safe keeping, then returned to the car to stand by the Seville emblem on the hood. Cadillac ornaments were in high demand in the Taipei black market and I sincerely hoped no one would make a try for it. They would end up dead.

It appeared I would not be strolling the streets of Taipei.

The shop was small, rather dark, but not dusty. There was no identifying sign, no prices – just a few objects visible. There were porcelains on small tables, with exquisite paintings of flowers or landscapes. A vase with golden carp swimming caught my attention and my thoughts shifted from the tragedy on the mountain to the beauty of the colors surrounding the fish. It was therapy. The shop owner having been carefully briefed, showed me his treasures of jade, porcelains, scrolls, cloisonné, and ivories, explaining patiently where they came from on the Mainland, how old they were and what he felt was a fair price for them. I couldn't help it. I was enchanted. China lay in my hand as I looked at a piece of lavender jade. It was cold, then as I held it, warmed to the heat of my skin. It held history in its carved translucence and I wished for it. But this was a day for household things and I reluctantly put it back in his hand.

I explored and my eyes returned to the vase with the swimming carp. The shop owner told me that Chinese artists never paint dead animals, fish or birds. They are always alive and moving. I studied the scrolls and porcelains and discovered he was right. A Chinese friend had recently told me I was born in the Year of the Tiger and as I moved to find a better light, a tiger in a scroll was walking down a path, right paw extended, his golden eyes on mine. The birds were poised to fly and the languid fish hung suspended in the soft green of the surrounding water. The vase needed a home and I had the place for it. I paid the pleasant man, thanked him and with a promise to return soon, left the shop. No one entered while I was there. It seemed to be an understood fact. When Missy's in the shop, you don't go in. What a solitary existence I was destined to have.

We visited three more places that gave me the chance to look at the local retail furniture and the car trunk filled up with one small table and a Korean chest inlaid with brass and an interesting lock. They would fill some of the empty spots in cavernous Quarters A.

I was tired. Seeing when you can't see is hard work and the day had been traumatic. I nodded to Sergeant Hsiu and we climbed the mountain. As we neared the site of the accident, tears traveled down my cheeks for there was a pair of shoes where the body had been. Using the rear view mirror, Sergeant Hsiu noticed my tears and explained that when someone is killed, they leave shoes there so the family can come and take them as a remembrance. His family didn't know yet. He had been a young man on a motor bike and now he was just a pair of shoes. The shoes looked lonely.

I needed to go home.

Mike was working on the pool with several other men. They were slowly draining it, channeling the water through a pipe and down the mountainside. The ground having dried out from the heavy rains was slowly absorbing the water. I needed company, distraction from the sadness of the day and putting on my floppy hat, I walked down to the pool and watched. The walls were green with algae. No wonder there was fungus medicines in the bathroom cabinets. What a monumental job it turned out to be. The draining had been going on for several days and soon they would begin scrubbing with bleach. Hogo was in attendance as always and I asked him to see that the men had a big pitcher of water and hot tea.

Mike waved when he saw me. " How was your shopping trip? Did you buy out Taipei?"

With a shaky voice I told him of the accident and my feeling of frustration and sadness at the unfeeling message of the pair of shoes.

He listened sympathetically, then said, "Mrs. Linder, I spent a great deal of time in Viet Nam during the war and while I was there, I met a family. I cared a lot about them, tried to see them as often as I could." He looked at the ground for a moment, then went on.

"Navy orders took me away and a couple of years later, I went back. I wanted to find them again. They were gone, no one seemed to know where, but I learned there was a chance they had escaped the country by boat." He was painting a picture in my mind and I guessed where he was going with his story." I had the same feeling of helplessness. The odds were they were all dead and if I had been able to stay behind, they might be alive today. Maybe they did get out by boat, but their chances of surviving were practically non-existent. Every time there is a refugee boat sighting, I go to the western Coast to see if maybe they made it. So far they haven't, but I'll keep hoping." His arms rested on his knees and his loosely clasped hands tightened.

Boat people. They were spread out all over the Southeast Asian seas, drifting with their last possessions, hoping to find a country that would let them land. They came from the steamy jungles of Cambodia, from war-torn Viet Nam and any place where despotism ruled. Modern-day pirates boarded their tiny boats, killed them, took their pitiful belongings and left them to the shifting currents. I knew some of these tragic people had landed on the western coast of Taiwan and I waited for Mike to finish his story.

" Americans tend to think that because of the numbers – the millions of Chinese here and on the mainland, life is not as important as it is to us. Don't you believe it." His jaw tightened. "Family has a lot more meaning with these people than it does in our country, or at least from what I've seen. What you saw today was just the accident. If the man has a family, tonight will be as sad as it would be in your own home under the same circumstances."

I knew he had a lot bottled up inside of him and I tried to lighten the moment.

I said, "As long as I've known about the Chinese, they've been described as inscrutable. Maybe we feel the way we do because of the lack of emotion they show on their faces. Mike, you spend time with them here, don't you?"

"Yes, I do. I'm comfortable with them. The people here are my good friends."

"I envy you. My life is so protected, I wonder if I'll ever have the chance to find good friends among the Chinese."

He grinned. "You will, Mrs. Linder. They're just waiting for you to get used to the place."

I was glad we talked. He told me a lot I needed to know as the afternoon wore on. Our conversation was one I would think of many times. The day had been confusing for me – one packed with emotions I had not anticipated having and I felt unsettled, but with Sergeant Hsiu and Mike around, I also felt secure. However, the growing awareness of the measures necessary to get me safely through a day made me uneasy. Sergeant Hsiu's dedication and protective talents were comforting, but I took that protection for granted and I was too ready to stretch the bands of restrictions. The serenity of this picture-perfect place was like an opiate and I had allowed myself to fall under its spell. My safety could not be solely up to them. Some of the responsibility must be my own. How I would accomplish that, I had not the faintest idea, but time would be the teacher.

It was 1977 and the twelfth of September was my birthday. I was not prepared for the way it unfolded. We had only arrived in July so I assumed we would have a quiet dinner on the porch, talk about the day and muse on having one's fifty-first birthday in such an exotic and beautiful place.

The doorbell rang at seven thirty A.M. Hogo opened the door and began to giggle. Standing on the front step was a person completely covered with flowers. We counted twelve bouquets, all from the Chinese generals, admirals, government officials and their wives. I was overwhelmed. Some of these people had met me, but a lot of them had not. Throughout the day, flowers and bottles of Chinese Kaolien brandy arrived. The front foyer looked like the San Diego Rose Show, and I could only assume that the story of my involvement with Kaolien had circulated and I was guaranteed a lifetime supply. The containers were ceramic and porcelain vases, painted with chrysanthemums, plum blossoms and bamboo, but if I had to drink the contents to display them, I would need more than a protector, I would need a keeper.

The day was one of surprises. Gifts arrived and I was astonished. I had often ignored my birthdays. With Jim gone, I found little reason to celebrate. That day was like any other day. But this was one I would never forget. We placed flowers everywhere. The bouquets overflowed into the library, the living room and finally, the porch. Having a brother who was a funeral director, I was accustomed to lots of flowers, but looking at this vast display, I knew he would smile and say it was one of his "better funerals." I also learned that having been born in the Year of the Tiger, was cause to celebrate.

I realized that thank-you notes would have to be written – by me. And each gift must be reciprocated with a gift as their birthdays came along. I did not realize at the time that the same procession of flowers and gifts would be repeated on our anniversary and at Christmas, not to mention Jim's birthday. That was the custom. I thought of my little cache of money put aside for furniture to fill the Quarters and determined that now was the time for a strategy meeting with Jim. Buying gifts for each one that had come to Quarters A on this day, would take all of my savings and then some. The meeting was held, my case presented, a decision reached and my furniture money was intact. The Navy would help, up to a point. Beyond that point, it was up to me.

At the September luncheon, the birthday congratulations continued and I felt humbled – and older by it all. One of the wives asked how I was getting along up on the mountain as several others joined us while we chatted. I mentioned that I was lonesome for my little white dog that was now with my mother. When my father died, Mother was not handling her grief very well. She looked lost and often disoriented without him, so I gave her our little Maltese Charlie, something to care for and worry about.

This started a general conversation about everyone's pets and I realized how important they were to these women and their families. To the children, their pets were as necessary as their friends because nothing is taken for granted in a foreign country. Your daily life is narrowed to your immediate neighborhood, the school your children attend and the Compound.

When lunch was announced, the word was out. Pat needed a dog. After talking to Jim, I posted a notice on the Exchange bulletin board in the Compound:

Lonely lady on mountaintop in need of husband-approved

little, white, fuzzy dog.

Call Quarters A.

CHAPTER NINE
CRUISING AROUND THE SOUTH CHINA SEAS

One of the perks of Jim's job was an airplane called The Blue Goose and she sat, bottom firmly planted on the runway, nose pointed to the sky. She looked like an old WWII movie plane, poised to climb into battle, her two propellers churning. There were a lot of flights under her silver belt and she had a comfortable, seasoned look. The interior had been modified – the bucket seats were gone and in their place were upholstered ones with a table for Jim to use for paper work. His command was widespread and as the U.S. protectorate, he would periodically visit the outer perimeters of the Republic of China, Taiwan. This included a chain of islands – the P'eng hus, between Mainland China and Taiwan in the China Straits.

I stepped off the plane and my hair went south. The wind was horizontal, steady and never let up. We bent into it and drove into a little town called Makung.

"Do you have to inspect the island in this wind?" I already had grit in my teeth.

"I believe that's on the agenda." He was hanging on to his cap.

"Try to keep your mouth closed or you'll have half of the P'eng hus in it. I'm working on the other half."

I kept my eyes at half mast to keep the dust out and noticed that many houses looked like bunkers – low to the ground with slits for windows. It was the only way to live in a place like this. The women wore towels around their faces and conical hats with only their eyes showing.

We were taken to the center of the town. Jim left for his meetings with the officials he had come to see and I began my walk-about with the wife of one of the military officers. She was pleasant, but understood very little English and spoke none at all. The village was small and by our standards, primitive. The wind was a tangible force that caused me to protect my eyes against the blowing dust and I wondered how long I could hold out before returning to the shelter of the plane.

Then I noticed something that looked like a bathtub with no legs. Looking around, I saw many of these and realized they were the overturned empty shells of giant turtles. This was the place that supplies the world with tortoise shell products. The mammal that lived in that house had to be enormous. I guessed this is where turtle or terrapin soup came from. I carefully examined the shells, imagining the size of the legs and head that plowed through the sea.

My eyes shifted to a table that held coral. The people of these islands also mined some of the most beautiful coral in the world. The divers did the harvesting and the artisans cut, cleaned and polished the pieces into works of art. There was every shade from the purest white to the deepest blood red. This was to be a day of great temptation for me. I bought a few pieces, then continued my look at this unusual town, but the air was thick with dust and I abandoned any hope of exploring and returned to the plane to wait.

I knew Mainland China lay to the west of these islands and it was not very far to the west. My questions had produced the information that communist China considered these islands as belonging to them. But Taiwan also laid claim to them and until China took them by force, they were under U.S. military protection. Like so many of the islands in this part of the world, they were scattered and vulnerable. Under the treaty, the United States defended them, collaborating with the military presence of the Republic of China, Taiwan as well.

Through conversations in Taipei, I was becoming aware of the fierce resolution of the ROC to hold onto its possessions in the face of incredible odds. The narrow band of water – from the western shores of Taiwan to the eastern coast of China was a dangerous place to be. The Taiwan Straits even then, were a source of animosity between the two nations. Shipping and trade had always been the lifeblood for these countries and obviously, to control the waters was to have the edge. Time was not to soften or resolve this push-pull of possession.

Later in the month, we flew to another group of islands that was claimed by the communist Chinese government, but under Taiwan and U.S. protection. They were the Chinmen Islands, or Kinmen as they were called after Chiang Kai -shek renamed them. Long ago, they were called Quemoy. These twelve islands were close offshore of Mainland China on the outer perimeter of a vast natural harbor. China's coastline is sprinkled with islands and this set seemed almost snuggled up to the great bulge of Goliath's belly. In the 1950s, China bombarded these tiny islands with artillery and the story goes that eventually, because of Kinmen's ingenious fortifications, the communist PRC (Peoples Republic of China) growing weary of daily bombardment that accomplished little or nothing, unloaded their ordnance every other day. On the alternate days, Kinmen bombarded the mainland. I found a certain humorous aspect to this story. It was an unusual way to wage war, but points were made. Taking the spent shell casings, the people on Kinmen made the unique Chinese knives found in most of the finest chef's kitchens around the world. A stunning case of "got'cha".

While we visited this tiny outpost, our hosts provided a telescope and we gazed at the communist mainland across the short span of water that separated the two political philosophies. A Chinese junk sailed serenely past my field of vision as I focused on the land. The beauty of the moment caught in my mind and I was back in Pearl Buck's China.

"Ah, Linder tai tai, please notice the village across the water." I could see one long street with typical Chinese buildings and in front of them were people, walking the length of the street, turning the corner and disappearing out of sight.

Nothing unusual about that, except that I realized I was looking at communist China.

"Linder tai tai, please to notice people as they come around corner of building at the end of street." The General moved the telescope a fraction and indicated I should look.

I obliged, but my eyes were in no condition to make out much of anything. "What should I be looking for, General?"

"If you look close, you will see them walk length of street, then turn corner."

"And…?"

"They will change their clothing behind fronts of buildings."

"Why on earth would they do that?"

"They will appear again at other end, looking like different people. Those are not real buildings."

"And those are not real roofs?"

"No. Today only six people changing clothes. Sometimes more. In holiday time, there are more."

"So today, there are just enough to make the "town" look industrious and prospering." I was beginning to get the drift. The General was delighted.

"Yes, this is done to show people on this Island of Kinman how good life is in communist China." He shook his head. I shook mine in wonderment.

The "town" looked busy, and just what every Chinese should wish for – especially those poor souls living on Kinmen. But they had been found out and thus became entertainment for the Kinmen population to watch them. That made two products at the expense of the communists on the mainland.

In retaliation, the Republic of China (the good guys) on Kinmen sent up weather balloons with cargoes of toothpaste, and toothbrushes, soap, games for the children, books – anything that spoke of a free and prosperous society and a perfect answer to the charade on the opposite shore. We were given tethers to hold and when the wind was just right, we sent our balloon off to China.

But it was by far the ceramics and porcelains created on this island that caught and held my attention. This was a collector's paradise with all the beauty and fragility of Chinese art. And what a dichotomy – a bombarded island producing the most delicate of porcelains. But it was symbolic of their culture – unexplainable to the westerner, but with its own inscrutable charm.

Taipei

Once again, Sergeant Hsiu brought the car around and we set off for downtown Taipei. As we passed the scene of the accident, I chose to look the other way and it helped. Of course, this good man noticed and I was rewarded with a brief nod and a smile into the rear view mirror.

In a small bookstore, I found a map of Taiwan and the surrounding seas and it became apparent that we were in a very strategic part of the world. Taiwan and the Taiwan Straits separated the North and South China Seas. Whoever controlled those waters would control the shipping and trade lanes of a vast area. China seemed the logical one because of its enormous mass of coastline, but Taiwan and the Straits stood in the way. The fortifications were beginning to make sense. How easy it would be for Goliath to squash David was it not for the United States' protection.

Although I heard more often, the name Chiang Kai-shek, the people spoke with reverence and devotion of Sun Yat-sen. He was the father of the Republic and in the early nineteen hundreds, worked toward a democracy instead of the dynastic rule the people had lived under for centuries. He introduced nationalism and a desire for the wellbeing of the Chinese people, insuring a vast following. He gave his people a glimpse of a different kind of future. For the Chinese on Taiwan, he was the catalyst that brought them here and kept them working toward their own democracy.

As I studied the mountains of Taiwan from my vantagepoint on Yangmingshan mountain, I felt like a flea on the back of an elephant; too much to learn and too little time to learn it.

The ubiquitous briefcase was open on the library table. "Pat, I have conferences scheduled in the Philippine Islands at Clark Air Force Base." His Joint Command included liaison with the Air Force and periodically, the two branches of the service met for team meetings. "There is a large Air Force hospital at Clark. Bound to be American doctors. Would you want to go?"

Enthusiastically, I said, "Yes. Very much." An American doctor – one I could understand. "But how do I make an appointment?"

"Skip will work out all the details and let you know."

That was easy.

The following week I was in Dr. Lin's office after my eight-floor climb. He was courtly, old-world in his approach to this patient with the unruly eyes. I was out of breath.

"Dr. Lin, I'm to accompany my husband to the Philippines and there is an American hospital there. Should I ask for an appointment for my eyes?" I had every intention of doing just that, but I knew the "face" thing was involved.

"Yes, Mrs. Linder. You meet American doctor. Good for eyes."

He did not say my eyes were bad enough to make this journey mandatory but by now, I had learned to go by my instincts and with his firm suggestion and my own knowledge of the changes in my sight, I agreed.

Skip called with my schedule. "Pat, I've been working with the Protocol Officer to make your appointments. His name is Bill Cutler and he will meet us at the plane."

"Great, Skip. I feel comfortable about this whole thing. Will Bill take me to the hospital?"

"Yes, and he will be with you throughout the day. You won't have to find anything on your own. He knew how I hated to be left alone when my eyes fogged up.

The flight down was a long one, even in the comfortable Blue Goose. We would remain at Clark for three days. As promised, Bill Cutler met and stayed with me as the doctors examined and re-examined my eyes. I had lived with this problem for five years. The original diagnosis was uveitis – an inflammation in the backs of both eyes that would eventually destroy my sight. The only treatment was steroid drops that together with the disease were causing cataracts to form and thicken very quickly. During those five years, I had been given every test known to mankind in an effort to find the reason why. Because we moved every year and each doctor wanted to do his own tests, I fell into the guinea pig category and finally called a halt when I feared my overall health was in jeopardy from the testing. To have an 'exotic' anything that can't be cured in the medical sense is to become a delight to the research department, but a threat to a doctor's professionalism and my next category was one of maintenance. I fell into it easily. Seeing a doctor every month was better than seeing one every week.

The doctors at Clark were intrigued and decided I should come back on a routine basis. Jim had told me of the MEDIVAC plane, which once a month scoured the South Pacific area for urgent or difficult medical cases and flew them to this hospital at Clark.

The term to go to the doctor meant a long flight on a four-engine plane equipped with stretcher-hammocks (usually filled), side seats, a week's stay on the Base with endless appointments, followed by another long flight back. It was not an easy exercise. I knew there were Guest Quarters – we were to stay in them for these next three days, but the thought of languishing in the Quarters or at the hospital for a week until the flight took me back to Taipei, left me limp. Bill listened carefully to the words the doctors used in charting my routine visits. He would be responsible for me each time I came. The doctors decided on a routine three-month visit with the good Dr. Lin taking care of me in the interim.

They also carefully explained to me in clinical terms the new twist to the disease in my particular case. The iris of both eyes was sealing down to the lenses and when the seal became complete, the aqueous fluid that passes through the pupil would have no place to go. The pressure would then build until it blew out the optic nerves.

I absorbed this new information, then asked," In other words, my lights go out – permanently."

The doctor smiled hesitantly. "I'm afraid so Mrs. Linder, unless emergency surgery is performed within a couple of hours." He looked at me steadily.

"I hope everyone in Southeast Asia knows how to do that, because that's where I'll be."

I'm not sure he was used to wisecracking Admiral's wives who were looking at total blindness. He looked serious and shook his head.

So I found myself living on the edge. But I had lived on that same edge in Europe, following Jim from port to port. The decision was made then to go ahead with my life as normally as possible, living with the chips, however they fell. Being raised in the Presbyterian philosophy, I had a strong sense of my own personal destiny and that included accepting what I could not change.

Our three days at Clark were busy, but we made time to visit Angeles, the town nearby. We walked the streets, returning the shy smiles of the Philippine people we passed. As we turned a corner, I saw a large building at the end of the street. The sign read *CALIFASIA* and in front stood a semi-trailer truck with BLOOMINGDALES printed on its side. The furniture money cache that I carried with me at all times – just in case, became warmer by the minute as I headed in a straight line for the entrance of the building. There was no discussion as to why and where I was going. BLOOMINGDALES said it all. We spent the better part of the afternoon choosing the pieces we needed and then made the necessary arrangements for shipment by boat to Taiwan. I considered it a most successful day.

Taipei

Taiwan was gray and I felt a little gray myself. The mountains wore the fog like a shroud and Quarters A was disembodied, hanging without an anchor. Tien Mou was only a suggestion of a shadow. As I turned my head to the right, two small white clouds drifted down the back yard, sailing over the pool then disappearing over the first terrace. They reminded me of cotton balls caught on the wind. Today, there was no Cultural College. As the fog had closed in, my spectacular view was gone.

This was a free day, but I was tired from the trip to the Philippines and welcomed the chance to kick back, read a book and write to the children. I missed them. It was coming onto Christmas and although we had spent other holidays apart in the past, this time I was grappling with a tangible hurt over the thought of being so far from them To me, they would always be vulnerable although in reality they were totally self-sufficient. They were born into a strange way of life that to them was normal. They bent with the wind. I took a little longer. In contrast, my childhood years were spent in one place with both parents constantly in attendance. I always felt uneasy about the life we handed our children. But they persevered, despite mountainous challenges and I knew because of that, as adults, they were stronger for it.

Jeff had written recently from Austin, Texas, where he attended the University. He assured me he was eating well, studying a great deal and getting his exercise swimming at Barton Springs, a natural fresh water stream that held great appeal to the students. I assumed they liked it for the swimming. A day later, the Armed Forces Stars and Stripes, the newspaper we received when outside of the United States, arrived and on the inside page was an article about Barton Springs in Austin. Apparently, thanks to a city ordinance or no ordinance at all, the female students had chosen the far bank to go topless. Not much was said about swimming. I cut out the article, slipped it in with my letter (and the ubiquitous monetary donation

– unasked for, I might add) and suggested that what mothers don't know was probably for the best.

The phone shrilled, breaking into my thoughts of the children.

"Mrs. Linder, it's Betty Collins." I didn't know this woman well. We had met only once, but the name was familiar. She lived near Shannon and Skip, a block from the Cultural College and taught in the American School in Tien Mou. She also taught English in a Chinese school and I admired her for her ingenuity. When I heard her message, I was stunned. With a quick and very sincere thank you, I hung up and called down for Sergeant Hsiu to bring the car to the front door as soon as possible. Within moments, he was there. I explained the call; we quickly assembled what would be necessary and headed down the vertical road, then took a left on the main road of Yangmingshan. Before the car came to a complete stop, I was out of the back seat, towels in hand and with Sergeant Hsiu helping me, we lifted the tiny body out of the watery ditch that ran by the side of the road leading to the Cultural College. There was still life in the little thing and as I held it close to my cheek and felt the soft breath, I knew it was mine forever. I had my little white dog. Someone had dumped four puppies in the benjo, which is the Chinese word for ditch and that's what she was--a benjo dog. The other puppies lay drowned in the standing water.

Later, Betty explained how, looking out her kitchen window, she saw several tiny, squirming puppies dropped near the road. To try for a rescue of her own would make her late getting to her school so she called from the Principal's office and knew I would come. On the spot, I named this wet, cold little bit of life that fit in my hand, Suzie Wong, after another survivor. Without warning, she wriggled out of the towels, landed on her four tiny feet and wobbled toward the car. Suzie preferred to ride – in a car – with a chauffeur.

She was a toy Japanese Spitz with fine, silky white fur, dainty feet, and a stub of a tail that would in time, become a fluffy plume that curled over her back. Her baby eyes were wise. She had escaped a watery death only to find herself in a nest of heaven and many times in our days together, she would get the best of me without my ever knowing what had happened. There was a permanent smile on her face and our friends, who came to the Quarters, were as charmed by her almond eyes as we were. The kitchen staff adopted her when we were off on official business. She loved the hustle of the kitchen pace and the smells of the cooking food. The guards played with her and she developed lasting friendships with certain ones. She was not only my friend and companion she became my protector. When our situation became desperate, she never left my side.

One of her favorites was 'Naldo. I'm sure he slipped her bits of food and she played him like a finely tuned piano. 'Naldo had steadily improved. We had our first dinner party for twelve and when the time came to move into the living room for coffee, I felt like it had been for forty. For his own esteem and my peace of mind, I wanted the party to be a success and as each course was served, I said a little prayer that the peanuts would be in the peanut soup and not in the Bernaise sauce. He cooked simply – my menu was tailored to his talents at that time and as we analyzed each recipe and discussed what could possibly go wrong, he finally seemed to grasp the importance of his position and became interested instead of just there.

The enlightenment of that first dinner party was something that occurred with Hogo. He had served and lived in the Quarters with Americans for twenty-three years. When I asked him to join me in the dining room to explain the table settings for the twelve dinner guests, he stood across from me on the other side of the long mahogany table. As I placed one linen and lace mat, silverware, napkin, wine and water glass and the plates that would hold the various courses, he nodded and giggled. Fifteen minutes before the guests arrived, I finished dressing and walked into the dining room for one last check. Something was not right. It took me a minute to figure out what was wrong. Everything was backwards, and because he had stood on the opposite side of the table, that's how it looked. I thought for a moment before I called him to make the changes. This was a test, my test as the hostess for these Quarters and the wife of the American Admiral. I rang the bell and he appeared.

"Good evening, Hogo. I just came in to check if all is well with dinner."

Giggle. " Yes, Missy."

"Hogo, it's not. All of the place settings on the table are backwards and I understand why there could be some confusion since you were on the opposite side of the table when I explained."

We eyed each other and I chose to be as inscrutable as he was.

" We have fifteen minutes Hogo, to change to the proper setting. Have Mama San help you, and please ask 'Naldo to come upstairs for a moment with his report on dinner."

He grinned, giggled again and called to 'Naldo to come see Missy. In a few moments, the table was perfectly set and the evening began. Later, in reviewing the successful evening, I knew I had established something with Hogo, or perhaps it was Hogo that established it with me. As long as I was here in this exotic country, I would be tested in one way or another on a daily basis

Hogo was an unknown to me. Because he was there in the Quarters, I had the opportunity to learn from him and about him. Wanting to understand the differences between West and East, I had only to observe him, yet I realized he was in the daily company of foreigners for so many years and wondered if any of our ways had become his.

They had not.

He was Chinese to the bone and a constant source of puzzlement. His story – what I could understand –- began in China when he served with the Generalissimo's Nationalist forces and in 1949, came with the Army to Taipei, leaving his wife and young sons behind. That was twenty-eight years ago. Comparing separations, his made our off and on, fifteen years apart because of Navy sea duty, look like a day at the beach. I wondered about the woman he left behind, never imagining I would find out on a very frightening day, months later. He had family in Taipei and on his day off, stayed with them. He told me of a relative who had been badly injured on the mainland during a battle. He lost his leg but held down some kind of job in spite of the disability. Hogo's life was a busy one, and I only had fragments of his history. In the end, they fit together like a jigsaw puzzle.

Once a year, Taiwan celebrates Confuscious' birthday. Prior to the day itself, the farmers begin to fatten their pigs for the competition. The heaviest sow on the island will be chosen, slaughtered, with the meat being distributed to the people. The skin will then be stretched and dried. During the auspicious celebration which includes parades of children, banners, songs, and finally, a gathering of all at the brilliantly decorated and highly ornate temple dedicated to this venerable philosopher, the pig will be brought in on a throne-like affair, carried on the shoulders of four men. Stretched and stuffed, the skin is the size of a small car.

We attended this celebration which began at seven thirty in the morning and were conducted to a fine place to observe the festivities. I noticed there were no chairs. We were to stand for the next two hours. Our places of honor were directly in front of the biggest gong I had ever seen, probably eight feet in diameter. I began my prayers. Please don't let them hit that gong.

They hit that gong - not once, but every time anything happened that needed introducing. There were many introductions that morning and I went home with a crashing headache. My ears would vibrate for the next two days. But along with the sound of the gong, was the memory of a pig the size of a car, the lovely singsong of children and white pigeons, released from their cages, soaring into a cloudless blue sky.

Jim and son Jeff at his Master's Graduation

Our daughter, Jamey

Jim and his granddaughters, Ashli and Anna

Our arrival in Taipei, Taiwan

Helen and Chris Soong, VADM Ted Snyder and the Linders

Hogo and Pat with a guard at the front gate

Julie, Pat and Mama San with The Girls

Jim with Suzie and Boom Boom

Ambassador Len Unger and Jim

Jim's Aide, Skip with Shannon and Pat

Pat and the Premier of the Republic of China

At Taroko Gorge fields of marble

Pat launching a message balloon to China

Helen Soong, far left and Queenie Yao, far right

Entrance foyer at birthday time

CHAPTER TEN
THE BAKED ALASKA

The black chicken foot stood straight up in the bowl of rice sitting in front of me. The old man across the aisle was sucking noisily on the chicken's other foot and he gave me a grin when he saw I had one, too. He had no teeth. .

"I can't do this, Jean. I've eaten a lot of strange things since I came here, but this is not going down on the list." It was the Iowa in me and I knew where those feet had been –padding around a chicken yard, picking up God knows what.

"But this is special and they'll be offended if you don't."

"Can't help it, my dear. I'll explain on our way home."

"All right then, pass it to me under the table."

I waited for the right moment when everybody's nose was buried in their rice bowls and slipped the foot into her hand. She sucked on it with obvious enjoyment, but not once did I wonder what I had missed.

Jean was a very special Chinese friend whose husband was in no way connected with the government or the military, so our friendship was on a different level. She was an elegant woman, highly intelligent and knowledgeable about objects of art. She mentioned once she had been approached to join Sothebys of London as an appraiser. We met as often as we could and she provided me with days that taught me things I wanted to know about this ancient culture.

This day found us in the outdoor Taipei market downtown. Under umbrellas, it was chaotic as women and men alike assessed, selected and argued over the price of something that they wanted to take home to their table. Drawn ducks and chickens hung from hooks, yellow in color – the longer they hung, the better they were. Fish were everywhere. There was every size from the tiniest to ones that looked like they could feed a family of twelve for a week. I was not fond of fish – the only kind I knew was the river catfish that twisted along the bottom of Iowa streams. The meat was sweet, white and tender and dredged in corn meal and fried in a hot cast iron skillet, those catfish were legendary.

Slabs of pork hung, slowly twisting as flies covered everything. The vegetables were scattered throughout and there wasn't time to see it all. After Jean made her purchases, we decided on lunch in a typical working man's restaurant nearby. This is how I liked it. We had "done lunch at the Ritz" and it was dazzling, but this held a different kind of promise.

We entered a narrow, long building with wallpaper that was no longer interested in adhering to anything, bare light bulbs and tables covered with oilcloth. At the door, a medium-aged woman met us and smiling broadly, proudly escorted us to stairs at the back of the room.

We were not dressed like the others and I felt eyes following us as we made our way upstairs. Everyone was bent over a bowl of rice. We found a table, sat down and immediately a bowl of what looked like water was placed in front of us. It was some kind of broth, chicken perhaps, but very thin. I was enjoying this whole thing. At last, I was seeing another kind of China. These were working people, taking a few minutes to put food in their stomachs before returning to their jobs. For many, their bowl of rice was their only meal of the day. I am not sure just what I ordered but after pulling the old "under the table chicken foot switch", the meal lasted as long as the foot had anything left on it. I worked away at the rice and wondered how late they served lunch at The Ritz. Of course the old man with no teeth witnessed the switch and grinned his vacant grin as we left our table. I tilted my head, shrugged my shoulders and gave him a wry smile. He laughed.

We had counterparts. Or perhaps we were their counterparts. They were high-ranking Army and Navy officials and our lives became woven together through our social activities. Of course Jim met often with the men in an official capacity and I occasionally lunched with the ladies, but our evenings found us on our way down the mountain to dinner parties many nights a week. This was not always easy for me. I am a solitary person who cherished time to myself and there was little of that.

Yet, these people charmed me. There was an unending graciousness that kept me at ease and made my attempts at the language and customs less of a struggle. I assumed there were comparisons made. Many American wives were on this island and the previous TDC Commanders' wives had come and gone, much as I would. The Chinese word for wife is tai tai, thus making me Linder Tai Tai. I often wondered how I measured up.

At the dinner parties, we always arrived promptly at seven. Our first one found me being tested again, this time by Jim's driver, Sergeant Fan. He was related to Hogo, but how closely, I did not know. When we pulled up in front of the building with the awning, Sergeant Fan cut the engine, jumped out, ran around the car and opened Jim's car door and waited for him to get out. Then he shut the door, walked around the car, opened his door in front and got in, leaving me cooling my heels in the back seat. I let myself out, decided I did not like Sergeant Fan and walked alone around the car to join Jim. He was being greeted and had not noticed the slight. I was not sure Sergeant Fan understood English, but somebody made the point for me, because it never happened again. Frankly, I was instinctively afraid of Sergeant Fan and had as little to do with him as possible.

Once inside, we were greeted by a receiving line, with the Chinese ladies in their ch'i p'aos, the Mandarin style – floor length, high collars and side splits on the skirts. They stood beside their husbands, ramrod straight, as they had at the airport when we arrived for the first time. Yet, with the ch'i p'ao's slim sheath of brocade, they were nothing but very feminine.

There was always a small glass of orange juice (I drank a lot of orange juice) and fifteen minutes later, on the dot, we moved into the dining area which contained a round table with a smaller movable one on top. In our country, we call them "lazy susans". Here, they were the only types of table used and once I attended a Chinese dinner, the reason was apparent. Courses were brought in and placed on the turntable. Then, in my case, the host for the evening filled my small plate with chopsticks flashing and the meal began. Sometimes there were fifteen or sixteen courses— once, I counted twenty-two with most of them meat in one form or another. The small wineglass in front of me was filled and kept filled with hsiao hsing, a delightfully light white wine that seemed to compliment every course.

There were toasts. Everyone was toasted and quite a few who were no longer there – in body or spirit. I learned to leave a bite or two so the tiny plate would not be filled again and barely sip the wine. One of our hosts had been so taken with my performance at the President's dinner when I had my first sip of Ksaolien brandy, that he had a small, exquisitely carved table placed beside and slightly behind my chair. On it rested a single bottle of that demon brew, should I desire it. I did not.

The food was unlike any I had ever eaten and once I learned not to ask what it was, it became addictive. My favorite of all dishes was minced pigeon served in small pancakes. The seasoning was unusual and I hoped for it with each dinner party. Always, there was a great fish, called the Yellow Fish, and I simply did not like it. It's large eye remained fixed on me as it twirled around the table, and as the chopsticks pulled chunks from its body, I waited for it to close in pain. Something called Drunken Shrimp had live shrimp jumping out of the hot oil as they cooked. It was a kind of culinary hot foot – big time.

Our second and much larger dinner party was coming up and I spent many hours with 'Naldo, going over the menu and explaining how things should look. When he was awake, his retention rate was marginal. Since I was not allowed in the kitchens at night because of the accumulation of guards, guns, the whole staff and the busyness of the place – it had been decided I would be in the way, I could only pray he would remember the most important things. The food was simple, good American fare with five courses, the last being Baked Alaska.

Once again, Hogo and I eyed each other across the table and I knew he would make no mistakes this time, after the table-setting fiasco. The linens were crisp and white and everything that could be polished had been polished. The mushrooms were carefully harvested off the wall and the dining room looked inviting with candlelight, crystal that sparkled and bowls of fresh flowers from Papa San's garden. I was pleased with the results and silently crossed my fingers.

A few years before, one of the galley stewards on Jim's ship showed me an ingenious way to make Baked Alaska. By imbedding the halved eggshells in the white meringue that covered the ice cream, little cups were created to hold the brandy for lighting. I carefully explained this to 'Naldo; we did one to make sure he knew what to do, then after it came out of the oven, perfectly browned, the brandy was poured (in one egg-shell cup, since this was a dress rehearsal), lighted—and we had a perfect Alaska. He followed me carefully as we went through each step and I actually felt confidant that at least the Baked Alaska would make it to the table intact.

The dinner went well. The soup was warm instead of hot, the roasts seemed a little dry, but no one minded. They knew this was our first attempt at feeding thirty people. But the dessert stole the show. After all the food had been served then removed, 'Naldo headed for the pantry to take down the bottle of Couvoisier brandy and prepare for the grand presentation. He was to open the pantry door, light the brandy and present the flaming dessert to the dining room.

Somewhere in between lunch and dinner, 'Naldo had discovered the delights of a good French brandy and when the time came to fill the little egg shell cups, the French brandy was in 'Naldo. All that was left was a bottle of Kaolien that went into the little cups. He then pushed the door open with his backside, ignited the Kaolien brandy with a match and the Baked Alaska exploded all over one end of the dining room. There was a hushed silence as vanilla ice cream, yellow cake and egg whites hit the walls and either hung there or slowly slid down to puddle on the floor. A bleary-eyed 'Naldo gazed solemnly at the mess, hiccuped and fled down the stairs to the kitchens below.

I rose to my feet, wiped a bit of meringue off my left sleeve and said, "Shall we move into the living room for coffee and check ourselves for meringue?"

Hogo was giggling non-stop and I wasn't sure he could manage the trays. I took one more look at the carnage and began to laugh. It was simply too much like an old Laurel and Hardy movie routine to do anything else. We all laughed and over coffee, stories were told of similar or worse experiences the ladies had lived through with their servants. It was a successful evening, relaxed and warm. I certainly was no threat to anyone as a hostess and seemed destined to provide interesting entertainment for dinner parties. The lichi nut episode at the President's house flashed across my thoughts and I could tell others were thinking the same thing. We grinned at each other and from that night on, I sensed a protective attitude towards me at the parties that we attended. This little twit needs all the help she can get.

I noticed one evening that the General seated next to me at a Chinese dinner party was drinking what looked like wine, but was actually very weak tea.

"General Wu, your wine is a shade darker than mine. Are there different varieties of hsaio hsing?"

"Ah, Linder Tai Tai, you have found me out. I will confess to you, but you must promise to keep my secret."

Of course I promised. Keeping a secret about the different color of a glass of wine did not appear to be much of a challenge.

"My doctor has advised me not to drink any more wine. It is not good for my liver. But I have made my wife my *dai byou* so she drinks for me. This way, we both drink to toasts, but I only drink tea."

I wondered about his wife's liver.

Another friend invited us for dinner not long afterward and the first course was bird's nest soup, but she hurriedly explained that the nests were washed and cleaned for days before making the soup. It is a very lengthy and complicated procedure and there would be no declining because of the cost of the dish. Damn that chicken yard. But I did what I had learned to do – concentrate on the conversation or the Chinese vases or the priceless scrolls on the walls and spoon it down. It was delicious and I felt honored to receive such a dish Later, I wondered if the little nests had been imported from the Mainland. Even though there was supposedly no contact with the communists, I was learning of a sub-culture of exchange in food and the art world. Some things were found only on the Mainland and occasionally on a dinner table, there were foods that came from far-western provinces. One such dish was tiny oysters half the size of my little fingernail. Being instructed to eat shell and all, I did and became intimately acquainted with the East Asian Confuscious' Revenge, the counterpart of Mexico's Montezuma's Revenge.

My alimentary canal was in a state of shock most of the time and when the stomachaches returned, despite my efforts to avoid MSG, I resignedly made another trip to the Dispensary. It had recently been discovered that there was plaster of Paris in the tofu that was often on the menu. Plaster of Paris meant the cook could shape the tofu into any design – vegetables, fruit, flowers – whatever fantasy occurred to their nimble fingers and while the results were sometimes astounding, what the tofu did to one's stomach was equally arresting. That, on top of the Boraxo the street noodle peddlers put into their noodles to make them whiter, convinced this Midwesterner there's no place like home – at least at mealtimes.

Throughout this culinary treat time, I was studying the Chinese language. Jim's office had made the appropriate inquiries and Sergeant Hsiu and I motored down the mountain once a week for an hour's lesson. It was difficult, challenging and maddening. I discovered I was a mimic. I could say almost anything and sound exactly like the Chinese, but I hadn't the faintest idea of what I said. Obviously, this could lead to any number of complications, so I studied hard. There was a problem. My teachers were different each time – all young people who spoke some English and wanted very much to find someone to practice on. I was a likely candidate because I found them engaging and a wonderful source of information about China.

We sat facing each other across a small table, language book between us. She had a delicate, flowerlike face with a small mouth and straight, black hair. We practiced words for a while, discussed (in English) the lesson and finally, I asked, "Carey, where do you live?"

"I come from Ma Ping."

"Ma Ping? I haven't heard of that place. Is it a suburb of Taipei?"

"Oh no, Linder Tai Tai. Is part of Beijing."

I studied this lovely child, guessing her to be twenty or twenty-two years old at the most, and knew that she had been born here on Taiwan, not on the Mainland. She was not old enough to have come in 1949 and the hostilities between the two countries made it impossible for people to travel back and forth.

"But Carey, how could you be from Ma Ping? You're not old enough."

"Oh Linder Tai Tai, my ancestors are there and so that is where I come from." Her face was a study in earnest pride. It was a lesson in single mindedness. These people who came from the Mainland to Taiwan were Chinese, not Taiwanese. Their ancestors belonged to the land that had known civilized culture for 5,000 years and in a sense, they had never left. There was pride in Carey's voice as she told me what the town of Ma Ping looked like, who her neighbors were, how the streets ran with water during hard storms. Her family taught her that Ma Ping was home and one day, they would all return to see those neighbors and visit the graves of their ancestors.

I knew that when Chiang Kai-shek brought his army to Taiwan, the goal was to return to the Mainland and if necessary, take China by force from the communists. The army trained constantly and became a strong army, dedicated and willing to sacrifice anything to regain their country. That training had lasted nearly thirty years with no battles to fight. Jim and I talked about their methods of training and the commitment they had to that single idea. My friend Jean taught me that China was the center of the Universe – had always been in every Chinese mind. Nothing was taken for granted here. These were essentially dispossessed people who had come as refugees and stayed to rebuild their strength and determination. How different from my own countrymen with their casual acceptance of the bounties their country provides.

He was a studious looking young man. His black suit was brushed, his shirt pressed and his glasses were firmly planted on the bridge of his nose. His eyes matched his black hair. We went through the motions of repeating the lesson and when he said a word I was not sure of, I replied, "Dzai shwo?" This is the phrase that means literally in English, "Say again?" I said it a lot.

He cleared up the point, then in precise and formal English said, "Linder Tai Tai, I am most interested in the manner in which a student in the United States attends college. I hope you could tell me of the classes and how they are taught. I wish to compare them to our classes in our Universities."

This began a lively discussion of the differences in institutions of higher learning (and gave him a chance to practice his English).

"Alex, depending on the degree you're interested in, a typical college course presents lectures, study from books, research in libraries, tests and examinations and often these examinations not only ask what the student has learned, but how he feels about it. That's called an essay question."

It was like turning on a light. He answered carefully, telling me that in China, knowledge is taught by memorization and then examinations to find out how much you can remember, with very little if any, opinions or philosophical thoughts. There were close to one hundred universities and colleges on Taiwan at that time but many young people were sent to the United States to be college educated. I am sure things have changed in the twenty-year interim, but this young man was hungry to express an opinion.

As the discussion flew in many directions, he made comparisons between Americans and Chinese.

"Even our faces are different from the people in your country, Linder Tai Tai, though it's sometimes hard to tell because all Americans look alike."

For a moment, I was speechless.

"But Alex, many Americans think all Chinese look alike."

"Oh, no. It's the other way around "

"Alex, you must be pulling my leg."

He looked stricken, horrified and I realized this was one phrase he had never heard before.

"Linder Tai Tai, I would never do that. I respect you and would never do such a thing."

"Alex, don't panic. I merely used a cliché you have never heard before." The explanation followed, clearing up the point of my leg being pulled and we talked about American humor.

"It is sometimes very difficult for Chinese to understand the humor of your country. We have one of your television programs that is humorous, but I don't understand why."

"Are you talking about "The Love Boat?" It was the only American program on Chinese television and it was chilling to think the Chinese were judging Americans by that program alone.

"Yes, Linder Tai Tai and is sometimes very hard to understand."

"Alex, I'm an American and I have that same problem. But don't judge us by that one program. It's what we call a "sit com", meaning "situation comedy." This began another lengthy discussion and we had gone long past our hour's time, but I wanted to pursue the point he made about Americans looking alike.

"Alex, when you say Americans look alike, what about their blond hair or brown, or red? And some have blue eyes, some brown or gray? Don't you see those differences? "

"No. Is hair different colors?"

"Yes Alex, and I'll make a deal with you. You begin to notice the differences between the Americans you see on Taiwan and I will try to identify what part of China the people I see come from. Deal?"

He grinned. That was a word he knew. "Deal."

Good lesson

CHAPTER ELEVEN
RENEE AND THE ROAST PIG

Our marriage was assuming a one-dimensional quality. We arose at seven, shared breakfast on the porch under the bugged fan while being waited on carefully by Hogo, then Jim left for his office and I prepared for my day. At six o'clock, Jim returned, we talked briefly about totally inconsequential things, dressed and departed for the long drive down the mountain to the dinner party of the evening. There was little or no conversation in the car, going or coming because Sergeant Fan understood English. Back at the Quarters, our chats were minimal and we retired for the night and started all over again the next morning. Boring.

On the few off nights we were home, we sat by the pool and in lowered voices, tried to communicate. Hogo was usually in attendance and we never wanted for anything but privacy. I was becoming impatient to be able to just talk to my husband about whatever came into my mind. He felt the tension and told me he was planning to do something to alleviate the situation, but he didn't tell me what.

Suzie was growing, fattening and promising to be an enchanting dog. Were it not for this little creature, the term stir crazy was appropriate to my lifestyle and the monitors of the fan bugs were probably mystified about my conversations with her. She was on friendly terms with the guards although not all of them pleased her. She slept in front of the French doors in our bedroom that opened onto the back lawn and sometimes in the night, I would hear a low growl as one of the men passed our door. One, she disliked intensely and would not go down into the kitchen when he was there for his meal. When he approached her outside, she bared her teeth. Some of these people ate dog meat and white dogs were a delicacy. At the time of Chinese New Year, we were advised to keep our dog inside or she would disappear into someone's stew pot. The guard may have had his eye on Suzie for his New Year's dinner – eating white dog meat was a guarantee for good fortune. Whatever the reason, she watched him closely.

So did I.

It was Sunday and Jim had bowed out of the ubiquitous golf game. I was delighted to have him home, but wondered how we would spend the time together. 'Naldo was providing our dinner, but everyone else was off for the day, including Sergeant Hsiu. If we were just staying home, it would be very quiet.

"How do you feel about taking the Seville out for a drive?" He had only driven it once since we arrived on the island and this seemed the perfect day to leave the Quarters and see some of the countryside.

We left by the front doors, walked around the house and down the steep driveway to the garage below. The guards watched our exit and when he backed the car around and went through the gates, they saluted. Jim acknowledged. We coasted down the vertical road to Yangmingshan with the intent of heading north, up the mountain. Waiting for us at the bottom of our road were two motorcycles that fell in behind us and sedately followed as we started up the mountain road. The guards had called the barracks and in the short time it took us to drive down the hill, the motorcycles were manned and ready to follow. No matter where we went, we would not be alone.

Walking up the mountain were young couples, picnic baskets in hand. I had heard of a beautiful park somewhere ahead and began to search my memory about festivals. Jim pulled over to the side and stopped to watch the procession. It was the Mid-autumn Festival and one that had great meaning for couples with marriage in their future.

They were young, dressed simply and quiet in their manner with a seriousness about their pilgrimage, as though the day would guarantee them happiness in their futures together. The symbol for this festival was the full moon with its circle of light representing the unbroken continuity of a marriage.

Finding the traffic too dense we decided to return to the Quarters, motorcycles trailing and I was depressed our afternoon together had ended so quickly.

We had neighbors across our little road. I noticed their home every time I left the Quarters. It was an Ambassador's residence and this couple with the name of Praetorius came from Praetoria, South Africa. The United States did not have diplomatic relations with that country because of apartheid, but they were our neighbors and although political philosophies created a problem in the circle of official socializing, it made no difference in our friendship.

Renee Praetorius was a tall, striking woman with dark hair and a penache that indicated travel and taste. I was intimidated until she unleashed her grin and we became good friends. Her husband Bill was a stocky man with an equally engaging smile and a florid complexion. We constantly worried about his blood pressure.

Bill insisted the name Preaetorius in Pratoria, was like Smith in the U.S. but there was nothing ordinary about this couple and their home To walk into Renee's long, airy dining room was to catch your breath, for everything there complimented the rest. She was hostess to many memorable dinner parties and I envied her for her chef – this was no mere cook. Occasionally at the end of a perfect evening, he would enter with a soaring chef's hat and a spotless white nearly floor-length apron to receive his compliments.

My first view of their home came the day after our tumultuous arrival, when I looked across the road and saw their uprooted trees in a tangle. The typhoon was particularly vicious on our mountain and they lost many of the big trees. It was one of their clay roof tiles that had blown into and broken our guest room window. This Sunday afternoon, after our aborted drive in the country, we called them to join us for a swim.

Renee did not care to swim, so the men splashed around, while we chatted. I told her of the debacle with the Baked Alaska and her eyes lighted up.

"My dear, do you want to hear the granddaddy of all chef stories? It's true and it happened to us."

The dripping men had joined us, and I said, "Of course I do. Is this going to take the edge off of my Alaska episode?"

"It will totally eclipse it."

Bill and Renee had been posted to the Belgian Congo early in his career and after arriving at the Quarters they would occupy, they settled in.

Soon, Renee was planning her first party. Somehow, a pig was located and she met in the kitchen with their Watusi native who cooked and served the meals. He measured a few inches over seven feet tall and his name was George.

Renee explained her instructions to this warrior. "George, after the whole pig is roasted, I want you to move it onto a silver platter, place an apple in its mouth and parsley in its ears, then carry the platter into the dining room and walk around the table for the guests to admire." Apparently, George agreed. "Then, you return to the kitchen and serve the plates there."

All went well for the first two courses – the soup was smooth and the fish perfectly grilled. When entrée time approached, George threw open the kitchen swinging door and appeared, all seven feet of him, holding the silver tray with the roast pig. But George had the apple in his mouth and the parsley in his ears. There had been a problem with translation.

"The silence was deafening. I could feel the blood drain out of my face and Bill's just got redder. George marched solemnly in his bare feet around the table, white teeth firmly clamped on that apple, with ears that looked like he was growing grass and disappeared into the kitchen."

I was having trouble containing myself and finally erupted with laughter.

Bill said, "Everyone's reaction, exactly." They both had been schooled in the British Isles and to hear this story in that particular accent only made it more hilarious.

Renee giggled. "Sometime later, the story appeared in Readers Digest. Friends of ours sent it to us and a member of the Embassy who was present at George's debut, told the story at a party in Madagascar. Someone must have sent it in to Readers Digest."

I could see Renee was enjoying the memory of it and my experience seemed tame in comparison. She was intrigued though, by the mushrooms on the dining room wall and we strolled into the house to examine our crop. She was not too interested in sharing the bounty.

As the men returned to the pool for another swim, Renee and I walked down the long slick hallway to our sitting room. As she reminisced about their experiences in the Congo, a shadow fell across her face. She quietly said, "The natives stormed our quarters and Bill and I had to run. We survived in the bush until we could get to safety. We lived through it, but it was a terrible time."

She talked sadly of the experience, then we went on to other subjects. This had been happening to women all over the world for centuries. But to see this elegant, poised and polished woman of such refinement talk of the horrors she lived through in the African bush country, made me realize the fearsome possibilities that anyone who serves in a foreign country is subject to. You are more than a tourist, you are the representatives of a government not always in favor. You are the tool insurgents or unhappy, dissatisfied people use to bring attention to their causes. You are there for the angry and fanatic and you are completely vulnerable. This was yet ahead for me, but it would happen.

Renee's story prompted other thoughts that evening as we sat reading in the library after one of Renaldo's unmemorable meals. Her accounting of their experience was in the privacy of our sitting room, so I chose to keep her counsel. Instead, I thought about the intense interest the Chinese seemed to have in children. As soon as we arrived, one of the first questions I was asked was about our children and how many there were. I happily answered their questions. By bringing Jamey and Jeff into the conversation, they seemed closer to me. They were never far out of my thoughts, but talking about them was a luxury.

To the Chinese, their children are their wealth. They are never taken for granted and although discipline is their first rule, their second is love of family. I had learned that from Carey who was convinced she would someday return to the Mainland to rejoin her family and neighbors. From Alex came the lesson of discipline without question. They grew up in a strictly controlled atmosphere and their seriousness was more than an unsmiling face.

At the language school, there were Chinese and Taiwanese, all ages, learning to speak and write calligraphy. One student was a woman in her eighties. She was studying Mandarin Chinese, the language she learned as a child when she lived on the Mainland. As the saying goes, *knowledge is power* and these people used their study to satisfy that craving.

Once a year, on the tenth day of the tenth month, October, the Chinese celebrate their Independence Day. *Double Ten* is marked by more than a week of celebration. We have our Fourth of July and they have their *Double Ten*. It commemorates the founding fathers of the Republic of China. For someone from the western part of the world, this provides a perfect time to see the many faces of Chinese culture. It's a joyous time with parties and dragon dances in the streets. With a renewal of commitment, the military parades not only have acres of marching soldiers and young women with banners and bright uniforms, but the weapons of war; tanks and guns. This was a country that was ready for anything. These were trained men, purposeful, dedicated and the product of strong leadership. And the threat was only miles away.

The finale to this week of celebration was a night of fireworks. Because they had invented the spectacular sport, their display overshadowed all others we had ever seen. We were led to an area on a flat piece of ground where a man sat at what looked like a giant organ. On a given signal, he began to play, but instead of music, the heavens lit up with great bursts of light. Brightly colored flowers unfolded against a black sky and shafts of silver and gold soared upward. Every conceivable shape and form in all the colors of the rainbow filled the night. It was awesome. The sequence had the elegance of oriental art but with the underlying feeling of force. It could have been a battlefield.

Thanksgiving was a few weeks off and I felt a little bereft. I tried not to dwell on our children and these holidays we had shared for so many years. They each had a special day planned, either in a friend's home or in Jamey's case, with her own children and a nearby family.

"Mrs. Linder, the Admiral and I have been working on something we think you might like." It was Skip, from TDC Headquarters "He wants to take you to the National Palace Museum Thanksgiving Day, if you don't have anything else on your calendar."

I had nothing on my calendar, and if I had, it was off, now.

"Wonderful. I can hardly wait and I'll bet you had a lot to do with it. By the way, I'm giving a luncheon up here next week and have asked 'Naldo to plan on fixing popovers. Any suggestions I can pass along to him?"

"Tell him to use both hands. But don't worry, I'll come up before and make sure he knows what he's doing."

Skip was an excellent cook, loved puttering in the kitchen and turned out wonderful dishes. He had been a godsend with 'Naldo. With his height and football-player build, he had only to make a suggestion once and it was done. But 'Naldo recognized he knew something about cooking and motivation was born. The preparation of Chinese food fascinated Skip and I knew that by the time he left for the States, he would be able to present a perfect Lemon Chicken in caramelized sauce.

Sergeant Hsiu was waiting by the car door and in a matter of minutes, he pulled up in front of the majestic Museum buildings with fountains, a long circular drive and terracing. The Museum itself was pristine white and light blue. Tilt-tipped roofs were edged with gold scrollwork. Sister buildings in the same architectural style and color stood on either side on the immense acreage. The mountainside was the backdrop and today, soft, wispy clouds drifted across its face. It was a work of art in itself.

We walked up the long flight of steps and waiting for us was the director and his staff. Introductions followed, then we were ushered into the building. I caught my breath. Everywhere I looked, was beauty. This was a formal tour, so we were assigned a guide, a tall, serious young man wearing glasses. His name was Thomas. After the introductions and small talk, he escorted us into the first room and I was lost for the rest of the afternoon. Scrolls, bronzes, porcelains, paintings, jades, all there to be studied and learned about. I would know China better this way than through any dusty book on politics or history.

I stopped in front of a scroll entitled, "Fei Chen-o's Killing of a Tiger." A tall, slender dark-haired lady of great beauty was walking toward a man (the Tiger) sprawled on a bed, sleeping off a night of too much of everything. In her hand, she held a long, thin dagger and eventually, it would end up in the "Tiger's" throat. The colors were black, white and gray, with curtains of yellow/gold and tiny touches of brilliant red. One small round bonsai pot of a jewel-like turquoise graced a corner. It was riveting. The story was clear and the colors were pure. Thomas noticed my admiration and offered to escort me whenever I found time to visit the Museum and wished assistance. Time permitting, this is where I wanted to be.

Several days later, my fingers went numb and tingled at the tips. A terrible headache and finally, a constant pain in my belly sent me to the clicking telephone to call and talk with Dr. Jim Ling, the head of the U.S. Military Dispensary. He advised me to come immediately and Sergeant Hsiu with concern on his quiet face drove me there.

It was a quick diagnosis.

I had acute MSG poisoning and Jim would probably have it, too. We had not been in this country long enough to build up an immunity and with our dinner and luncheon schedules, we were receiving liberal doses of the white powder daily. Dr. Ling gave me a prescription and told me to do my best to avoid the lethal powder, beginning at home. There was nothing

I could do about the official parties – what was served was what I ate – but at least I could police the Quarters' kitchens again and find out what was being put in our food. I had been told of the lard and MSG, but nobody said it was poisonous.

The rest of my day was open because of the trip to the doctor, so I rested, took the medicine and when the symptoms began to abate, I felt my way down the stairs to the kitchens below. It was afternoon, the guards had gone back to their posts after lunch. Hogo was in his room by the garage and Mama San was in her little laundry room, watching Chinese television while she ironed. 'Naldo was nowhere to be seen – probably asleep under a bush. I explored and quickly found a large pot the size of a soup cauldron full of white powder. Feeling like a police detective, I touched, then tasted. Having never tasted straight MSG before, I had nothing to compare it to, but I couldn't resist playing Sam Spade, even with a lingering stomach-ache. Mama San found me poking around in her domain. With hand gestures, I pointed to the powder, held my poor aching stomach, clasped my pounding head and finally, shook my hands and said, "Mama San, I sick. MSG. Bad stuff. No more in food." Fingers to mouth like eating and face screwed up in pain. It was quite a performance.

She watched, entranced and said, "Okay."

The following week, the Ambassador's wife, Anne Unger, invited me to attend a Chinese cooking class downtown at the YWCA. With the good Sergeant Hsiu at the wheel, we stopped at a stop sign and while waiting for the light to turn green; I looked idly out my window at the myriad shops that line Chung San North. For some, it was impossible to know what they sold. Their signs were in calligraphy and nothing appeared in the windows to identify the merchandise. But next to the corner was a larger store with a sign three feet high and running the length of the building. It read: V. D. Clinic and I realized this was the Chinese way of treating a whispered-about or ignored subject in our own country. They advertised. A few months later, as I sat waiting at the same stop sign, the sign now read: ViDal Sassoon Barber Shop. Waste not, want not – that "V.D.." came in handy. I could only ponder if the Clinic had run out of patients or just moved to a new location.

The cooking class was a one-day affair and there was a lot to be learned. Thirty of us sat on graduated seats, looking down on a very long table with a sink on either end. In front of each sink, stood a young Chinese girl. In the middle, stood a tiny woman of indeterminate years with a wok-style pan, a pair of chopsticks and a large spoon. Everything else was food to be prepared. In three hours, she cooked and served thirty people six courses, explaining in excellent English as she worked each step and something about the food itself. Chicken, pork, beef, shrimp and lobster were given exotic sauces and crisp vegetables as their complements. The girls at the ends of the counter were the clean-ups.

When the time came to toss in the MSG powder, she explained a little of its history. Originally, MSG came from the lotus root and would in no way be harmful to the digestion. But the Chinese discovered another and more lucrative use of the organic root and produced instead, a chemical replacement, which could have severe and painful effects on anyone not used to it. I knew all about that.

The food was delicious and I nibbled at it, trying to sidestep the tingling fingers that always served as a warning. The preparation had looked so easy. But after all, it only took three people three hours to do. What I remembered from the jumble of foodstuffs, the pouring of oil and the flashing of chopsticks was – you can fashion tofu into any conceivable shape from pork chops to rosebuds and sometimes, as one of the mysteries of the Orient, cornstarch will not thicken for the chowder. That bit of information was delivered like a "Confuscius say" and I never doubted it for a moment.

We simply ate less of everything, for Jim had developed the same symptoms, but not as severely. His twenty-eight years on ships had guaranteed him a cast-iron stomach and until the doctor lowered the cholesterol boom, he ate whatever was put in front of him. I marched down the steps one more time to remove the large pan of congealed lard that lubricated everything we ate and we began a slow, but steady recovery.

One thing that abounds in this part of the world is the parasite. Taipei had a Naval Research Unit and the officer-in-charge invited us to visit his laboratory. I had no idea what I was getting into and should possibly have inquired, since my stomach was still slightly queasy. But on our first free morning, I joined Jim at the Compound for our trip into the bowels of Taipei to make our call. I remember jars; little jars, big jars, jars of unusual shapes and all filled with completely unrecognizable and disgusting-looking things. Kurt Sorenson, the director of the Research Unit, explained these were parasites that had been removed from peoples' innards and in some cases, the innards themselves. Some were several feet long and looked like what they had been – living organisms until they were removed and placed in these jars for posterity (and this unsuspecting Admiral's wife). My stomach began to churn.

"I would like a promise from you both that you will stay away from sushi and any kind of rare meat." Kurt spoke seriously and after what we had seen, there was no doubt in my mind that I would obey him to the letter.

"Kurt, is this sort of thing more prevalent here than in other places?" Jim was very interested in what he was seeing. I made a mental note to ask him if any of his people had dealt with it aboard ship in the Mediterranean area.

"Actually, no. The waters and the land have become so polluted worldwide, the problem exists almost everywhere. These creatures are unwittingly consumed and begin their life growth where they shouldn't be."

I vowed on the spot that even if it caused an international incident, I would never eat sushi or rare meat again. My stomach continued to churn.

"Remember that Sunday in Washington, DC, when we took the children to the Army Medical Museum after church?" Jim grinned as he said it and I felt a chill go down my back. A friend had made the recommendation and the children seemed interested. They thought the two-headed things in jars were "neat" but I only lasted twenty minutes. And here we were again, staring at the indescribable.

We went next to the snake room and I fervently wished to be home with a good book. Yet, it was interesting and after I learned the story about Taiwan, the island of snakes, and how it came to be that way, my respect for these people who live today with another nation's cruelty, increased. The Japanese had occupied the island for fifty years, having taken Taiwan and the P'enghu Islands from the Chinese in 1895. At the end of World War II in 1945, the Japanesee were forced to give Taiwan and the P'enghus back to the Chinese, but before leaving, they delivered their final cruelty to the Taiwanese people who had never ceased their resistance to Japanese occupation. Poisonous snakes were released throughout the island and over the years, proliferated and here they were – in more jars – a testament to man's inhumanity to man. I had heard a sketchy account of this history when we first arrived and I noticed the snake chart on the back of our bedroom door, but this was reality and there would be no more walks in Papa San's flower garden.

The other side of the snake coin could be found in downtown Taipei's Snake Alley. Typical of the enterprising and practical Chinese, poisonous snakes were gathered up and sold. There were baskets of the writhing creatures waiting for selection on a busy side street. The custom was to pick out your snake, pay the vendor, then he took it from there. The snake was held up for the customer's inspection, slit with a sharp knife the length of its belly and the bile was gathered in a cup. Something was mixed with it; perhaps hsaio hsing wine or Kaolien brandy and on the spot, consumed by the customer. Since this was hearsay and told to me in great detail, I can only imagine the scene. But the aphrodisiac effects of the potion guaranteed a thriving and lucrative business, at the same time, ridding the Island of at least a portion of the snake population. Not too different from the chef's knives from Kinman.

I was greatly relieved when we said goodbye to Kurt and his bottles. An American luncheon was scheduled for the next week and I planned to check out the menu very carefully. Even cooked, I no longer had any interest in clams, oysters or shrimp. In time, my knee-jerk reaction might fade a little, but the image of those bottled creatures still haunts me.

The Wives' luncheon entertainment for the afternoon was Chinese music and my first exposure to this art form. We had attended the Chinese operas, but this was a small group of women, playing various instruments and since I had read that only in Taiwan women are taught to sing in voices that resemble musical instruments, the program promised to be interesting. I did not realize it would also be funny in a macabre sort of way. To the American ear, female Chinese singers sound somewhat like bagpipes. But in Taiwan, the art of this type of music, is the last true example in all of China.

After our lunch, about ten Taiwanese ladies in traditional long dress costume, came into the dining room and gracefully seated themselves on the floor, each holding the musical instrument she played. Some held long flutes traditionally, as we know it in our country. One was played like a clarinet. The stringed instruments resembled a Russian balalaika, and a small lady with bent head, played on something that looked like a banjo.

A man with a long stick entered last and took his place behind the group on the floor. With a thump of the stick as a signal, the music began and at first it sounded like an orchestra, tuning up. Nothing matched. Suddenly, the man reached over the group and smacked one of the players on the head with his stick. She winced, tucked her head down and continued playing. I was so startled, I simply watched. Again, he smacked another and her reaction was the same. We realized that as the players made mistakes, he used the stick. He resembled someone playing a xylophone and for a moment, it was hilarious, but as women, we were appalled that this man could hit these ladies on their heads; yet this was China and they did things differently here. Talk about harassment in the workplace.

When it was over, the players got to their feet. The man came around them, stood dead center and bowed. My inclination was to take aim with my piece of pound cake. But discretion overcame me and I merely applauded like all the rest, if only to let the ladies with their sore heads know how much we appreciated both their musical talent and their monumental patience with their insufferable conductor. However, that afternoon became a hot topic of conversation among the wives for a long time.

CHAPTER TWELVE
SLAKE SOUP, HEN HAU

The days folded into each other. The routine was set and I complied, sometimes chafing at the sameness of it, but more often, trying to extract anything new that would help me to understand this country and its people. A trip to southern Taiwan was laid on. We would fly down in the Blue Goose and inspect the industrial part of the Island. Not that Taipei was without industry. The yellow, brown haze of pollution confirmed that. But southern Taiwan, particularly the Kaoshung area, held the heavy -duty realities of a country in a defensive mode. Steel mills, petroleum - cracking plants, cement factories and shipbuilding were there to inspect. With hard hats and comfortable shoes, we covered the waterfront.

I had not counted on the pollution. Assuming the air would be clean from the ocean winds, I was unprepared for the murk that greeted us as we stepped off the plane. The smog was a combination of the many industries' effluents and I realized this would be a long three days. But we were here, with people to meet and places to go. Good friends, Queenie and General C. Y. Yao, accompanied us on the trip. Queenie as the Executive Assistant to a high ranking official in the Koumintang, would be showing us the Export Zone.

Touring the shipyards, I was shocked when I saw the size of the oil tankers being built. "How long are those monsters, Skip?"

"I would estimate them at about one and a half times a football field." He should know. Skip was a football player from college days. "They carry a crew of only seventeen people to man them."

"Seventeen people? Are you serious? It takes three thousand for an aircraft carrier."

"That's what the briefing said. There's a small area for the crew. All available space goes for oil storage tanks."

There had been in the recent past, a shipwreck of one of these ships off the coast of Taiwan and the beaches on the west side of the island were fouled with oil and would remain so for years to come. But they would build as long as the orders came in.

Satisfying a lifelong ambition to visit a steel mill, I donned a hard hat, smock and glasses and watched the fiery liquid stream out like the spewing of a tiny volcano. At the cement factory, I found a bathroom and washed out the layer of concrete dust that had accumulated inside my lower eyelids.

The important thing was that all of this was going on. A tiny island was fighting for its life and not just leaving it up to someone else to guarantee. They had to choose between turning over a clean island to the communists or keeping a dirty one. They had chosen to hang on to what was theirs. It was exciting to see survival in progress and the inconveniences became unimportant.

We were driven south of Kaohsiung, close to the end of the island. I stood on a hill and looked out over the sea. In the far distance, almost obscured by haze were the Philippine Islands. The Pacific Ocean and its seas are so vast, that to glimpse one country from another was a unique experience.

A series of tiny coral atolls called the Spratly Islands are positioned midway between Vietnam, Maylasia and the Philippines. I heard them mentioned many times in Taipei and when I asked where they were and what they were, I learned they had belonged to Nationalist China before it split with China in 1949.

Jim was well informed on the Spratlys. " Everybody claims them; China, Vietnam, Maylaysia, the Philippines and Taiwan."

"But why? If they're just chunks of coral, what's so important about them?"

"Like the Matsu Islands, they're a bone of contention because of their strategic placement. They built submarine bases there during World War II."

I thought of the P'enghus, controversial because they were smack in the middle of the shipping routes. Even Japan had held the Spratlys for a while, but finally gave them up. Now, in 1978, they contained only military garrisons, but because they sat on the greatest oil and gas reserves ever discovered on earth, they provided the flashpoint for territorial war. In 1988, China and Vietnam would go to war over the Spratlys and seventy people would die. On the map, they are labeled "the Spratlys – disputed," indicating everybody wants them, everybody claims them and Taiwan is on the list. For international intrigue, you can't beat this part of the world.

Kenting Park was an oasis of beauty with sand dunes that reminded me of the North Carolina Outer Banks. Our hotel was comfortable and I wakened early with the mist still drifting like fog from the breaking surf. As I stood at the window, marveling at the beauty spread out before me, indistinct figures seemed to be moving in slow motion. The mist gave them a disembodied look like a scene from an old movie, shadowy and slow. I was seeing Tai Chi Ch'uan for the first time and it was a moment of complete mystery. Their movements were seamless and serene – fluid and sensuous. As the mist cleared a little, the people emerged. They were young and old, quiet and unsmiling in their concentration of this ancient exercise. Then the mist closed in again and they were gone from my sight. It was a diverse country; the thundering industries and the languid silent beauty of people moving as one.

Breakfast that morning was, to say the least, unusual.

"Jim, did I miss something? There are peanuts on my plate. Shouldn't we have had these last night with our drinks?"

"I noticed them when we came in the dining room. Everybody has them. Must be the customary breakfast." Unflappable, as always.

"Would you like to comment on the pickle on the side?"

"You're right. It is a pickle."

"And….?"

He grinned. "So eat the pickle. I don't know why it would be there if you aren't supposed to eat it."

Bowls of gruel were served. It tasted just like the word sounded. I practiced my 'pick up peanuts with chopsticks' routine, ate the pickle, closed my eyes and finished off the gruel.

The morning was spent touring. Lunch was a laid-on affair – an official do. There were generals I had never met and one sat directly across from me at the round table. Normally, the spouses sit across from each other at official functions, but today we were doing it a bit differently. I chatted as much as my limited Chinese would allow with the people on either side, then looked across at the gentleman facing me. "Ni hou ma?" I was inquiring how he was, the equivalent of hello. He smiled, complimented me on my Chinese, which was ludicrous since that little phrase was nearly the extent of it. I smiled, said, "Seay, seay" (thank you) and the soup was served.

"You like slake soup?" He was trying to use his English, but it was difficult for me to be sure of what he was saying. However, I remembered a fish called "hake" I had eaten in Spain and the name was very similar. If this was the same kind of fish it certainly got around. We were a long way from Barcelona.

Smiling, I answered, "Yes. Slake soup hen hau." (very good). He smiled broadly and began spooning away at his bowl. So did I and it was very hen hau. We smiled again at each other and as I chewed the bits of meat, the light bulb went on in my brain and I realized I was eating snake soup. The meat was not fish texture, but more like chicken. I put down my spoon, contemplated my next move, saw him watching me and resumed eating.

Next on the list was the Export Zone. This vast place consisted of endless lines of factories and barracks. Canon cameras were put together, Parisian designer gowns were made, German fur pelts were shaped into coats, golf clubs manufactured, TV sets assembled. The list was endless. We saw rows of buildings, peopled by rows of young men and women, doing assembly-line work. This was where *Made in Taiwan* began.

In the fur factory, the air was filled with hair. The young girls bent over their patterns and Queenie explained that the designers from Europe brought their pelts and designs, took up residence for a year while they taught the Taiwanese how to cut, let-out and sew the furs into coats. There was every kind of fur I had ever seen and some I had only heard about.

"Queenie, this is so impressive. I am simply amazed these young people can learn such an exacting art." She looked pleased at my compliment, so I gathered my courage and went one step further.

"Queenie, is it possible on Taiwan to buy mouth and nose masks like the doctors wear?'

For a moment, she looked puzzled, thinking I was asking if they made them here in the Export Zone. But then she followed my eyes and I was gazing at the hair-filled air that surrounded the girls at the tables. They needed masks, because without them, all that hair was going into their lungs. Like conspirators, we smiled at each other. I had done the face thing properly.

One week later, Queenie called with the information the girls were all wearing masks and she thanked me for the idea. Sometimes in the rush to become strong, little things fall through the cracks.

It was a good trip to Kaohsiung. There were others as time passed; some I went along and some I missed. We were there during the next big earthquake in Taipei and returned to find Quarters A standing like a rock. And we were in Taipei when a worse one hit Kaohsiung, destroying nearly all of the huge cranes used in the shipyard. But Jim was to have a final visit there a year and a half later; one unlike any he had ever known.

It was the one that nearly broke our hearts.

Calls were waiting for Jim when we returned and one of them made him smile, but I was not enlightened as to why until the next night. Around five, Mike drove into our driveway in a little car. Jim followed in the official car behind him. The little car went down the driveway to the lower level and soon Mike came to the door and said "Hi, Mrs. Linder. I think the Admiral has a surprise for you tonight, and I think you'll like it. See you soon."

And he was gone, catching a ride down the mountain with Sergeant Fan.

Jim came into the house. "Did you see Mike drive in?"

"Yes, I did, but he left with Sergeant Fan. Who belongs to that funny little car that drove past the windows?"

"It's ours and let's go sit by the pool."

He was still in uniform, but he was also excited so we hurried down to our chairs on the back lawn. Hogo immediately appeared, seemed startled by Jim's appearance, quickly brought his drink, giggled, then disappeared back into the house.

"It's our ticket to some privacy. We're going to take weekend drives and see the countryside without the motorcycle brigade behind us. The Cadillac gives us away with the *001* license plate, so maybe with this car, they'll let us alone."

I was ecstatic and terribly grateful to this man for his thoughtfulness. I would make a list of all the things we could talk about, since they had been held in reserve for so long.

"We have a little car and on Sunday, we'll pack a lunch, take Suzie and head for the beach on the western shore." He was thoroughly enjoying his surprise.

It sounded like a piece of heaven.

I don't remember the rest of the week. Christmas would soon be upon us and I had shopped every chance that came along for things to send to the children and friends, as well as the gifts for the Chinese admirals, generals, government officials and their wives. I was given my allowance for these official gifts and having an Exchange to shop in helped, but it never covered the costs and I was constantly juggling accounts to remember everyone on the list.

The family and friends would receive the exotic Chinese things and the Chinese, the American goods from the Exchange. It was a very confusing time. One guestroom held mounds of holiday wrapped boxes that would go into bigger boxes for shipping and the other guestroom held mounds of holiday wrapped boxes that would go into the car for delivery to our friends in Taipei. By the time Christmas came, I was fuzzy on what had gone where, but with Mike and Sergeant Hsiu's help, it all worked out.

The invitation read *A Christmas Luncheon at the Hilton, followed by a fashion show.* So I joined my Chinese friends to see the latest in what to wear.

The spacious luncheon room was beautifully decorated, as was all of the Hilton. We took our places at the assigned tables, close to the runway and Dim Sun, the equivalent of our canapes and hors d'oeuvres were served. I had become quite attached to certain offerings on the platter and today it seemed like every province on the Mainland was represented. The selections were endless. Szechwan, Hunan, Kangsu, Chekiang and Cantonese cooking are each different from the other. To quote the Chinese philosopher, Lao Tzu, "Governing a great nation is much like cooking a small fish." To the western mind, that translates to "in governing a country, just the right 'seasonings' and adjustments need to be made for successful results." Wise man, Lao Tzu. If he were alive, he should take on our Congress.

The Chinese for centuries have relied on food as a medicine and that dates back to the Shang Dynasty, sixteenth to the eleventh century BC, some 3,500 years – give or take a century or two. We are just becoming aware of these same values as a resource for good health. I wonder where we've been all those years.

The decorations were as enticing as the food; vegetables carved into swans, birds and chickens. The swans were actually doing a courting dance in the middle of the platter. It could have been the entertainment for the afternoon. Some talented man in the kitchen had carved a long fish net out of one carrot, then draped it over a serving table. The music began and the show was announced.

They came down the runway – tiny, perfect Chinese dolls, not in traditional Chinese dress. Instead, they wore Parisian haute couture and looked stunning. This was as good if not better than fashion shows I had seen in Paris, Rome or Florence, Italy. Their flower-like faces were still as they walked with the swift, long-legged strut that only a professional model can do. On their feet were ankle-high boots with ankle socks. And they got away with it.

I looked around at the women in the audience and realized a great number of them had been to Paris and not for its chestnut trees or the Louvre. These were ladies with beautiful clothes and jewels, enjoying themselves, knowing they looked smart and fashionable. It was good to see yet another side to these people. They may be refugees from their homeland, but here on this island, they had the freedom to go where their passports would take them.

It was a purely female afternoon with the brilliant colors of the food, the charming French arrogance of the little models, the jewels and gowns and those busy swans in the middle of the table.

Suzie was alternating between ricochet and window-licking. She loved the little car, but on her third pass through the front seat, I snatched her in mid-air and sat her firmly on the back seat.

"Suzie, you are driving us crazy. Now you sit there and be quiet."

She was absolutely still, her almond eyes glued to my gaze. She sat like a coiled spring, but Suzie always sat like a coiled spring. We regarded each other for some moments, then she grinned and I was lost.

"All right, window-licking, but no leaping around."

She had won again – and knew it. Sedately, she marched across the back seat to the window and pushed her nose against the cool glass. Sergeant

Hsiu would shake his head tomorrow when he washed those windows but Suzie was everybody's darling and lunchtime would find her curled up on his lap, automatically forgiven.

This was our Sunday getaway to the western coast. Suzie and I were more than just excited. She knew something was up when I crept down into the kitchen in the early morning to make a picnic lunch. She chased her tail until she ran into the table leg, smacked her head on the rung of a chair and after finding Mama San's crochet yarn, rolled it under my feet. I finally put her on top of the big air conditioner outside the back door to keep her from ending up in deep trouble. She and Jim inspected the car and neither of us was sure we could make the trip with this whirling dervish but her grin put her in the car and on the back seat.

I looked forward to a whole day of clean ocean air. With rocks to sit on, a beach to walk, nobody following us, and the sight of wheeling birds over the water, the kinks of the past few months would smooth out. My list of topics was firmly printed on my mind.

As we sat out of sight in our little Toyota, ready to escape, Jim gunned the engine and we tore up the driveway and out the open gates before anyone knew what was going on. There was nobody in the house to give us away and we raced down the mountain to the Coast road with no motorcycles behind us. There was a heady feeling of freedom and I knew this was a good day. Jim would probably be scolded by whomever scolds Admirals and I would be labeled as the perpetrator of the crime, but on that particularly beautiful Sunday, neither of us cared.

Yangmingshan wore the brown sleeve of pollution as the smog crept up the mountain and I hoped we would not be here when it settled over Quarters A. We had friends who lived on the way down the mountain and as we passed their houses, we noticed they were dimming out as the yellowish, brown air crept up to and past them on its silent journey.

My eyes were beginning to rebel because of the murky air. Dr. Lin had done his best, but I knew another trip to Clark Hospital would have to be scheduled after the New Year celebrations.

The drive was spectacular – rugged mountains, flat plains and terraced hillsides – everything that the Mainland had to offer, including the rural population with their primitive carts and oxen, conical hats and gray clothes. This wasn't the teeming, noisy city with a sea of cars, bicycles and people. Instead, it was what I had always imagined the real China would look like – landscape that had been here for millennia and would be here for the next one. The colors of the mountains were subtle, pastel and shadowy. Everything looked like the paintings in the Palace Museum.

"Jim, when you can, look over to your left. See the dots on the sides of the mountains? They look exactly like the paintings I've been studying. I thought they were an artist's interpretation of mountains, but they're not. Those are trees and bushes, but they look like dots."

" You like the Museum?"

"Very much. Tuesday, Thomas took me downstairs to the workrooms where they are reproducing some of the pieces in the Museum for commercial sale. There were tables of young artists, shaping and painting the ceramic pieces and I was fascinated with the precision of their work."

155

"What do they do with them when they're finished?"

"Export them, I guess. I saw some pieces in the Museum gift shop and they are probably downtown in the better shops. Do you remember in the porcelain section of the Museum, the small bowl called Ju ware – the one that was my favorite of all the porcelains?"

The color was gray green and so thin, the bowl was almost translucent. I thought at first the piece was Celadon, the color was similar – just a little grayer.

"I asked Thomas about it and he said that particular piece of porcelain is the most valuable one they have. It's such a small bowl."

"Has Thomas told you abut the jades?"

"Some, but I'm to take a lecture course in a week, so I'll know more then. I already know which piece of jade is my favorite."

"Let me guess. It's the yellow jade seals and the most valuable of all the jades. Right?"

"Right. And the value has nothing to do with it." (I've been known to go for the expensive stuff without even realizing it.) "The workmanship is like nothing I've ever seen before, and the butterscotch color is so unusual. They look good enough to eat."

Suzie heard the word 'eat' and placed her chin on the seat behind us and whined.

Jim said, "Suzie, don't whine. I don't like a whiny dog. We'll be there soon and have our picnic." Jim was the one person she didn't test and the whine was swallowed.

"Thomas told me the Museum was built against the mountain and has caves behind it. He said there are enough treasures stored in there to change every piece on display once every six months for the rest of my lifetime."

"Did he tell you the story about getting the treasures from Beijing to Taiwan?"

"No, but I'll ask him next time I'm there." I had no way of knowing I would sit spellbound as the man responsible for the transporting of thousands of paintings, bronzes, jades and artifacts told me his story. But today, I could only marvel as I imagined the prodigious effort that went into such an undertaking.

We were anxious to see the beach and talked about having our picnic on the sand. But as we cleared the top of the hill and looked down at the western shore of Taiwan, all we could see was black. The rocks, the sand and as far as the eye could see were black. Tar and oil covered nearly everything. The shipwreck off the southern coast had leaked oil that found its way into the northern currents. Our day at the beach became just the length of time to spread the tablecloth on a small patch of clean sand and have our picnic. Suzie wanted to run, but we knew getting the oil off would be hard on her, so we packed up quickly after lunch and resumed our drive.

Before we left, I looked out at the Taiwan Straits and made a mental note to ask Mike, the next time he was at the Quarters, if this was where he came to meet the boat people.

"I need to go back to the hospital at Clark, Jim. The pollution is bothering me a lot now and they asked that I return as soon after the first of the year as possible."

"All right. I'll have Skip check on the MEDIVAC plane schedule and call you tomorrow."

How I hated this link to incapability that just wasn't me. I railed against it in the privacy of my thoughts and had been known to kick the wall when words on the paper wouldn't come into focus. Yet, if my lot was to stumble through life, running into walls and falling off of curbs, I would do so, but until they assigned me to the rocking chair on the porch, I would leave my mark. There was so much to do, and although I sometimes felt I was running out of time, every moment would be made accountable.

"Jim, this may sound really stupid, but what do you do? I know a lot about parties and extracurricular things, but I don't know what you do. Am I out of line in asking?"

"You're not out of line at all. I haven't wanted to discuss anything at the Quarters because it's not for just anybody to hear."

"I realize that and you know I'll keep it to myself. For instance, remember when you went down-island last month, before our trip to Kaoshung? What was that all about?"

"The usual. We visited the Chinese Marine Headquarters and had briefings on their readiness and material requirements. Then we witnessed a parade celebrating their Marine anniversary."

"How do they compare with our Marines?"

"They were proud and well informed about modern warfare tactics. They seemed pretty dedicated." He grinned. " But, I noticed they lacked air conditioning in their barracks and it reminded of my days at the Naval Academy."

"But you were younger then and didn't notice it as much."

"I was younger then, but I noticed."

He went on to say he had also visited the Naval base and their Naval Academy facilities in the south part of the island where there was a small number of diesel submarines that were predominantly used as training ships. He was briefed on their tactical use of the boats in naval warfare in this region.

"You're talking about the Taiwan Straits?"

"Right. But these ships were not capable of conducting combat operations."

"But with their shipbuilding industry, can't they build their own combat ships?"

"They don't need to. They can obtain current submarine technology through other sources more economically."

Of course. Countries had been buying or leasing older ships from the U.S. for a long time. I remembered seeing U.S. destroyers and other combatant ships in Spain and Greece.

"They are also very interested in our training methods. It's one thing to have a ship, but without training, it's worthless. You can't run a boat on instinct."

There were more questions, but I wanted to talk about the children and the ride couldn't last forever. We chatted about their letters, what their Christmas plans would be and Jeff's progress towards college graduation in May. There just wasn't time for this kind of talk during the week and although we had learned to get ready for a party in twenty-two minutes (which included a shower and in Jim's case, a shave), we found it hard to talk about our children in capsule form.

I questioned Jim about the people in TDC and the Embassy. Some I knew well and some I would never know at all. I needed background to understand the undercurrents that are always part of a command. Jim supplied what he could and we traded opinions about them. We weren't playing the game of gossip. Things are said that point out problems or potential problems and we learned to take advantage of these observations early in his career.

Our day alone was coming to an end. We drove slowly through a little village with small gray houses and no sidewalks and I studied the faces of the people we passed. There were differences. I could recognize Mongolians and Taiwanese now. Most of the people living in the outlying rural areas were Taiwanese and had probably lived there for generations. It had been a perfect day, with only the oily beach as a disappointment. We stopped in different places to look at the terraced hills and the sleeping mountains. Each time, Suzie ran and explored until she was completely worn out. On our way home, she lay curled in my lap, asleep.

CHAPTER THIRTEEN
THE MAH JONG CAPER

Hogo came hurriedly down the hall to the sitting room where I was checking the clothes for the party that night. Mama San waited to take the jade green mandarin ch'i p'ao downstairs for pressing. Hogo was excited and of course, giggling and he told me something was at the front door for Christmas and I had better come because he didn't know what to do with it. His excitement was infectious and I hurried after him, mindful of the ice-slick hall floor.

Beyond the red doors, stood four men with two of the biggest Christmas trees I had ever seen outside of the one at the White House. They were a gift from the Chinese government and the next move was up to me. I stood dumbfounded while everybody giggled, including Mama San who brought up the rear. She tapped my arm and when I looked at her, she pointed to the two French doors that led onto the porch. Of course. It was the perfect place – one on either side and the soaring ceiling would probably accommodate them if the men cut a little off the bottoms. That done, they were carried in and set up on the wooden stands that came with them. They were awesome.

I stood across the room and looked at the effect. Suddenly, the room filled up and the thought occurred to me that if I left the trees there, I could forget buying any more furniture. Then the needle situation came to mind and I dismissed the idea as a bad one. They were stately, perfect in shape, deep green in color and smelled like the mountains. I would enjoy

161

every minute they were in the house. Mama San had remained in the room, patiently waiting my return to the business at hand in the closet in the sitting room. She had her inevitable ball of white cotton yarn in her apron pocket and the little crochet needle threaded through it. I never knew what she made with that yarn, but it was what she did when there was a free moment downstairs. An idea began to form in my mind and I said, "Mama San, what do you make with that needle?" I touched the needle and looked inquiringly into her round, smiling face.

She took it out of her pocket and we both examined it. " Things." Not much information there.

"Mama San, you know snowflake?"

Big smile. "No".

Another game of charades; I pointed to the mountains, she nodded, I wiggled my fingers like snow coming down and clasped my arms with my hands to look cold.

A dawning. Then I took the yarn and needle and pretended to crochet. She found that very funny and we both laughed. Finally, I drew snowflakes on a paper from the library, laid the needle and yarn on the pictures and asked, "You can do?"

Big smile. "Okay."

Three days later, I had crocheted snowflakes of every shape and description and I couldn't turn her off. The project threatened to become a blinding snowstorm until Hogo helped me out and together, we convinced her that a tree could only hold so many of her lovely little snowflakes. Sergeant Hsiu became involved when I wondered about buying her yarn downtown and gave him money to find what he could. He arrived at the Quarters with a large box of the cotton yarn and told her it was hers; no matter how much or how little she used. She made me feel like I had given her the world. And because she liked making the snowflakes, they eventually became a source of income for her. She found a buyer in Taipei and off they went.

That took care of one tree and the other stood untouched until I was in a shop downtown a few days later and there for the incredible price of one dollar for a box of twelve, were crystal tree ornaments; icicles, little houses, snowmen, angels, sleighs, reindeers and Santa himself. Next to the display was a nativity scene beautifully carved out of wood. It was perfect except for one detail. Joseph was Frosty, the Snowman. Just a religious misinterpretation between cultures.

Although Christianity was widely accepted on the Island, the old ways of Buddhism still existed. Ornate Buddhist temples, the Chinese equivalent of baroque art, graced Taipei's streets in direct opposition to its concrete skyscrapers. It was the sign of a democracy in the making – religious philosophies coexisting side by side. One of my Chinese friends laughingly referred to "the others" as closet Buddhists. And among the Buddhists, I imagine "the others" were called closet Christians. Taoism and Muslim beliefs were also followed. It was a mixture. There were both Protestant and Roman Catholic churches on the Island.

One day, I saw two young men in black pants, white shirts and black hats, pedaling their bicycles up Yangmingshan. They were Mormons, doing their two -year missionary work on Taiwan. I had no way of knowing, but I could only guess that religious freedoms either didn't exist or had gone underground on the Mainland. Communist societies were not known for their interest in the church.

The trees were duly decorated and admired by all. I tucked our family pieces amongst the snowflakes and the result pleased our Chinese friends. But Christmas isn't much without the children and even as the gifts rolled in (and out). I found it hard to drum up any enthusiasm for the day.

TDC was giving its big, annual Christmas party at the Officers' Club and there was quite a stir when President Chiang Ching-kuo gave an affirmative answer to our invitation. He was the son of Chiang Kai-shek and we were surprised and delighted to know he would be there. Not long after we arrived on Taiwan, Premier Chiang Ching-kuo had changed his title to President, making me wonder what happened to the delightful man we had met the night of the lichi nut episode. Plans were made for a special evening.

Things went fuzzy for me late in the afternoon of the party. As with any physical problem, there were good days and bad days. This was not a good day. When the mists closed in, I floundered and this would be one of those evenings.

The long silk suit with the fur collar was laid out on the bed and I dressed quickly. We were due at the Club in plenty of time for the President's arrival. The receiving line was forming as I automatically took my place next to Jim. Shannon was on my right, with Skip to Jim's left. As people came through, Skip spoke their name to Jim who in turn told me. Shannon was there to help me if I needed her. I had missed lunch due to a lecture at the Museum, so a small plate of food was placed behind me on the low window ledge. We were ready.

My feet hurt.

Receiving lines are a necessity in officialdom, but to the person standing in them, they are endless and close to a punishment. I put on my receiving line face as the first guests stood in front of me and through the fuzz, tried to identify them if only by their voices. With Shannon's help, all went well for a while.

Then I heard Jim whisper, "Here he comes."

Obviously, the President had arrived and was being escorted through the line. I finished my conversation with the person in front of me and braced as the next person moved into place. I looked up at the medium height shape that had light reflecting off of the medals and buttons, took his hand and before Shannon could stop me, said, "Mr. President, we are so honored to have you here tonight."

A soft voice that was decidedly Chinese said, "Ah Linder Tai Tai, I am only his aide."

The President was having a long conversation with Jim. He then moved in front of me and once again, I shook the hand of a medium height shape in a dark suit – no decorations – and graciously said my piece. Whether he had caught the little amusement that had just occurred, I never knew. We chatted for a few moments, he was courtly and charming and then he was gone. Shannon in all her wisdom handed me the plate of food and I wolfed down two pieces of something before the next handshake. Somewhere during the evening, I kicked off my shoes which lowered my skirt three inches, giving the impression I was standing in a hole, and continued smiling. We shook a lot of hands.

All in all, it was a good party. The President did not mingle, but left after speaking to the Ambassador. He was an elderly man, not always in good health and I had heard him described as fragile, but for that night, he was just a medium sized shape in a dark suit.

The haze had cleared a little by the next day when I walked into the living room on my way to the porch for breakfast.

"Jim, would you have Skip call me today about my trip to Clark Hospital? I had a hard time last night and even if they can't do anything, I'll feel better, knowing I've made the effort. The doctors did mention they wanted to try some new treatments." More guinea pig stuff.

"I'll have him give you a call. Can you wait to go until after the Chinese New Year celebration?"

"Probably, but it should be soon." That holiday was still weeks away and I could feel a sense of urgency building.

Skip called later in the morning and after checking with the schedule, found the MEDIVAC plane would not be coming through until later anyway, so I was stuck. Back to Dr. Lin.

Chinese New Year is celebrated sometime after our New Years day, and falls on whatever date the Chinese calendar finds appropriate. It is not only colorful, but also busy with parades, boat races and the inevitable parties. These customs were all new to me, so I enjoyed the many ways they have of celebrating a better year to come. One of the wives told me that on the day the New Year begins, merchants try to get rid of their inventory, thereby ensuring a profitable year ahead. I never figured out the reasoning behind this, but we all took advantage of it. I paid a call on the furniture stores in Tien Mou and found good bargains. Slowly, the Quarters were being furnished and with the pieces coming from the Philippines, I was almost finished.

During the time of Chinese New Year I was invited by an international group of ladies to play Mah Jong. an ancient Chinese game which I had first learned in Greece. Instead of cards, there are tiles, no partners and, it could be called a mind-stretcher, dating back thousands of years. The Chinese eventually ruled it illegal, not for the money lost in betting, but for the time wasted in the marathon games the Chinese prefer to play.

We met at Suzanne's house that sat on top of a hill with a very long flight of steps leading up to the front door. The group had been playing for several years since coming to Taiwan and I looked forward to these afternoons. The tiles were sometimes hard to see but they were patient with me and their efforts helped me.

Sergeant Hsiu dropped me off and I asked him to return in three hours. I climbed the long flight of steps, greeted the ladies and we began. On this particular day, there were eight people playing at two tables covered with Mah Jong cloths. All was ready. We played for an hour, then stopped for cakes and coffee. As Suzanne stood up, she glanced out the living room window and froze.

"My God, there's a police car at the bottom of the steps and a man coming up here. Grab the table cloths and throw everything on the bed in the bedroom."

I was completely mystified, but did as I was told. The tables stood accusingly empty and we all resumed our seats. In the back of my mind was the thought that Jim would not be happy, finding his wife in jail and I was glad Sergeant Hsiu was not at the bottom of the steps, otherwise the man on his way up would either be dead or crippled for life. After all, Linder Tai Tai was up there.

The bell rang and Suzanne primly opened the door. The man said a few words, Suzanne swung the door wide and invited him in. He found himself looking at eight extremely innocent-looking non-Chinese women and asked, "You ' pray' Mah Jong?"

Suzanne answered, "Why yes, officer. I do know how to play Mah Jong."

She turned to one of the other ladies and said, " Janine, would you bring in the coffee and cakes? Maybe the officer would like to join us in our dessert."

He panicked. "No, no. Lady call, say neighbor 'pray ' Mah Jong. No good. 'Pray' Mah Jong ' blake' law."

We were being raided. Sergeant Hsiu, where are you?

"But officer, we were just going to have cakes and coffee before we go on with our meeting."

He was beaten and he knew it. "No, no. I go now." And he did. The lady next door had heard the tiles clicking (she must have had her ear against the window) and jealous because it was illegal for her to play, she called the cops. The police didn't know that this was a gathering of international women who, inside their homes, can play anything they want to. The game resumed.

These were interesting women. They came from Lebanon, India, Holland, South America and the United States. Their husbands were with international firms, placed in Taiwan and were often there for years. They made lives for themselves, as women tend to do wherever they are. I knew something about that and welcomed the easy acceptance I found with them. There were no judgements of each other and no one appeared to be competing with anybody.

They talked often about the trips they took off the island and I realized in time, they were describing the answer to island fever, the prototype of cabin fever. After so long on an island, a woman needs to leave it, if only for a few days. I knew that when the pleasures of learning about another culture wore thin, I too, would need to get away. Some far-sighted soul energetically made arrangements with airlines and travel agencies throughout Southeast Asia to take care of this situation and offered at a low cost, trips to Hong Kong for three or six days, depending on the condition of one's checkbook. These trips came at regular intervals and in time, I knew more about downtown Hong Kong than I did downtown Taipei. I could freely walk the streets and poke around in little shops, try out my pigeon Chinese, eat Dim Sun, have tea in the lobby of the Peninsular Hotel and watch the movie stars stroll by. It was frothy and fun.

There was a shop in Hong Kong I particularly liked. A friend gave me directions and after searching the streets, I found a long dark, flight of stairs that ended in a tiny, dimly lit hallway containing only a door of heavy iron latticework that was the granddaddy of all security doors. I didn't know what to do next. There was no bell and to knock would leave me with bruised knuckles. While I pondered my next move, the door opened and I was face to face with a woman who was straight out of China or an old Hollywood movie. She wore a floor length black satin Mandarin ch'i p'ao and her black hair was drawn back and held with jade hairpins at the base of her long neck. She was rail thin. I introduced myself, feeling short, blonde and very Western and gave her my credentials, including the person's name that had steered me into this dark hallway. We studied each other and after a proper amount of time had passed, the door swung open.

"Please – you may come in." Her voice was a perfect match to the rest of her and I walked into Old China. The room was large and every inch filled with treasures beyond my imagination.

"I've never seen anything like this; so many beautiful things. How did they all get here?" It was a frivolous question, but I had to start somewhere.

Cautiously, because I was still a stranger to her, she answered, "The family who owned this business fled the Mainland and brought their heritage with them."

Boldly, "Are you of that family?"

"Yes, I am." Nothing more. Her back was ramrod straight and her chin, slightly elevated. She looked like a member of the family.

We moved slowly and silently through the crowded aisles. Some objects dated back hundreds, and in some cases, thousands of years. They were priceless and they offered me a glimpse of what the Mandarin class had enjoyed as their way of life before the communists reduced China to communal rule.

That afternoon is firmly imprinted on my memory. These were not just museum pieces – these were the everyday articles that were used and taken for granted. I fell under the spell of Coromandel screens, black lacquer on one side and gold leaf on the other, with Chinese landscapes made of inlaid jade and coral, hairpins of polished silver with carved heads of rose quartz, and Imperial jade, the darkest and most valuable of all jades. I touched three inch -long fingernail sheaths, lacquered with lovely designs. At first, I was stunned by the luxurious quality of what I saw. Many things were simply things – beautifully carved or inlaid with precious stones, but I hadn't a clue what they were used for. Their age made them primitive, but their beauty was timeless and I could only marvel at them and wonder what their place had been in a household. Then I called on what I had learned about China before and since coming to this part of the world. The class system was clearly defined as it had been for 5,000 years. These were the "haves". The "have nots" were still in the fields.

As I moved into a small room that contained articles of clothing embroidered in gold and silver threads with buttons of jade, I saw the tiny shoes that were made for bound feet. The Dragon Lady was within calling distance "Would you answer some questions I have about this?"

"Yes, Westerners are often curious about that custom."

171

I asked about the practice of foot binding. It was ancient and done for two reasons; tiny feet made a girl more marriageable, since it was practiced mostly by the upper class. The lower class women needed their feet for work in the fields. The other reason was given in a flat, emotionless voice.

" With bound feet, the pain kept women from running away from their husbands, since marriages were matters of arrangement."

Her face was totally expressionless as she spoke, but her black eyes betrayed her feelings. One could only imagine the desperation of a young girl, married against her wishes to a cruel or old man for family financial purposes. It had been done for centuries in nearly every culture, but holding that tiny shoe in my hand, the abject cruelty of it was appalling.

Watching me, she opened a book sitting next to the shoes and I was looking at photographs of women's feet that had been bound. I was horrified. First, the toes atrophied, then eventually dropped off, leaving only an arch and a heel which in time, disappeared. What remained was a tiny stump, no shape or form. Just a bone with a skin covering. The skin looked pale and delicate. The pain must have been indescribable and lasted the length of time it took for the metamorphosis. This, to keep a woman at home.

My feminine instincts showed in my face and my eyes teared over the agony they had endured. I felt a soft touch on my arm and looked up to see this elegant woman's eyes which now held interest. This short blonde Westerner felt something besides curiosity and she responded by motioning me to follow her. We walked into a room almost filled with one bed that could have been a house built of rosewood, beautifully carved, with cabinets and cubbyholes.

"These cabinets hold tiny objects, carved out of jades, ivory, quartzes – all precious and semi-precious. Her husband provided these things and this is where the new bride spent her time. Since she was unable to walk, she sat on the bed and played with them. That was how she put in the hours of her day." We looked at each other and it was obvious we both deplored this barbaric custom.

On the bed was a basket with its own compartments. "This is the bride's wedding basket and she brought it with her at her marriage time. It contained her favorite things from home." The carved ivories were tiny animals or figures of people – a perfect flower bloomed in the soft pink of rose quartz. Thus, she spent her days counting, touching, stroking these inanimate little objects that gave her nothing back. Class had its restrictions.

This elegant lady and I were friends before the afternoon ended. She sensed my interest in learning all I could and explained many things as we drifted through the rooms filled with China. There was little I could afford, but she helped me choose a carved piece of sandalwood with a woven satin cord that was once worn on the belt of a Mandarin warlord. I promised to return on my next trip to Hong Kong. She said she would wait for me.

Taipei

In the bookstore, I picked up a book in Chinese and for a moment studied the calligraphy, realizing that I should be reading from back to front.

Early calligraphy was found on animal bones and tortoise shells. I had seen some of these in their Museum of Natural History a few weeks before. The curator guided me through the earliest archeological finds and there was a scientific beauty in the simple carvings. They were a form of pictograph and eloquent in their simplicity. He told me calligraphy was the only language that began with pictography and is still used in modern day. To me, it is an art form. The heavy, slashing line that ends in a lyrical shadow carries a full story.

When my tour ended in the antiquities Museum, the curator, elderly and scholarly, ushered me into his office/study that was piled high with books, magazines and newspapers. Dust was everywhere, but it was obvious he knew the exact location of each piece of information. As I sat down in a somewhat rickety chair, I noticed shelves on the wall that held small, three legged bronze wine vessels that are almost symbolic of China's bronze period. They looked authentic and I asked about them. His answer was riveting, considering the political situation between the ROC and Mainland China at the time. An arrangement had been made, whereby artists on the Mainland mined the metals necessary to make the bronze alloy from the place the original bronzes were cast. They then shipped it through the underground to Taiwan. I understood. For these displaced Chinese without their ancestral heritage, the answer was to recreate it, faithfully following the rigid rules of the ancient art. It was important to know it could still be done. When I asked the curator what he would do with the finished vessels, he answered, "They will be destroyed. We only needed to know the process can be properly accomplished."

My thoughts drifted back to the book in my hand and I opened it to find a full-page map of Taiwan, set in the surrounding seas and again, I was struck by the vulnerability of this tiny island. The immensity of China to the west and the slim body of water separating the two only made more poignant the uneven odds. But I was getting to know these people and their determination. I laid my index finger on the Taiwan Straits and it filled the space. It was such a short but important distance, west to east. I purchased the book, not to read, but to enjoy the beauty of the calligraphy and study the map that could hold the key to Taiwan's future.

The next day was the National Palace Museum's scheduled lecture on jade that I had anxiously waited for. Most of the lectures were presented in a small amphitheater type classroom with graduated seats, a screen, podium with a light and a lecturer. The rest of the room was pitch dark, canceling the opportunity to take notes.

Sergeant Hsiu dropped me at the door and assured me he would be waiting there to pick me up. No matter how long it was, he was always close by. Thomas was waiting inside the museum and escorted me to the classroom. We chatted as we walked down the corridor and after I was seated, he waved a goodbye and disappeared into the museum.

A young woman came in. I guessed this very business-like lady, dressed in a starkly plain black suit to be somewhere in her late twenties or early thirties, but she could have been fifty. Age is difficult to guess in China. She was a no-nonsense lecturer. The lights went out, the screen lit up and I settled back to look at China's treasures.

The slides began with the early jades – four thousand years ago. They were primitive, simple but with the hint of beauty to come. As we marched through the dynasties and their representative pieces, I could see shapes emerging, carvings that were slight and simple and the beginning of an artistic idea. The Chinese people love their jades. For centuries, the stone has been a symbol of survival. They worshipped it as holy and pure and used it in their quest for power and position. As a military wife, I was intrigued by the jade piece called a Tiger Tally. When broken in half, one side was given to the military leader and one to the Court. If the pieces fit when the Court sent an order out to the battlefield, the commander knew the word came from the Emperor. I tried for a comparison with my husband and the Pentagon's method of communication and realized there was none.

I had always thought of jade as jewelry – valuable trinkets. Instead, a procession of musical instruments, axes, ink stones, flower holders and perfumeries flashed by. I was dazzled. White, blue, lavender, yellow, brown, green, black – all jades and carved into incredible shapes and forms. Brown jade was used in the shaping of the insect called a cicada. These were used on the eyelids when preparing the dead for burial. Jade is one of the hardest of stones and very difficult to cut. Yet here was a life-size Chinese Cabbage, resting on a polished teak base, its stalk of the purest white, graduating into the deep green of the leaves at its top, with a grasshopper, hair-thin antennas waving, nestled in the lacey leaves.

When the artist first sees the stone he is to carve, he has no idea what is inside the gray, rough rock that looks like any other rock. Yet, the cutter has an instinct about this. As he uncovers the jade inside, he must choose the subject matter. There is no way to know if the jade changes color, as it often does, or if he has a pure piece of one color. In the case of the cabbage, the combination of skill, wisdom and pure serendipity produced an incredibly perfect and priceless work of art.

As I learned the four thousand-year history behind this remarkable stone, I automatically made the analogy with the Chinese people. Like jade, they had survived down the long march of dynasties. The uniqueness of the stone could be compared with the uniqueness of the people who found the rough rocks in the mountains and the rivers and considered them "the essence of heaven and earth." It was the symbol of power, but also the symbol of Chinese civilization.

A simple piece of smooth, dark green jade flashed on the screen which the lady at the lectern identified as the toy of a Chinese boy-child given to him to play with. The next slide showed a piece of broken roof tile and she ended the lecture with the words, "This is what the girl-child receives as her toy." Her light went off, the room lights came on and we all blinked, not just at the lights, but at the clear message.

After the lecture, I wandered into the Jade Room and stood in front of my favorite glass case. On black velvet, with a light from above, sat the three Yellow Jade Seals of the Ch'ing Dynasty. The artist had found a large block of solid yellow jade and from it, carved three one-inch square solid blocks joined by one continuous free flexing chain. I could see no break – just a piece of continual carving out of one piece of jade that had a soft, almost liquid look and the color, instead of yellow, was a warm, glowing butterscotch. The years of work that went into this one piece of jade were a hallmark of patience, skill and inspiration.

Thomas joined me and I realized he had been standing near the door, waiting for me to come out of my reverie. As a young man who spent every day in the Museum, studying and learning, he knew that appreciation and understanding take time.

"Did you like your lecture, Linder, Tai Tai?"

"Yes, Thomas. It was very enlightening. Have you heard that lecture before?"

"Yes, and you are correct. It is very enlightening." Our eyes met and when I chuckled, so did he.

"Aren't you glad you were born a Chinese boy?"

"Yes, Linder Tai Tai, I am very glad I was born a Chinese boy. But my piece of jade was not Imperial jade as the one in the picture."

"It should have been."

We left it at that.

CHAPTER FOURTEEN
AN AFTERNOON WITH THE YUANS

The word finally came in on the MEDIVAC. I was to fly to Clark Air Force Base in the Philippines in two weeks, which gave the office time to set up my schedule. The Guest Quarters were waiting and there were appointments and more tests. Skip called with further information.

"Pat, the Admiral has a conference in Subic the end of your week at Clark."

Subic Bay was the U.S. Naval Base on the western coast of the island of Luzon where I would be. I had often heard of Subic when Jim was flying in the Korean and Viet Nam wars. The U.S. had major naval and air force bases in that area and in later years, would give them up when the leases ran out. At that time, it was inconceivable that such huge bases would be turned over to the Philippine government, but there were even stranger things yet to happen.

"What are the plans, Skip? Will he be going down in the Blue Goose?"

"Yes, he will, and instead of picking you up at Clark, we'll arrange for you to fly down to Subic and meet him there, then you can go home together. We thought you might want to see the Base."

Dear Skip. I had been looking at military bases for the past twenty-eight years, and one more I could pass on without a quiver, but there would be old friends to say hello to and new friends to meet and of course, the Station Boutique that was a shopper's paradise.

179

"Sounds interesting and I'll be ready to hitchhike down, if necessary."

I had no idea how they would accomplish my journey from the interior to the southwest coast. The jungle was dense between the two places.

"Let me know if there are any other arrangements you need at Clark. The Protocol Officer will meet you with your medical appointment schedule. Remember him? His name is Bill Cutler."

"Yes, I do. I liked him and I'm glad you asked him to help me."

Skip chuckled. "Oh, he'll help you all right."

And what was that all about?

"Almost forgot, Pat. You and the Admiral are to visit the ROC National Assembly on Thursday."

"Fine. I was hoping for that. Are you going along?"

"Oh yes."

"Good." Why did I always feel safer when Skip was along?

Thursday at the Assembly meant I should head for Suzy Chen's Little Body Shoppe in Tien Mou today. I called for an appointment for everything and why not? Suzy's was a beauty shop and upon entering, the customer was seated in a chair and "done" from the top down. One young Taiwanese girl shampooed the hair, one did the cutting, another set it and meanwhile, there were girls on each hand and arm, manicuring and massaging. Each foot and leg had the same treatment – and this for five dollars. They operated like an assembly line but I actually felt more like Gulliver and the Lilliputians by the time I was ushered out the door. Suzy was an enterprising woman and with the number of Americans and Europeans in the area, she would obviously be able to retire at an early age.

I called down for Sergeant Hsiu to give him the schedule for the afternoon and asked Hogo to send Mama San to the sitting room.

I chose my clothes for the trip to the General Assembly and they needed her touch. On one occasion, I dressed for a luncheon and as I tiptoed down the slick hallway, she noticed a wrinkle in my skirt. It was back to the bedroom while she dispatched the crease. I wasn't allowed to leave the house without her inspection, which was a good thing because some days, I couldn't tell if there were spots or creases or if the tops matched the bottoms. She accomplished all of this with a big smile that always made me feel cherished.

Mama San pattered in, we discussed the choice in hand gestures and one syllable words and she pattered out, dress over her arm. Sergeant Hsiu was next, standing inside the big red doors, patiently waiting to be noticed. Each day, my admiration for this man grew. He was so dedicated and my life was easier because of him. Having been on my own for so many years, I reveled in the feeling of protection.

"Good morning, Sergeant Hsiu." He nodded in answer. Suzie had wakened from her morning nap on the foot of our bed and came sliding down the hall when she heard his name. He smiled, ruffling her ears and she closed her eyes in ecstasy.

"Sergeant, did Hogo tell you about Suzie and the fish pond?" We were standing in the hall with the stone pond in front of us. He shook his head. In pigeon English and the ubiquitous hand gestures, I told him what his little companion had done the day before. It had been quite a sight, seeing the little white dog balanced on the tips of her tiny feet on the slim piece of stone, nose pointed at one of the golden carp as they swam lazily around the pool.

As I came into the room and saw her, I was so startled, I said, "Suzie, WHAT are you doing?"

Still on tiptoe, she very slowly turned her head, looked me dead in the eye, decided her next move and fell into the pool. It was a calculated, thought-out decision and as always, she won the round. I was laughing so hard, she knew she was safe from a scolding. Hogo and I scooped up the fish, he added some water then mopped the stone floor. Suzie, buried in a towel, grinned all the way to the kitchen.

Sergeant Hsiu was delighted with the story. He picked her up and said something in Chinese. Suzie looked like she knew a secret.

I gave the sergeant his driving schedule for the afternoon and after lunch, we drove down the mountain to Tien Mou to get me worked over. I liked to drive through this tiny village. The shops and houses were old and quaint. It was a typical Taiwanese town with a big tree in the middle of the road. Sergeant Hsiu kept me in his sights if I wanted to stroll and although my back tingled, knowing someone was watching me, it was not the tingle of fear.

Suzy the hairdresser pounced as soon as I entered the upstairs shop and the girls scrambled for their positions. The shop was plain – most interiors were – often with just a light bulb hanging from the ceiling in the center of the room. But Suzy had "westernized" and there was more light and an amenity or two. The process never took long. With so many people attached to or working on one's movable parts, the whole thing was over within an hour. Each person had to be tipped and by the time I laid it all out on the counter, the total cost was close to what I would pay in the United States.

The sergeant didn't seem to mind waiting and he always nodded approvingly when I came out. I sometimes wondered what he thought when I went in. Was the change that great?

Jim's office could have been in Norfolk, San Diego or any American base. It was plain, business-like with no frills. The military is not much for chintz curtains. Since it was a Joint Command, each branch had a smattering of women on its staffs. This was before the great influx of women into the military that came in later years, and the women attached to the TDC were no-frills ladies. Always, the feeling was of serious dedication to their jobs. I " helloed" my way to Jim's office and after a round of greetings, we left for the official car parked downstairs.

As always, I kept busy looking at as much of the passing sights as I could see while Jim and Skip conducted TDC business and a briefing about the National Assembly. We would be escorted around and shown the chamber and the voting procedures. I was greatly disappointed that the Assembly was not in session, but it was vacation time for them, just as we have in our own Congress. This visit held a particular fascination for me because I had served on a U.S. Congressional staff on Capitol Hill in the late sixties and early seventies. Jim was in the Pentagon for a two-year tour of duty and I fell into the job by chance.

The offices of the Indiana Congressman I worked for were in the Longworth Building. I let the images of that time fill my thoughts. There were protestors on the Mall and on the steps of the Capitol. Some had clothes on and some didn't. Viet Nam was still raging, as were the dissidents. Often, the rhetoric on the floor as well as in the galleries was emotional, sometimes, even vitriolic. Because we had just come from a nightmare tour of duty, with Jim flying in Viet Nam I often found it difficult to listen to the steady stream of hatred that poured out of the mouths of those protestors who knew nothing about what was really going on in that other part of the world. It was a lesson in control and the recognition of every American's right to the First Amendment, but I often wished they would just take the time to read the rest of the Constitution.

During those days, card-carrying Communists served in the House of Representatives. One California Congressman placed the American flag outside his office, upside down, with the Stars and Stripes puddled on the floor of the hallway. It was a divisive war and those were divisive times. Yet, I felt a kind of wonder at the freedoms my country allowed and the people enjoyed.

The official car pulled up at the National Assembly and after our greeting by an impressive group of Chinese politicians, our escort, a smilingly pleasant young man, ushered us into the large room that was the chamber of the government. The electronic voting boards were high on the walls in the corners and there was a sense of waiting. I had known that same feeling the times I stood in the empty chamber of the House of Representatives in Washington, D.C. It was after all, just the shell that housed the dynamic and sometimes uproarious spirit of a democracy at work. This room would fill and the hum of discussions and arguments, passion and anger, would express the excitement of their democracy just beginning..

"The National Assembly meets here with 314 members. Originally, the capital of the Republic of China was Nanking, China, and our Constitution was adopted before the ROC moved to Taiwan, where Taipei became the temporary capital."

The young man was impressed with his visitors and appeared mesmerized by the medals that marched up Jim's tunic. He had studied our biographies carefully and his eyes returned often to the Navy Cross at the top of the bank of the colorful awards.

"The members of the National Assembly are elected by popular vote and serve four-year terms. The Assembly itself has the power to amend the Constitution, change the Republic of China's borders and impeach the President. It is made up of five Yuans."

I was making mental comparisons and these could be compared to our three branches of government; the Executive, Legislative and Judiciary.

"There is the Executive, Legislative, Control, Examination and Judicial." All but two sounded familiar. So I asked.

"Would you describe the Control and Examination branches, please?"

185

He seemed startled that the woman in the group would speak. After seven months in an oriental environment, I was getting used to the "seen but not heard" philosophy for females.

"Yes, Linder Tai Tai. I will be very pleased to tell you of this. The Control Yuan has the power to impeach and censure the President and the Vice President and to conduct government audits."

Ah – the GAO, Government Accounting Office, that watches the watchers and lowers the boom on whomever deserves it.

"The Examination Yuan is in charge of our Civil Service," he continued.

And if their Civil Service is anything like ours, their bureaucracy will burgeon like the hydra-headed monster and will need more than an examination to keep it under control.

It was an afternoon that evoked many memories of my days on the Hill. Our democracy would soon be two hundred years old; theirs was just beginning. New political parties were emerging and the press was flexing its muscles. It's exciting to see a country waking and stretching, testing new waters, trying new ways of governing. The autocratic rule of Chiang Kai shek was moving into the twentieth century and would feel the shove of demanded democracy. The fundamentals were still there; the pride of all that is Chinese, the ability to survive for five thousand years, the eternal need and love of family, but with it, the determination for self-governing. They would stumble along the way, make mistakes and feel the pain of losing, but they would continue the climb and in time, be looked upon as the economic miracle of this century. I felt a deep pleasure at being on scene to watch.

Clark Air Force Base, the Philippines

I was packed and ready by 5:30 Monday morning. The trip to the airport would take over an hour and with plane stops all over the South Pacific, you were either there when they loaded or they took off without you. I was there.

As we dropped Jim off at his office, he said, "Are you sure you packed everything you'll need for the week?" My faithful reminder.

"As Mother used to say, everything but the kitchen sink." He knew I dreaded this week and tried to lighten my mood.

"I think you'll enjoy it. You might even be surprised by a few things." He and Skip had acted like co-conspirators all week. I knew something was up, but couldn't imagine what.

"Are there any secrets or surprises you two should let me in on?" They both grinned and Jim shook his head.

"No, no. Just relax and enjoy the week."

How does one enjoy a week of being prodded, poked and punctured with needles?

In 1972 when the doctors had first discovered this serious disease I carried in both eyes, Jim's reaction was one of anger. He had taken command of the aircraft carrier Forrestal and since the doctor's office was on the Naval Base where the ships were berthed, I frantically found my way there after hearing the verdict. I ran up the gangway and asked the officer on the Quarterdeck to please find my husband. I needed to talk to him.

They escorted me to his stateroom and I waited a long ten minutes for him to come in.

"Jim, I've just come from the doctor and he says I have a serious eye disease in both of my eyes. I couldn't wait for you to come home tonight. I needed to talk to you now."

"What do you mean? What are you talking about?" He was angry. I was stunned.

"Jim, I can't help it. It's something that has just come out of nowhere. They don't know why." Immediately on the defensive, I imagined he was thinking about the complications this would cause. Command of an aircraft carrier is an awesome responsibility and one that demands total attention at all times. Having a blind wife who would be left alone for long periods of time was not in the scenario. I could feel the same anger building in me.

Many years ago, early in our marriage when we were starting our family, Jim received orders to Korea. His combat tour would last nine months. He said something that at the time, I thought was cruel. "Remember Patti, there is no such thing as an excuse."

I stared at nine months alone in a strange place with a two-year-old and another on the way. It occurred to me that I should have married a farmer who only went out to the bean field in the south forty and was home by dark.

" No such thing as an excuse". Okay, Buster, we'll see how long I last.

188

It served me well. When the car had a flat tire, I didn't say, "I can't do that because I don't know how." I learned how. When the grocer overcharged me, instead of being too embarrassed to confront him with his mistake, I marched back and demanded restitution. And restitution was made. I grew up very quickly, not being able to excuse my inadequacies. It toughened me, not that any sweet young thing wants to be toughened, but Navy life demanded it, and since there is no such things as an excuse, I made it through the nine months successfully and presented him with a son, besides.

As we lived together and apart, I slowly realized that the reaction I had labeled as anger was really fear, instead. There is a kind of courage a man must have when he leaves his family and all of his worldly goods behind for months, sometimes years at a time. There are many unknown factors that cannot be planned for and not every wife is obedient like the old-fashioned marriage vows require. So you recognize the anger is really fear, and comment to yourself, "No big deal". The old worries are put aside, to be replaced by a whole new set to chew on.

Jim was uneasy about my first trip off the island alone, so we kept the conversation light as Sergeant Fan steered the official car through the tangle of traffic. When Jim climbed out of the car and straightened to his full height, I looked up and said, "Remember dear, there's no such thing as an excuse, so eat whatever Hogo puts in front of you."

We both grinned and he disappeared into Headquarters. Skip looked a little puzzled but I didn't enlighten him. Everyone has to find his own answers. We were still hunting around for all of ours

The flight down was over four hours long and tiring. But I had never been on such an errand and there were things to learn. The plane was a prop plane – no swift jet to whisk us there. This particular flight had one attendant and only one stretcher case. The rest bided their time like I did. It was tedious and for those in pain, the trip must have been endless. The impression was that we were passing over the entire 7,100 islands of the Philippine chain before reaching our destination.

The sprawling Air Force base came into view and we all breathed a little easier. Clark had a population of 14,000 people. Many were Filipinos employed by the U.S. Government. A military base, like an aircraft carrier is a city within itself. Most of the amenities necessary for living were available, thereby ensuring the personnel prices they could afford.

I looked down on the precisely placed hangars that from this altitude reminded me of Monopoly buildings. Military installations in the tropics have more trees than bases in the States, giving them an atmosphere of a small town. But a Base is a Base and they all have a similar business-like look. The plane landed and taxied into place. We staggered off, stiff from hours of sitting and as I put my foot on the runway, the young man I met on our previous trip stepped forward and reintroduced himself.

"Mrs. Linder, it's good to see you again. How was the trip? Was the plane comfortable?"

I had the impression if it wasn't he would do something about it.

"I have a car waiting and by the way, please call me Bill."

"Everything was fine. Very professional and a godsend for those of us in the outer regions. And I'll call you Bill if you'll call me Pat. Skip said we'll be seeing a lot of each other this week and when you call me Mrs. Linder, I feel like I should salute."

He put his head back and laughed. ""Pat' it is when we're not around the doctors. They know who you are and expect formality."

"I can live with that and I don't want to rock any boats. After all, they have the needles. Are we going first to the Guest Quarters? I would like to unpack and freshen up before we go to the hospital."

"I'm here to take you where you will be staying."

He had the same look on his face that Skip and Jim had in the car. How many people were in on this, and when was I going to find out about it? He stashed the luggage in the trunk of the car and we drove off. Most of the buildings looked alike, but as we drove, I noticed we had left the business end of the Base and were winding down a street of houses.

"Neat place for a hospital – right in the middle of housing. And Bill, this is not the way to the Guest Quarters."

"No, Pat. It's the way to our house. You are to stay with the Cutler family this week and we come complete with children and dog."

I was overwhelmed.

"It's all been arranged. Mary and the kids are waiting to meet you. We figured you would be tired, so I'll go over the hospital paperwork with you and get it back to them for your first appointment in the morning."

"Bill, I don't know what to say. I didn't expect any of this and its almost too good to be true."

"It's our pleasure. I talked it over with Mary after your last visit here and we decided you should be with us and not stuck in those Guest Quarters all by yourself. Skip and the Admiral seemed very pleased about it. We're just glad you can be with us."

God is good.

They charmed me. It was a busy family, with something going on every minute. The flight down, the grind of hospital paperwork with print too small to see, left me frazzled. I met Mary, a small, pretty, dark-haired lady who looked like she had always belonged to Bill. The children were in and out for introductions and the biggest German shepherd I have ever seen stood guard over the whole family. I named him Dear Beast and we became friends, which surprised me because I had always been afraid of big dogs. My two much older brothers had lolloping Great Danes and Irish Setters around the house and because I was very little, I was usually flat on the floor with one or the other standing over me, jaws ajar and tongue dripping. Looking up at the underside of a Great Dane does not have a calming effect on a four-year-old and I was always glad to be somewhere else when large dogs were around. But Dear Beast had his charm.

Mary settled me on the couch on the porch after Bill left for the hospital with the paper work and I was immediately asleep. An hour later, I awoke to find the big shepherd (he was the length of me when he stretched out), snoozing companionably on the floor by my side. I was on his territory and rather than argue the point, I concentrated on how to cement our friendship.

It was quite a week. I hardly noticed the strange things the doctors were doing to me; the usual round of blood tests and countless hours spent in a chair with people peering into my eyes, followed by endless consultations and speculations. I was bored with the whole thing by the end of the first hour.

When I wasn't at the hospital, there was time to more thoroughly explore the nearby town of Angeles and the contents of the shops. Some were small and rickety, some were filled with unusual articles made of the many types of shells found in the waters surrounding the islands. The embroidery work was exquisite. I spoke with a tiny young clerk who answered in the patois of Tagalog with its rapid, staccato clicking and the idiomatic English that found its way into their language during World War II. It was a fast, confusing jumble of words, but we managed the transaction and our granddaughters would enjoy the exotic things I found for them. The furniture store was next and I asked to meet with the manager to discuss our furniture that had arrived by boat a few weeks before.

"I couldn't be more pleased with the way our table and chairs turned out. But I must tell you that instead of four chairs, you sent five and since they fit around the table, I will keep the extra and pay you for it today."

He seemed astounded that I was offering to pay for their mistake. "Mum, you must keep the chair as a gift from my company."

It was my turn to be astonished and we parted friends. My future dealings with this company would be easier and there were more sales ahead. He knew that.

Bill showed me the sprawling Base with its many streets of housing, the hangars, commissary, exchange and the things that make a military installation in a foreign country the vast city it is. Twelve years later, the nearby volcano Pinatubo would erupt and cover Clark Air Force Base and the town of Angeles with half a billion tons of volcanic ash and cinders. Typhoon rains would sweep through like a tidal wave and in the year and a half following, one thousand people would die as a result of the massive mudslides and floods that buried fifty villages. Following the eruption, the U.S. abandoned Clark Air Force Base for all time.

Dr. Franklin, one of the eye specialists I met during my days at the hospital, asked about my care in Taipei. I told him about Dr. Lin.

"Mrs. Linder, I will be traveling to Taipei next month to treat the military dependents who can't get down here to the Philippines. Do you suppose there is any way I could meet Dr. Lin? I would like to compare notes on Chinese medical procedures."

"I see no reason why not. I'm scheduled for an appointment with Dr. Lin the first week of next month. Would you be there then?"

"Yes, I can come then. It would actually be more convenient for my schedule here."

"Good. I'll call his office when I get back to Taipei and confirm the appointment. I'll mention you will be with me, hoping to meet Dr. Lin. And by the way, please try to join us for dinner at the Quarters."

"I would like that very much. I'll look forward to meeting the Admiral."

Everybody always says that. With such a fumbling wife, they probably want to see the paragon of patience who lives with her.

Many of the large military hospitals scattered throughout the world sent doctors to outlying areas as collateral duty where military personnel and their dependents were stationed. I had no idea at the time how this would impact on me at a particularly frightening future time.

There was a party at the Officers' Club and the Cutlers insisted I join them. I hesitated, being a complete stranger to all but my host and hostess, but they would not hear of me staying home with just Dear Beast for company. The Club was done in the style of the tropics with bamboo and waving palms. This particular night's menu was Mongolian Barbecue, something I had never heard of.

"Mary, I'm curious about the Mongolian end of the barbecue tonight. Why Mongolian?"

Mary grinned. "The story I've heard is bizarre. During Ghengis Khan's rule when the Mongolian's were raping and pillaging, they slung leather pouches over their horses' rumps. And they carried big shields. They gathered up anything they found during the day – chickens, milk, roots – anything edible and put it into the leather pouches. Then at night, when they made camp and built their fires, they put their shields on the fire, emptied the pouches, let the stuff cook a while and that was dinner."

I could imagine the condition of the ingredients, including the churning effect on the milk during a hot day.

I hadn't the faintest idea what to expect, and it was an unusual evening. The atmosphere was easy, laid-back and the food was superb. We each took a plate, loaded up the many items we wanted, handed it to a chef, who stir-fried the whole thing and gave us a steaming, aromatic mixture of meats and vegetables on our shields.

The entertainment for the evening was a small band of Filipinos playing gongs and chimes. It was called Kulintang and derives from Spanish music. There were only a few notes and lots of rhythm, reminding me of the steel bands we had heard in the Caribbean. Four young native dancers brought long wooden sticks and placed them on the ground. Two moved the sticks in time to the music that had picked up speed and one at a time, the other two dancers jumped in between the moving sticks. One mistake and someone's ankle would be in a splint for a long time. It was exciting and I shouted encouragement like everyone else.

"Bill, do they ever miss?" They looked so fragile to be doing anything that dangerous.

"I've seen the dance many times and so far, no misses."

They knew I was enjoying the whole evening. Bill and Mary had many friends and I met them all. I was just "Pat", a visitor from Taiwan and I answered their many questions about that exotic place.

During the night, a storm moved in. The rainy season had supposedly come and gone, but this was a maverick and tricky at that. I had two final appointments at the hospital, then Bill and the official car were waiting to take me to the airfield to board a helicopter headed for Subic Bay where I would join Jim. I hated to leave. It was a wonderful week, in spite of the needle pricks and hospital waiting rooms. I couldn't help the tears in my eyes when the children and Dear Beast lined up to tell me goodbye. I felt a little like General MacArthur when I said I would return, but then, this was the Philippines.

The helicopter was as big as a building. The designation told me it carried cargo and from the size, any kind of cargo. My luggage was put under a seat but when I turned to give Bill a hug and another thank you, he looked worried. The storm was increasing and although we had been cleared for takeoff, I knew he didn't like the way it looked. An Air Force Colonel climbed into the plane and helped me aboard.

"Don't worry about her. We'll get her to Subic." He shouted to Bill over the howl of the wind and the engines.

I only had time to wave and throw Bill a hasty kiss before the big Mickey Mouse earphones were clapped over my ears and we moved away.

We headed west toward the coast. The Colonel, taking out a pad of paper and pencil, wrote, "Don't be frightened. The weather should be better in a short time."

I nodded, realized I was frightened, excited and having the time of my life. A helicopter moves differently than a plane and the sensation is a lot like being on a roller coaster. Where you go next, only the pilot knows.

I took the pencil. "My name is Pat Linder."

He nodded.

I continued writing. "I'm glad you're here, but I'm not afraid."

"Good for you. Neither am I." We looked at each other and laughed. We were both scared and knew it. The helicopter bounced and skidded in the driving wind and rain and the jungle below was impenetrable. I realized if we went down, nobody would ever find us. Those trees below resembled a green tarpaulin, making a search party hard pressed to ever figure out where we were.

We were over the island of Luzon where battles had been fought during World War II. A short distance to the north were Bataan and Corregidor and to the south, Mindinao. I closed my eyes to stop the world from gyrating and found LIFE MAGAZINE pictures of the killing battles, infamous enemy treatment of the Allied soldiers and the native people filling my thoughts. My brother was somewhere in the South Pacific during my teenage years and as the reports came in with their bloody descriptions, I feared for him. The names of the battles were firmly imprinted on my mind. I doubted they would ever completely leave my thoughts.

Hanging onto the bucket seats, I never noticed how insufferably uncomfortable they were. There are no soft spots in a cargo helicopter. It's all metal and because of my size, there wasn't a lot between my bones and the seat.

The flight took on a surrealistic quality as the pilot diverted to miss worse weather ahead. I felt caught in a vacuum, suspended for an indefinite time with only the muffled hum of the engines that made it through the thick pads of the earphones. It was too bumpy to write, so we both sat quietly and waited for the end – either the trip's or ours.

The sun suddenly broke through. We were out of the storm. There's one to tell the grandchildren. The Colonel and I exchanged notes again.

"I'm to attend a meeting with your husband at Subic."

"I'm glad you weren't along just to keep me from falling out of the helo."

He laughed and so did I. We both looked comic with our big earphones. I was grateful I hadn't panicked or lost my lunch in his lap. After all, "there's no such thing as an excuse."

CHAPTER FIFTEEN
TAIWAN

'MAYDAY! MAYDAY!'

I jerked awake. The Blue Goose was churning its way across the China Seas, headed for Taipei. The speaker in the cabin of the plane picked up what came through the radio and we were instantly awake. Jim headed for the cockpit. The Philippine Islands lay behind and both of us had dozed off, worn out from the week's activities.

A boat was foundering in the choppy seas below. As I watched out the window, the plane began to circle the area, every eye searching for a tiny object in trouble. We made as many passes as possible, but there was only so much fuel and we were a long way from home. Jim finally returned to his seat.

"Did you see anything from the cockpit? I couldn't make out anything from this side of the plane."

He moved across the aisle and continued to scan the waters below.

"No one was able to spot anything that looked like a boat. We don't know how big it is and if it's a fishing boat, it may be too small for a visual sighting, but we've radioed our position and the message we received, so if there are other boats in the area, they may be able to help."

We both lapsed into silence – Jim, with his memories and I with my imagination.

Once, years before in the Pentagon, an Admiral had a small plaque on his desk that read, *Protect me, Lord. The sea is so great and my boat is so small.* I had since seen other interpretations of that same request, but they all boiled down to the insignificance of man in the vastness of the oceans they travel.

I looked down at the great stretch of sparkling water below us, so deceptively beautiful, and knew that under that benign mantle lay treachery and power. Having my husband on the oceans of the world for most of our married life, I learned early to respect the possibilities of an anonymous death. When the sea claims a victim, there is no body, no closure, no final chapter; just a written or spoken word that delivers the verdict and changes lives forever.

As we came through the great red doors, Suzie took a running jump and glued herself to the front of me. We staggered into the living room and she became a squirming, squealing, leggy ball of ecstasy. Mama San 's bath, earlier that morning left her soft and silky and I could smell the talcum powder. I was glad to be home – even the glassy hall floor looked inviting.

A pile of invitations from Jim's office waited for me, but I was too weary to deal with them now – tomorrow would have to do. I walked out onto the long porch and gazed at the mountains cloaked in the late afternoon purple haze. They slumbered; here today, here tomorrow. I knew now what the lower mountains to the right of Tien Mou reminded me of. Their crests bore the profile of Kuan Yin, the Goddess of Compassion. She lay on her back with her quiet face pointed to the sky. My pursuit of information led me to a picture of this gentle lady and Hogo confirmed that my imagination was not playing tricks on me. I found the sight of her perpetually comforting as I began each day with a glimpse of her serene face.

Three guards passed below me on their way to their posts. Usually it was one, sometimes two. Must be a rumble or trouble of some kind. I would check with Jim.

Dr. Joe Franklin from Clark Hospital made his scheduled visit the last of the month and Dr. Lin indicated he was anxious to meet him. Joe joined us for dinner the night before my appointment. Dinner was on the porch and the view provided the evening's entertainment. The men talked of the medical arrangements on the island and Jim said," Pat tells me that the doctor has equipment she has never seen before, but he never uses it."

I explained my curiosity about the situation. Joe asked questions and I knew he would find a way to help Dr. Lin. "I've wanted to ask him why he doesn't use the machines, but I'm afraid I will get into the 'losing face' thing and I don't understand enough about that to do it gracefully."

Joe laughed and said he would be careful when he asked his questions. We met the next morning at the hospital for the ten o'clock appointment, introductions were made and the two doctors lapsed into that world that does not include the patient. I had been there before and whiled away the time by memorizing the charts. Once in a while, a little cheating is good for the soul.

"Dr. Lin, your equipment is superb." Dr. Lin glowed. "May I try some of them on Mrs. Linder?"

Dr. Lin looked hesitant. Joe reached down, plugged in the machine and with my head stuck against the eyepieces, made the necessary calibrations and adjustments as he peered into my eyes. He then turned the machine over the Dr. Lin. " Take a look. You may want to make your own adjustments, but this is a beautiful piece of machinery."

Dr. Lin took his place, gazed back at me, turned a knob and looked up with a beatific smile. Nothing more was said and Joe methodically went through the same procedure with the other unused equipment. It was a dandy morning. I had another thorough examination, Joe met and liked Dr. Lin and Dr. Lin knew all there was to know about the newest innovations in eye testing. Face was saved and for once, I didn't mind being the guinea pig.

The following weeks were spent in the Blue Goose, flying around the Island. Topographically everything that could be found in China could be found in Taiwan, only on a smaller scale. The sea, of course, was just as important as the land. The coasts were fished and provided the people with their favorite food. In T'aichung, we inspected an immense harbor being built, using the latest construction technology. When finished, international trade would flourish, but as I looked out at the water, I was looking at the Taiwan Straits with China a few short miles away. The Chinese pride in this amazing accomplishment was infectious and I brushed away the undercurrent of fear I always felt when I looked toward the west. In the distance were tiny islands that belonged to the Republic of China and were as controversial as Taiwan. They shared the same vulnerability of their mother island.

The land of Taiwan rolled, plunged, shot to the sky and tumbled to the plains. Terraced hillsides dropped like solid waterfalls and gorges of marble slashed through the high peaks of the mountains where there was still snow, feeding frigid streams that raced through them. In central Taiwan, the East-West Highway, a masterpiece of engineering, snaked through the Taroko Gorge. The sheer walls of marble gleamed from the cuts made to lay this highway through Taiwan's highest mountains that filled the center of the island and left only the outer edges for man to live.

At a future time, grapevines would be planted for wine on the sunny side of the lower slopes. Apple trees bore fruit that resembled pears, sweet and bulging with juice. Large white onions lay in piles near a field, recently harvested. Brown-skinned peanuts could be found in all the markets. Every inch was utilized – either with natural beauty or the man-made beauty of growing food and building the infrastructure of the Island. Nothing was wasted.

We were driven or flew from place to place. Always there was a delegation to meet us and offer lunch or dinner depending on the length of the trip and the tours. Sometimes we spent the night in the best hotel available, but none came with enough light. I needed light to see through the scar tissue that continued to build from the ongoing inflammation. The bare bulb in the ceiling just didn't do it, but often I was so weary from looking at what was on the agenda for the day, I simply fell into bed, grateful for the darkness.

In central Taiwan, we were introduced to one of the nine tribes of aborigines. These people were smaller in size than the Taiwanese and their skin color was almost the same as mine. They were charming people – happy and playful. They spoke the Formosan language and we joined them as they danced to their native music. Jim, in full uniform, towered over them. We were in a circle with ten other people who were dressed in ornate and colorful costumes. When the dance finished, we were each handed babies to hold while pictures were taken. Jim looked acutely uncomfortable. The tribe was communal and everybody belonged to everybody. Later, we would see them in Taipei dancing, as they entertained the assembled dignitaries. I liked them. Their happy faces always produced an answering smile.

Despite the whirlwind traveling and new sights presented to us at each stop, Jim had a distracted air about him. I noticed it at other times when he appeared to be intent on his job, but thinking of something else. Although, because of his career, we spent many years apart, I had a sixth sense about him.

After the central island visit, we drove to Keelung by ourselves. The city is just east of the northern tip of Taiwan and has a busy harbor. The movie Sand Pebbles was filmed in the downtown and harbor areas and as we drove into the city, I looked to the west and saw hillsides covered with shacks and bits and pieces of houses that gave it a distinctive ghetto look. It was an accumulation of the very poor.

We needed this day to ourselves so I tried to use the time wisely.

"What's bothering you, Jim?" Blunt and to the point.

He was a man of few words and I knew I would hear only what I should hear, which was probably not much. But I found it important to let him know I noticed his mood changes and was there as a listener.

"I'm disturbed about the level of protection of Taiwan."

"Even with what we saw in Kaoshung?"

"That's just a beginning."

I tried to reassure him. "But they have us."

"*Us* will probably go away some day and I don't know what will happen to them when that time comes."

We were parked on the side of a city street with the teeming mobs of people hurrying around us. Ordinarily, I liked to look at their faces and play the guessing game of what part of Asia they came from. Today, I felt the seriousness of Jim's concern and concentrated instead on his words and even more intently, on his unspoken words.

He said, "To try to explain some of this, I'll have to go back to the war in Viet Nam. Do you remember that communiqué I handed you after I returned from my first combat tour over there?"

Remember it? I will never forget it. We were sitting on the bed with family papers that needed going over and a packet of Jim's messages from his office to check before returning to his squadron the next day. It was good, having him back in the casual atmosphere of family life. The preceding year when he was flying strikes over North Viet Nam had been a year of living hell with fear as its hallmark – the knot in the stomach kind. I never knew if he was alive or dead and wondered how I would ever tell the children if the news was bad.

He handed me a paper out of his message packet. "Remember that newspaper article you got so upset about – the one that described my squadron's raids on the series of bridges in North Viet Nam?"

I wasn't just upset, I was livid. The American press had seen fit to print the whole colorful story of the raids that wiped out the enemy's major supply route and had therefore, provided the enemy with Jim's name as the man who had led the raids. I took the paper from his hand, tried to make sense out of the message abbreviations and finally found the core. It was a thank you from the Chinese communists to the U.S. press for providing them with Jim's name and an assurance they would be waiting for him with a welcoming committee should he ever return to North Viet Nam. Once again, the coldness of fear covered me for I knew, as only a wife's instinct can tell her that her husband would indeed, be going back again.

"Oh yes, I remember that piece of paper – but what does that have to do with Taiwan?" I really did not want to dwell on those terrible days of the sixties and hoped to pull him back into the present.

"The Chinese Communists and Russia were supplying the Viet Cong with weapons and ordnance – most of it pretty sophisticated stuff."

We were still in the Cold War during those days and anything Russia could do to annihilate us was worth their careful attention.

Jim continued, " China's interest was, I suppose, territorial – the more countries they could add to their list of colonies, the stronger they would be."

"So that makes three communist countries in league with each other."

"That makes lots of troops, many weapons and ordnance. When the war ended and we pulled out, we gave them the wherewithal to use what we left behind – and we left a lot."

"Are you getting around to telling me that China has all of that and could use it against Taiwan?"

"Why not? I'm sure it was divvied up among the three countries and along with the physical elements of war was the technology that made it all work."

My God. The weapons of war, some even our own, to be used against this tiny country, should it come to that. But why did that surprise me? Hadn't we given Japan the scrap metal necessary to produce what they gave us in return – Pearl Harbor? No wonder he was worried.

"Won't we always be here for them?" My protective instincts were heating up.

"According to what I hear in the weekly Team meetings at the Embassy, we should all be paying closer attention to what's going on back home. There are some pretty serious economic problems and under the Carter Administration, the interest rates are going off the charts."

With all of the swirling activity of this place, I had forgotten about the jigsaw puzzle that is Washington, D.C. and had assumed if we could take care of ourselves out here, they could do the same back there. I should have known better.

Jim's long fingers tapped the steering wheel as he looked out the front window of the car. "Our foreign policy is directly tied to our own economy and that has to be our first priority. The military's primary objective here is protection against the enemy – and on a proximity basis, that would be China. State sees it as a diplomatic problem – one that can be solved by talking. You know how I feel about that."

Indeed I did. A dichotomy would always exist between the two. So often in the past, the talking had led us into convoluted situations that could only be resolved by the use of force, leaving the military as the bad guys.

"But Jim, there has to be both or the world would have destroyed itself centuries ago."

"I agree, but we're in a push-pull situation now with Taiwan. We're their umbrella of protection, but the question is, will our own economic problems override that?"

Was this another definition of the handwriting on the wall, I wondered? "Anything more you want to tell me?"

"No, I'd better not."

I let it drop. At least I had the answer to my concern of his distraction. And I certainly had enough to mull over in my own mind, not that there were any answers. Not now.

But I couldn't let it go until I asked, "One last question and you don't have to answer it if you don't want to. What happens if we're not here for them?"

"The supposition is immediate invasion by the Chinese communists – but that's based on Taiwan opinion. Nobody really knows until it happens."

We resumed our drive that led us down to the waterfront of this busy harbor. Overlooking Keelung on a hill high above our heads, I saw an immense statue of the Kuan Yin, Goddess of Compassion and Protection. Her face was peaceful, benign as it is always presented.

Lady, you have your work cut out for you.

209

I answered the jangling telephone, waited for the clicks to stop, almost said, "Hello, boys, how's it going?" but didn't and instead said, "This is Mrs. Linder."

"Mrs. Linder, this is Jim Ling at the Naval Dispensary."

"Dr. Ling. I haven't talked with you for quite a while. How are you?" Amenities.

"Fine, thanks. I wonder if I could ask you to come in today or tomorrow to talk over the results of your tests they made at Clark when you were last there?"

Oh grand. If I were smart, I would pack the bag this afternoon and head for parts unknown. I hated listening to test results. In Norfolk, five years ago, the Naval hospital notified me by telephone that I had some fatal blood disease with two weeks to live. As my grandmother would have done, I cleaned out the closets, wrote a will leaving everything to the children and sat down to examine my life. Then I got mad called the doctor, demanded another set of tests and found that because of a lab mistake, some other poor soul instead of me, should be making out their will.

I seated myself in front of Dr. Ling's large, paper-filled desk. He was pleasant but serious. Down to business. "Pat, you have gout."

I felt my jaw drop.

"I have what?"

"Gout."

"Are you serious, and if you are, how did I get that?"

210

" One of your blood tests taken at Clark indicates you have gout and I suspect it's from the many Chinese meals you've consumed since coming to Taiwan. Too much meat. It creates an acid that affects your liver and simply put, that's what we call gout."

"But I always thought portly Englishmen with cigars and a glass of Madeira had the gout. I'm just not the Henry the Eighth type."

"Probably all of those hsaio hsing wine toasts that go along with what you're eating brought it on so quickly."

I thought of Sun Yat Sen, the Generalissimo and Confuscious and decided they owed me one. "Are any of my inner parts affected? I haven't noticed anything different on the outside."

"There is some liver damage, but that will repair itself over time. My recommendation is that you eat less meat and cut down on the toasts. "

"Now Dr Ling, can you see me saying to my host, 'Gee, I'm really sorry, but I can't toast the Generalissimo tonight because I have the gout'?"

He grinned. "I would like to be there when you do. But you must change your intake or you will have really serious problems."

I thought of the Chinese general I caught drinking tea instead of wine and decided we should have a little chat. I won't snitch on him if he will fix me up with the wine server. As for the meat, instead of two bites on my little eight-course plate, I will only eat one and if necessary, drop it into my purse on my lap. After all, these people were used to seeing things drop out of sight while I was eating. They were the same people who had watched the lichi nut find its way down my dress front at the President's dinner party.

On the way home, after assuring Sergeant Hsiu I was all right and there was nothing to worry about, and receiving one of his rare, illuminating smiles, I thought about this latest twist. President Nixon had gone to China and made all those toasts. I wondered if he went home with the gout. Actually, gout would have been better than a presidential resignation. Isn't gout the symbol of the good life? Will I end up in my wing chair with a swaddled foot resting on the Queen Anne footstool? It all seemed so absolutely ridiculous. And I knew I was not going to pass this little bit of information along to my husband – he had enough on his mind.

As luck had it, the Chinese general was very gracious and understanding and he tipped off the wine server. We toasted each other with a wink and a grin. His wife continued to be his 'd'ai biao' who drank for him and I never inquired about her liver. But the word must have circulated, for without acknowledgement, my servings of meat became much smaller and the problem was solved without comment so Jim never knew. In our country, it's called thoughtfulness. Out here, it is an unspoken kindness that is a symbol of the depth of friendship and to be on the receiving end of that is humbling.

Spring was coming to Taiwan. As I padded onto the porch in robe and slippers one morning for a cup of Hogo's coffee, I drew in my breath in amazement. At the foot of the back lawn, beyond the swimming pool, stood a plum tree in full bloom. That fragile little thing had flowered overnight and was the first to show blossoms. No wonder the Chinese artists place plum branches in so many of their paintings. To them, the tree is the symbol of moral integrity, one's good personality, and the blossom is an example of simple beauty. The yearly lesson learned is that something so fragile can survive the cold and snows of winter. My next trip to the Museum would be a study of the paintings, both on scrolls and porcelains, of the plum branch. Because of our traveling, my Museum visits were fewer than I hoped for. Yet, while attending a party at the American Embassy a few weeks before, I became more determined than ever to spend time there.

The Ambassador's wife, Ann, introduced me to a quiet, unassuming man of indeterminate age, and I assumed he was older than he looked. His name was Dr. Na Chih-liang, the Curator of the National Palace Museum at that time. He told me that in 1933, the decision was made to pack up the art treasures into nearly 20,000 crates and move them out of Beijing because of the threat of destruction from the invading Japanese army. By foot, the crates were carried on the backs of peasants on a 12,000-kilometer journey around China for sixteen years, with always the threat of acquisition from both the Japanese and the Chinese communist forces that followed the Japanese rule.

When Chiang Kai shek came to Taiwan in 1949, American warships helped in the transporting of troops to the island. The Chinese brought as many of the treasures as they could carry, more than half a million artifacts that were then stored in a cave dug into a hillside for protection against raids from the Mainland. Eventually, in front of the cave, the National Palace Museum was constructed as the permanent housing for the works of art.

213

I had to imagine the rationale for this incredible effort. When an enemy culture invades a country, often the first thing to go, besides the people, is the history and art of the victim society. It was a given that the Japanese forces would destroy as much of the Chinese culture as possible.

The Chinese communist forces would of course, want the wealth of the treasures to remain in their own country. But ideologies clashed and those treasures of China are safely stored in a cave and an imposing building on Yangmingshan Mountain. I knew of the Nationalist's Chinese dedicated desire to return to their country and to turn it into a democracy and I assumed the treasures would only go home when that goal was achieved.

The sixteen-year foot march was a miracle of endurance and determination. It was also a logistics nightmare. That this frail man could accomplish so much in his one lifetime made me realize what a privilege it was to speak with him and my days at the Museum took on new meaning.

In the early 1970's, the Peoples Republic of China – communist China – sent an art exhibit to the United States for viewing and we attended the showing held in the National Gallery of Art in Washington, D.C. The exhibit consisted of recently uncovered works of art and historic artifacts that spanned thousands of years of history. As we stood, gazing at a tiny curled-up leopard, enameled in its exact color and with emeralds for eyes, a man sharing this stunning piece of art spoke softly, "The Chinese were doing this when the Greeks were still on their hands and knees."

And Jim's comment was "They were doing this when everybody was still on their hands and knees."

We moved to the bronze statue of a running horse with only one hoof resting on the back of a swallow. The artist had made a statement on the dynamics of balance and one day a copy would rest on my own table. But it was the Jade Princess that once viewed, never leaves the memory. Her body was totally encased in jade, cut in one-inch pieces, and held together with bands of gold and gold knots, forming jade chain mail. The soles of her shoes were solid pieces of jade, cut in the shape of her foot. There was simply no word to describe the opulence of the lady in the glass case. She was a princess and her burial suit clearly spoke of her importance both in life and afterwards.

The schedule read, "trip to Hong Kong: Conference with Naval Attache." This would be our first trip to the British island together. Jim was there many times during the Korean and Viet Nam wars and I had my one brief visit of three days on the Kowloon side earlier in the year.

I was excited about it and wanted to know more.

"How long will we be gone – a week, six days, five, four?" He nodded on "three" and I sighed. Can't accomplish much in three days.

"I have to be back for another visit down island. It's a must."

"All right, but can I do some things besides sit in hotel lobbies or Consulate waiting rooms while you have your conference?" Great wads of my life had been spent staring at carpet patterns or generic paintings on the walls. Not in Hong Kong.

"I'll see that Skip makes up separate itineraries for us both."

I had heard that one before and would wait and see before letting anticipation set in.

Jim's responsibilities included meeting with the U.S. representatives in that area because of Hong Kong's proximity to Taiwan. We stayed on the Hong Kong Island overlooking a deep, well-protected harbor and there was to be no strolling this time. It was quite different from Kowloon on the land side. I missed the chance to look in windows and walk the streets, teeming with people. There were over six million inhabitants in this tiny place and at certain times of the day, it was preferable and safer to be inside. Neither Jim nor Skip had the time to keep a protective eye on me so I accepted their instructions.

The Naval Attache's name was Jack Dewinter. There was no U.S. Embassy in Hong Kong., but a set of Consulate offices. Jack and his wife had their home high up on a mountain, which was not too unusual considering the topography – everything seemed to be built on a mountain. They were a gracious couple and we liked then. Jack insisted he would meet us at the airport when we left to return to Taipei. Although we told him not to bother, he said to expect him. That would have its own set of consequences.

Skip dropped me at an inside mall, a safe place to shop then drove Jim to his meeting. Two hours later, I was gathered up and we set off for the New Territories. It was a long drive that included skirting a 72-hole golf course.

Jim was very interested. "Is this all one golf course, Skip? It's been going on for miles."

"Yes it is, Admiral and I don't believe it doubles back."

"Too bad there isn't time to schedule a game."

I stared at him and said, "Are you serious? It would take you two days to get around seventy-two holes."

"Only because I'm out of practice." He looked smug. I chose not to bust his bubble.

When we stood on the high hill overlooking the New Territories, I realized I was looking down on a vast plain that was communist China. For a moment, I felt the immensity of that country The mountains behind the plain were like the ones in Taiwan, but I had no friendly feeling when I looked at them.

"Pat, this is the Guondong Province of China." Skip had done his homework.

"And that's part of communist China, isn't it?"

He nodded. Enemy territory and my always-active imagination served up more menace than the bucolic scene deserved. Mist hung at the base of the mountains like thin smoke and the land was silent.

The whole area was also heavily patrolled to stop the migration out of China. People swam the South China Sea to leave the Mainland and reach Hong Kong. The need to escape the harshness of life under communist rule motivated thousands to leave their homeland. I saw all I wanted to and was ready to return to Hong Kong.

There was a shop I noticed as we were on our way up the mountain. My request to stop was greeted with a sigh but accommodated. In the yard of the tiny place were replicas of Chinese bronzes – bells, pots, rice servers, all crafted in a back yard forge to exactly resemble museum pieces. The three of us fanned out, looking at each piece while the driver remained with the car. In a tiny back room with shelves on the wall, I found the Flying Horse with his hoof on the swallow's back. I could feel excitement building. Skip had been following me around in case I picked up something too heavy to carry.

"Skip, it's the Flying Horse. I can't believe it. And it's for sale. Look, the balance is the same as the original. Where's Jim?"

I hurried to the front of the shop, "Jim, please come. The Flying Horse is in one of the back rooms and it's a wonderful reproduction of the one we saw in Washington, D.C. so many years ago." I pulled him along toward the back of the shop.

We threaded our way through a group of British tourists into the little room only to find the horse gone. Skip had obviously moved on to more shopping.

"Oh no. I can't believe it – my horse is gone and there was only one."

Jim patted my shoulder. "It looks like one of the British group found it after you did and snapped it up."

I was devastated. We wouldn't be back here any time soon, if ever and my disappointment was clearly visible.

"I've seen everything I want to. I'll wait in the car." Disappointment had dampened my desire to buy anything. I needed to pout.

Skip had obviously found something for Shannon. He placed the package in the trunk of the car and we made the long drive back to Hong Kong. Jim and I picked out our restaurant for the evening and returned to

218

the hotel an hour later. As Jim opened the door to the room, I saw the result of a grand conspiracy on the coffee table in front of the couch. The British were innocent. Jim and Skip were the culprits. They had managed to pull it off and my Flying Horse would go home to Taipei with me.

Our time was up and we climbed into the car for the drive to Kai Tak International Airport. I wondered if Jack Dewinter would be there. I wanted to tell him about my new acquisition and thank him for his hand in our itinerary. As we waited in the chaotic main section with people rushing by in all directions, I looked up to see Jack who did not see us.

"Hi Jack," I called to get his attention.

But along with his attention, my words also alerted the security force and we found ourselves surrounded by very serious, unsmiling Chinese in police uniforms. Anything even suggesting a highjacking, was excuse enough to take extreme measures. However, Jack's arrival, Jim's uniform and Skip's size plus my fluffy head of hair made us the most unlikely of suspects and the rumble was quickly over. Although the men were gracious and forgiving about it, I know Skip wished I were a poodle in a cage instead of the Admiral's wife.

CHAPTER SIXTEEN
GRADUATION

It was a soft, spring afternoon. I had nothing on my calendar, so I stretched out on the porch couch, faced the mountains and reread Jeff's letter. Suzie draped herself across my legs and was softly snoring before I reached the bottom of the page. Our plans were to return to Texas in May for our son's college graduation and I began to count the days. I missed the children more than ever before and didn't know why. In years past, we were separated with thousands of miles between us and their absence was a tangible hurt. I never adjusted to the rationalization of birds leaving the nest, it was natural and necessary, but nobody ever convinced me that the hole in my soul could ever be filled by anything other than my children. Jeff, being our youngest and the last to leave the family must have known this, for during one of his years in college, he sent me the poem by Khalil Gibran that makes the analogy of the parent being the bow and the child the arrow. You can hold the bow, pull back on the string, but sometime, you must let the arrow fly.

"Suzie, I know you're asleep, but why is so hard to let the arrow fly?" Her eyes opened at the sound of her name, she sighed and resumed her nap. The bug monitors would probably report that I was beginning to talk to the dog and what I was saying made no sense at all.

The trip back to the United States promised to be long and arduous. I listed the stops and the list grew every day. When Jim came home at 5:30,

I reminded him there was no party tonight and we would be at home for a change. 'Naldo's menu looked interesting – he was improving, slowly and within another year or two, I might be able to relax during one of our dinner parties.

The evening was too beautiful to stay inside on the porch. Hogo had anticipated our desire to be out in the spring air, so the pool furniture was freshly cleaned and Suzie's potato chips were waiting for her.

"There was a letter from Jeff today. Graduation is the last week of May and I've made a list of the stops we'll need to make."

Jim nodded and looked at the mountains.

I continued. "I don't know what your itinerary is, but there's Jamey and her family, the graduation, a visit with my mother and your father and since you mentioned going to Washington, D.C. for briefings, I should try for an eye appointment at Bethesda Hospital."

Jim continued to look at the mountains.

"Dear, if you are waiting for the mountains to move, the last I heard they are stationary." I felt uneasy.

"We will have to miss Jeff's graduation." His voice was soft but unyielding with information I did not have.

I knew that voice because I had heard it many times in the past. It carried the sound of no compromise. I was seeing only his profile and the strength of his face was very evident. His jaw was set, the straight line of his dark brows was down and his full lips had thinned. His eyes, always the foreteller of his moods, were narrowed. I felt like the enemy.

"Please tell me you're not serious."

"There's been heavy message traffic this week and I am required to be in Washington in mid-July."

I was waiting for him to face me squarely and tell me the reasons why. His eyes stayed on the mountains.

"Jim, I don't usually say things like this, but what you've told me is unacceptable. I will not allow it to happen." I steeled myself to say something I really didn't want to. " All my married life, you and the Navy have told me what I can and cannot do, usually at the expense of our marriage and our children. I have no intention of giving chapter and verse on the inequities we've put up with, but you cannot tell me I must miss our son's college graduation."

He looked at me and there was anger in his face. "I will do what I have to do. We can't afford two trips back and my orders are to be in Washington in July." His jaw was set.

"Then I will go without you." It had happened in the past. It would happen again.

"You can't make the trip alone because of your sight and you know it. Besides, your presence will be needed here." He looked back at the mountains.

I could feel anger and frustration welling up. Suzie, snuggled up against me in the chair, sensed something was very wrong, put her head in my lap and I burst into tears. These damned eyes. When I need you, you aren't there for me. Oblivious of the guards and Hogo, I ran up the stairs to the French doors of our bedroom with Suzie on my heels, flung myself on the bed, covered my head with a pillow and cried it out.

222

That I had any tears in me came as a surprise. My two older brothers had shamed me out of them as a child and Viet Nam and the Sixties left me drained of tears and emotions. The life we lived demanded control and weeping was a luxury that only made me weak and defenseless. I couldn't afford to indulge myself like this – but I did, for the first time in many years.

Later, I paced the room, trying to figure out what to do. I had traveled without Jim many times in the past – all those years in Europe – but I could see. Now, I was an accident waiting to happen. I tried to imagine the trip in my mind – first, changing from international to domestic in the Honolulu airport was a living nightmare with 20/20 vision. With my sight, it would be a recipe for disaster. Then graduation in Austin, but Austin was difficult to get to. That left the month of June and part of July to kill until the Washington thing. I couldn't see well enough to go visiting and I was too independent and proud to beg everyone's help.

I thought of his words, "Your presence will be needed here."

Dammit. I knew I was beaten and once again, would do what the Navy and my husband told me to do.

I tried to imagine why Jim was so unreasonable and assumed Taiwan's future had something to do with it.

Aloud, I said, "Taiwan's future can go to blazes. My son's graduation is the beginning of his future and my future is to share it with him." I was oblivious of the listening device in the fan and later, when I remembered the words I had spoken, wondered at the impression they made on the monitors. But to the Chinese, they were a woman's words, spoken in anger and therefore, of no value.

I walked down the glassy hallway, through the living room and onto the porch, seething. A very quiet Hogo waited on us and we ate in silence. When 'Naldo appeared for our assessment, I complimented him, but he too, knew it was a difficult time and after a timid smile, hurried back down to the kitchen region below.

No one had ever seen me truly angry before. I kept my cool through bad dinner parties, misinterpreted directions, too many guards and the frustration of never being able to talk freely. My sense of humor usually took me through whatever problem I faced. Tonight was different.

I felt empty. My anger drained me, leaving a void, and suddenly, I was too tired to deal with anything more. I crawled into bed and slept like the dead until morning.

Jim was gone when I awoke and Suzie was sitting near the French doors, watching me.

"Hi, baby. Have you been waiting for Mom?" She blinked. "Come on up. I need a hug."

She was on the bed before I finished the invitation and I held onto her, rubbing my face in her fragrant fur.

"What to do, Suzie – what to do?"

There was no answer to that, but I did know I had to get a grip on myself. I climbed out of bed, checked the calendar on my desk and automatically laid out the clothes I would wear for the morning brunch at the Club. Getting through that would take some doing. Admirals' wives aren't supposed to have any emotions and I sometimes felt like a plastic wind-up toy, complete with hat and gloves.

Mama San came in to check me for wrinkles. Her face was impassive, but before she left, she placed her hand briefly on my arm and it helped.

My mind swirled all day, wondering what kind of a conversation we could have tonight on our way down the mountain to another party. Thank God tomorrow was Saturday. Maybe we could get away on our own and have this thing out.

There was no conversation that night. We simply looked out the windows and thought our own thoughts.

Jim played golf on Saturday and that meant seven more hours of silence unless I talked to Suzie, the monitors or myself. Trying to recall every word for hidden meaning, I went over in my mind the conversation of the day before. We learned to speak in double entendre – the Chinese did not always understand and sometimes, we could get an entire conversation going that we understood, but nobody else did.

Obviously, this was another "no need to know" situation that left me completely in the dark. I sat at my desk and idly watched the geckos scurrying across the wall. The little chameleons moved quickly, then stopped with heads raised and round eyes watching. They were such a part of the house I seldom noticed them.

On a piece of paper, I wrote:

Heavy message traffic.

I have to be in Washington in mid-July.

I will do what I have to do.

Your presence is needed here.

You can't make the trip alone and you know it.

We can't afford two trips back.

I crossed off the last one. If we had to mortgage the house, we could find the money. The Navy paid my way out and back – when the tour of duty began and when it ended, nothing in between, but we both knew that was not a valid reason.

He was probably right about my not being able to make the trip alone, but ways to overcome that problem could be found. I studied the first four reasons: Was this double entendre talk? The Chinese are watchful people and expressions speak as clearly as words. His seriousness that bordered on threat was firmly imprinted on my mind and I tried to put the two together. It didn't work. I was still too angry.

He returned from his game late in the afternoon and there was no small talk.

I said, "I don't know what you have planned for tomorrow, but if it's another golf game, cancel it. We need to talk and don't ask me what about." My fuse was getting shorter by the minute.

"I'll call the General."

"Do that. And thank you."

In our get-away car, we headed out of town, no particular direction, just out.

"Am I to be given any explanation about your decision or is this another 'no need to know'?"

"I'm afraid that's what it is."

226

"Take it or leave it. Those are my choices?"

"I'm sorry Patti, but it has to be that way, at least for now. I'm just as frustrated as you are knowing I will miss Jeff's graduation."

I wasn't hearing him. "This makes twenty-nine years of the 'no need to know' philosophy and we all have our saturation point. I just reached mine." Careful, don't back yourself into a corner you can't get out of. "I'm not asking for state secrets or 'your eyes only' stuff. I'm asking for a logical and truthful explanation of why our son will graduate from college with none of his family present."

"When I am ordered to do something, I do it, no questions asked." His jaw clenched again.

My response was swift. "And no quarter given."

This whole conversation was degenerating into a potential blow-up with only one outcome. I wanted it to stop, to go away, to let us alone. I wanted the Navy and its demands to fade into oblivion.

I wanted to see my son.

"However you choose to do it Jim, by telephone or letter, the message *will* come from you. I won't speak against you to Jeff, I never have, but my only request is that you tell him in such a way that he will have a minimum of hurt. And if you can get him to understand, then someday, maybe he can explain it to me."

End of conversation.

As always, stress caused my eyes to go haywire. I made the appointment to see Dr Lin, climbed the eight flights and stared into the machines.

"Mrs. Linder, your vision no good today."

"Dr. Lin, my vision is no good – period." The good doctor hadn't the faintest idea what I was talking about.

He walked away and stood for a few moments with his back to me. Then he turned.

"Linder tai tai, I want to put you in hospital and give you typhoid fever."

Dear God. The whole male world had it in for me.

"Dr. Lin, why would you want to do a thing like that? I've had shots to keep me from having typhoid fever. And you say you want to give it to me?"

"I think maybe high fever kill inflammation in eyes."

"But with that kind of fever, I could have brain or heart damage."

"Meyogwanchi." That's the Chinese word for "never mind."

I slid out of the chair, shook his hand and said, "Dr. Lin, don't call me, I'll call you."

He wrote into my record his latest recommendation and I wobbled down the eight flights of stairs to Sergeant Hsiu waiting for me at the bottom step. He stayed close beside me in the throng of people, milling around the lobby, then helped me into the car. Thank you Lord, for Sergeant Hsiu.

On the way up the mountain, my thoughts strayed to my own college graduation I missed in order to be in Annapolis for the Naval Academy Ring Dance, traditionally held during a Midshipman's third year. We were engaged and would marry, following Jim's graduation one year later. My father was disappointed that I chose not to walk across the stage – logical, since he had paid for four years of college and would be deprived of seeing me receive my diploma. But my parents understood that after a four-year engagement that only allowed thirty days a year of being able to see each other, we needed every chance to be together. They bowed gracefully to my decision, but I was beginning to understand their hurt and disappointment.

Marriage at the Naval Academy was strictly forbidden until after graduation and should a Midshipman marry in secret during those four years, it was grounds for immediate and automatic expulsion. We chose to abide by the rules. As one thought leads to another, Jim's graduation took its place in my mind. June Week with parades, tennis matches, sailing on the Chesapeake, chapel services and tours of the grounds, made the week an immersion in the ways Naval Officers are taught and trained to serve their country. It was colorful and exciting when the Midshipmen's hats were thrown into the air to be replaced by their new officers' hats. Jim had his parents, my parents and me to share it with.

Comparisons are deadly. I was relieved when we pulled into the driveway and Suzie was waiting for me.

May rolled around and as the date approached, I often found tears close to the surface. Jeff knew through our letters that we would not be there for his big day. I knew from past experience that with time, the anger would fade as we fell back into the routine of the marriage we had grooved throughout the years. The hurly-burly of loving children and grandchildren would warm the coldness and fill the void, but for now, I was stuck with the void.

On Jeff's graduation day, we hosted a dinner for eight at the Grand Hotel. Three influential Texas couples were passing through Taipei and it was up to us to entertain them. Following dinner, as we strolled through the lobby of the Grand, one of the wives asked about our children.

We traded information and when she heard our son was attending the University of Texas, she asked, "How much more time does he have before he graduates?"

I looked at my watch. "About twenty minutes."

She studied me for a few moments, saw my brimming eyes, reached for my hand and gave it a gentle squeeze.

CHAPTER SEVENTEEN
BOOM BOOM

I looked down on clouds like clabber milk. Washington, D.C. lay ahead and I felt stiff and sore from endless hours on an airplane. Our altitude put us above the clouds so I had to imagine the Rocky Mountains, the prairies and the sprawling cities along the way. It was good to be in my own country again, but I knew cultural shock would set in the moment we walked into the airport.

The pace was the same. People moved quickly, intent on making a plane or finding a phone. The colors caught my attention and I knew I was in the United States, instead of any other country. In Europe and the Far East, people dress in more subdued, almost somber colors. My tired eyes took it all in and I was home.

Washington in July has its drawbacks, but it was close to the Fourth and the city was full of people, anxious to see everything the Capitol had to offer. Families ambled along the sidewalks, pushing strollers while children darted in and out, shouting advice or threats to each other.

We sat on the grass of the Mall in front of the Smithsonian. With us was an American friend from Taipei who happened to be in Washington on business. We ate hot dogs, dripping with mustard and cooled down with sodas. The shade of the big trees broke the pulsating heat coming from this city of concrete and marble.

I cherished the sound of it. Everyone had an opinion about everything and gave it freely. Arguments sprang up like mushrooms, were explored then

231

discarded for the next topic. More than I thought possible, I had missed the free flow of conversation I could understand. Eavesdropping, I found these ordinary Americans to be well informed and articulate. Soft-spoken visitors from other countries viewed the scene, as one would study a painting. It was a perfect time for this American to return to her country.

Jim's briefings began the next day and my appointment at Bethesda Naval Hospital turned into five days of more testing at the National Institute of Health. As they hung things on my eyeballs, I thought lovely thoughts. My Victorian mother practiced that art each time she had a physical.

At last it ended, with no new conclusions or treatments and we left Washington for the round of visits with our families. In Texas, Jeff was my biggest surprise. He was in no way disturbed about our absence at his graduation ceremony.

"Actually, it was a relief because I had a new job and attending graduation is optional now. You don't walk across the stage anymore, and they send you your diploma." I could see no hint of hurt.

They needed new rules for such a large graduating class so Jeff spent that special day, working. If there was disappointment, we never saw it. I don't know what Jim's explanation of our absence was, but Jeff put us at ease.

We lunched in a tree house restaurant and ate sprouts, Jim looking somewhat uncomfortable. Any college town has its individuality and Austin was no different. I listened to father and son argue a question, prepared to intervene if Jim's brusque manner hurt our son, only to have Jeff assure me he could take care of himself. He had changed and grown this past year. The arrow had left the bow.

On the plane to our next stop, San Diego, I asked Jim to explain to me now why his presence was necessary in Taipei during Jeff's graduation.

He pondered my question, then obviously decided I was due an explanation.

"The Republic of China is very touchy at this point and they're sensitive to any kind of changes in our routine."

"Do you mean in relation to the treaty?" I asked.

"Yes. Two trips back by either one of us would have seemed impractical and I had to be in Washington in July. There was no other way."

"You couldn't have told me that and saved the anger?"

"No, I couldn't and I'm asking you to forget the reason why."

We were back to the Navy memo talk and I gave up. Jeff had not been hurt and that's what mattered most to me. I didn't consider it a very good explanation, but obviously, the situation was much more complicated than I had previously thought.

I subsided and watched the clouds drift by.

In San Diego, our granddaughters once again proved their abiding affection for their roaming grandparents. We did the zoo, ate peanuts and cotton candy, strolled hand in hand on a beach touched by sunset, and promised to return. They never doubted us.

When we arrived in Taipei, after our absence of three weeks, I wanted to crawl into my Quarters A bed and sleep for a week. Suzie bordered on hysteria since our arrival and where I went, she went. The summer was a lonely time for her. The staff had taken their vacations during our absence and often, there was only Hogo babysitting the Quarters and the dog. I kept her close to me and with Jim's increasing preoccupation, I leaned on the little dog for companionship.

In the middle of the pile of correspondence on my desk was an invitation to tea from a French Vietnamese friend. Marie France was married to an Irish businessman and I found her a delight to be with. *Tea* means a cup and saucer, little sandwiches and cakes with a sit-down conversation. This differs from a tea which means standing around, sipping, munching and talking while somebody pours. I preferred the sit-down kind. As stated in the invitation, on Tuesday afternoon, Sergeant Hsiu delivered me at the door promptly at three.

Marie appeared, carrying a white ball of fluff that snored softly in her arms. In her lilting, musical French accent, she smiled and said, "Ah Pat, we are so glad you are back from your treep. I do not think you 'ave met Boom Boom, our leetle dog."

The ball of fluff stirred, turned its head, looked me in the eye and sneezed. Boom Boom was a white Chinese Pekinese with a nose that was only good for sneezing or snoring. Marie chuckled, put the little thing into my arms and said, "You mus' get to know each other."

I juggled my purse and this silky dog that promptly went back to sleep on my chest as we edged into the living room. I greeted two more

234

mutual friends, sat down where Marie indicated, adjusted the dog, was handed a teacup and saucer and tea began. Boom Boom snored throughout and I managed the refreshments without spilling anything on the lump in my lap.

"Pat, did you know my husband is being posted to Hong Kong?"

I did not. "Will you be moving, or will he commute?"

"Ah, we will move in three weeks and we have a very pretty apartment waiting for us."

"Oh Marie, I truly hate to see you leave."

"My dear Pat, we have heard about your Suzie Wong and I wish you to take Boom Boom to live with you and Jim. She will be a playmate for your Suzie."

I froze.

"Marie…." Boom Boom stirred, laid her head on my arm and resumed the soft snoring.

"I cannot take my dear leetle dog with me and my heart is breaking."

Well, we certainly can't have a broken heart. Carefully, I set my cup and saucer on the Louis XV table next to my chair.

"Marie, I don't know what to say."

The other two ladies were watching with smiles on their faces and the possibility I had been set up crossed my mind.

"Dear Pat, say you will. Boom Boom and I will be so 'appy." Her tiny French face with the slightly upturned eyes could have charmed a

Chinese dragon. She clasped her slender hands where I assumed her heart was and smiled. I was lost.

"Oh Marie, I'm probably going to be in deep trouble if I do, but so be it. Your baby can join our family."

What was I saying? I tried not to think of Jim's reaction. When I should be thinking about the future, I wasn't.

Marie's eyes misted and she came to my chair, knelt and in the customary French way, we touched cheeks. She lifted Boom Boom out of my lap and held her close. I felt a little misty, myself.

"She is such a sweet leetle baby. You will love her jus' like I do."

"I will, Marie. That's a promise. We will do everything we can to make her happy."

"There is one leetle thing she does that is so funny. Instead of squatting, she lifts her leettle leg when she pee pees."

Any dog that's as confused as that belongs in our family. I wondered briefly if B.B. would teach Suzie how to lift her leg or if Suzie would teach B.B. how to squat. Either way, it promised to be entertaining.

When I walked out the door with Boom Boom in my arms, Sergeant Hsiu's eyebrows shot skyward.

"Don't ask, Sergeant. Just tell Hogo when we get home, there will be four for dinner tonight."

Once again, I flipped the switches on the air conditioners in the bedroom area. None of them uttered a sound. I tried one more call to the Chinese Colonel in charge of maintenance at the Quarters and was given the most polite of continual run-arounds. It was hot. I was hot, and more than a little exasperated at the lack of interest I had just received. Calling Skip would solve nothing. He would go through the same wickets, spend time that should be spent on official business and end up as frustrated as I was.

I marched down the glassy hallway with Suzie and Boom Boom sliding along behind. The three of us went to the porch and I positioned myself under the bugged fan, looked up and said, "This is Admiral Linder's Tai Tai and I want these air conditioners fixed NOW or I shall call the Admiral personally and tell him to have the Taiwan Defense Command take care of it."

The two guards on their way to their posts stood riveted, watching this lady talk to the ceiling fan with both dogs looking up to see what I saw. The message must have created a sensation somewhere because the phone rang. Hogo answered and reported repairmen would arrive shortly and fix the problem, chop chop. The three of us marched back down the hall to the sitting room and I left the dogs chasing each other while I took my morning shower.

Boom Boom's arrival had created somewhat of a sensation with everybody in the house. Mama San eyed her like she was a big bug, Hogo giggled non-stop for ten minutes and the guards just shook their heads. Suzie backed up when I came in the front door, then stood her ground. I put Boom Boom down, walked to Suzie, held her and talked to her, then let her go. She headed for the porch and the little Pekinese did the same. From then, on, whatever Suzie did, Boom Boom did, and they looked like they were glued together. After Suzie got over her astonishment, they retained their individuality on leg-lifting versus squatting. Each afternoon, both of them waited by the great red doors for Jim's arrival after work and followed him down the slick hallway, little white rumps switching and feet sliding. Boom Boom's short Pekinese legs often went out from under her as she hurried to keep up with Suzie and she would skid the last few feet, making a catapult entrance into the room. She was a natural clown. A bundle of silky white fur with a squashed-in nose and sinus problems. Her world was Suzie Wong. We named them The Girls and Jim was as charmed by them as I was.

I finished my shower and was just reaching for a towel when I heard voices in the bathroom. I peeked around the shower curtain and found three Chinese workmen, squatting in front of the air conditioner, studying it.

I cleared my throat. They stayed.

Ignoring me completely, they chattered to each other and fiddled with the dials. Grabbing my towel, I wrapped it around me and sat in the bathtub. This should teach me not to talk to the fan. Eventually, they moved as a group into the bedroom to fix the next one and I escaped into the sitting room and quickly threw on a robe. The two machines whirred and cool air began to circulate. There was a lot of door slamming that morning as I moved from room to room, trying to get dressed. The dogs were enchanted, watching the passing parade. At last, the job was completed and the three men left with smiles and giggles.

Our "do" for the evening was a reception at the Grand Hotel for the Flying Tigers. I looked forward to meeting these men who had flown for Claire Lee Chennault in 1937 during the Chinese war with Japan. They were volunteer pilots, and their job was to defend the Burma Road and

238

"fly the Hump," the Chinese supply route from India, over the Himalayan Mountains. Chennault later became a Major General in the Air Force and his Tigers flew P-40's during World War II. As a teenager, I thrilled at the movies about these brave charismatic men.

They were older, but still with the flair that comes from living a dangerous life. I knew Jim felt a certain camaraderie with them and we found the evening relaxed as though meeting old friends. General Chennault's widow, Anna, made the introductions and I realized we were meeting real American heroes.

The next morning, 'Naldo brought the menus for the week to the sitting room for review and we talked about the next party coming up. He was improving with each meal he prepared and I let him know we were pleased with his efforts.

"Mum?"

"Yes, 'Naldo?'

"Mum, I'm gonna' get married."

I thought about this for a while, then said, "'Naldo, what about your wife in San Francisco?"

He looked surprised, then thoughtful. "I forgot about her."

"'Naldo, I think you should give this more thought. It's not really a good idea to have two wives. Besides being illegal, it could get very complicated."

Now I knew why he was always sleeping. I knew nothing about the poor soul in San Francisco, but she took a chance, letting him out of her sight.

"All right, Mum. I'll think about it some more."

When he left, maneuvering carefully down the hall, I moved to the wing chair and picked up a novel, sitting on the table. The Girls were wound around each other in the middle of the oriental rug and as usual, Boom Boom was snoring.

As though someone put his foot in the back of the chair and kicked hard, I flew out of it and landed where the dogs had slept. They were on their feet and staggering around the room. Another earthquake – and totally different from the others. They climbed into my lap and we rode it out. The beams into the mountain held fast. Once again, Quarters A came through with a minimum of damage.

We were scheduled to visit President Chiang Kai-shek's shrine and resting place near Lake Mercy, and the drive there was through bamboo forests. The trees are graceful and from them comes the saying, "bend with the wind". Their flexibility belies their strength and every part of them is utilized. I was involved in a Chinese ink drawing class with an older woman who was a well-known artist. Her introduction to bamboo, the part it played in ancient art up to the present time, and the very brushes we used with handles of bamboo made the tree more than just a symbol. Like the plum tree blossom, it stood for something. I had not lived in Taiwan long enough to know the whole philosophy behind the symbolism, but one had only to look at it to know the message: survival.

We stood in a long line and waited our turn to pay homage to the Generalissimo. Once a year, this ceremony is repeated and each person moves to the position in front of the shrine, bows at the waist, then moves on. The crowd was large and the bows were like a prayer and we were both tired when we finally reached the car waiting for us. It was an unusual afternoon, the first connected with death in any way and I recalled the description of Tomb-Sweeping Day, a festival celebrated between spring plowing and summer weeding. Families go together to the tombs of their relatives, sweep and clean the area and spend the day, picnicking and visiting with the families of the nearby tombs. We had seen the procession as they walked up Yangmingshan Mountain to one of the several cemeteries found on the sides of the hills.

A Chinese friend explained the custom of waiting for the best time for burial. The deceased is often kept for months, sometimes years until the right moment. I wondered who chose the right moment. To this westerner, accustomed to the swift dispatch of our loved ones, it was difficult to understand, but I filed it with the other many things I would never fully comprehend.

It was a busy month of visits to places Taiwan is famous for. Touring with a group to a monastery, high in the mountains, I stumbled onto an exorcism. A prickle of fear touched me as I quietly backed away from the highly charged atmosphere. The participants were oblivious to their surroundings and would never have noticed me, but I felt embarrassment at witnessing such raw emotions.

In another area, the monks in their saffron robes were seated for their noon meal and the women of the village cooked and brought the food to them. I thought they were serving pork chops but found instead, it was tofu, shaped and colored to look like chops.

241

We journeyed to Sun Moon Lake, with a tiny island in its center and a favorite for newly-weds because of its incredible beauty. On Lin Shan Mountain, we were guided into a forest of square bamboo and I placed my hands on the trunk of a four-sided tree. With each place we visited, I was amazed at the similarity of the landscape to the Chinese paintings, both ancient and contemporary. This was not just any country's landscape, this was Taiwan, and unique.

Another trip to Hong Kong was laid on. This time, I went with the shoppers. A new MacDonald's was open and the line stretched for blocks. Happily, we joined the throng and waited our turns for a MacDonald's hamburger, fries and a milk shake. It was a touch of home.

The rickshaws were quickly being overcome by the onslaught of automobiles, pedestrian and the ubiquitous bicycle traffic. We were due to return to Taipei on Friday and I would have just enough time to get from the airport to the Quarters to change for a reception that evening. As we sat in our assigned seats, waiting for takeoff, a passenger discovered he had left his passport in the terminal. We settled in for a wait and I began to feel uneasy about the lost time.

He returned, we taxied onto the runway, but the plane turned and taxied over to a corner of the airfield away from the other runways. Then we sat. A "cherry picker" trundled out to our plane and the pilot told us we had a kite on our tail and it must be removed before takeoff. It could only happen in Asia.

When I finally arrived at the reception in my traveling clothes, Jim quietly asked me why I was late.

I merely said, "I had a kite on my tail."

Knowing me, he kept his questions until later.

CHAPTER EIGHTEEN
HOGO

Hogo's face was like a thundercloud and there were no giggles as he served breakfast. Jim was scheduled for an early meeting, so it was just Hogo, The Girls and I.

"Hogo, are you all right? You look so sad today."

He stopped serving and looked at the mountains. Then, in an angry voice, he said, "I find out wife in China marry man three weeks after I come Taiwan."

"You mean in 1949?" I was aghast. That was nearly thirty years ago.

"She marry man, take my three sons with her. I send money every month for…." He counted on his fingers. "…twenty-nine years. And she marry other man."

No wonder he was out of sorts.

"How did you find out?"

His face was getting darker as he spoke. "Brother's son, David, come Taipei and tell me."

"Hogo, I am so sorry. What a shocking thing to find out. Is there anything you can do?" It was a meaningless question, but I had to say something.

"No." And he stomped down the stairs to the kitchen.

I didn't know what to do with this piece of information and decided to leave it for Jim to ponder. Family was everything to these people and when Chiang Kai-shek brought his army to Taiwan, they left wives and children behind. Because of the lack of money, the majority of the troops could not bring them over at the time, and like Hogo, many sent money back to their wives to save toward finding a way to come and resume their marriages. After the two million left the Mainland, the communists sealed the borders and the families could not get out. But in Hogo's eyes, he had been betrayed and I had to agree with him.

A few days later, he came to my sitting room and began the conversation with, "Missy, okay brother's son David come live here?"

It caught me by surprise and I waited to gather my thoughts before responding. "You're asking me if David can live at Quarters A?"

His face was completely impassive. Looking at him, the word 'threat' edged into my mind. "Hogo, I do not make the decisions about who lives at Quarters A. Because of security, that's something only the Chinese government and TDC can decide."

"He stay in my room. No bother anybody."

"It's not a matter of bother. I'm sure he's a very nice young man, but you must speak to Commander Wright about this."

He turned and abruptly left the room. Hogo had changed. I actually missed his nervous giggle and there was more anger in his face with each day that passed. He did his job, but I knew he was furious about his wife and when they told him that his nephew could not live at Quarters A, I wasn't sure what he would do.

The mountains looked pretty serene. I was glad something did.

Jim was late, coming home and when he did, his face rivaled Hogo's. He was angry and I wondered what questions I could ask that would even get an answer.

"Can you talk about it, or are you just going to grind your teeth?"

After nearly thirty years, his moods were familiar to me and I knew he preferred the straightforward approach.

There was no party that night and he called down to 'Naldo to hold dinner until seven thirty. He gave me the "let's take a ride" look and we went down the stairs to the garage area. Not a word was said as we climbed into the little car and sailed out the front gate, Jim saluting the startled guards in a way that indicated there was to be no escort.

We didn't have much time before dark, so he found a small side road, pulled onto it, parked and shut off the engine. It reminded me of our courting days in high school and I giggled. He looked puzzled and I explained my memory. There was a vestige of a smile and the tension eased.

"What is it, Jim?"

"Things are not going the way they should." His jaw was squared.

"What things?"

"I'm being cut off at the pass. I can't do what is necessary to keep this island protected and every way I turn, there is an obstacle put there by our *policy*." He tapped the steering wheel with his fist.

"Our policy?"

"The U.S.Government's policy; the State Department, the Carter Administration, the Defense Department. It's as though they're in league together and I'm the only one who doesn't know what the score is." There was hurt and frustration in his voice. But more, there was anger. "I've been given a job to do and I'm not being allowed to do it."

I shifted in my seat to see his profile. "Any idea why?"

"Remember your question about the 'handwriting on the wall'"

"Of course. And I remember your answer. Does this have to do with the Treaty?"

"I personally think it has everything to do with it, but it's like throwing a punch at a cloud. Whatever I ask, I'm given the diplomatic run-around and I'm damned sick of it." His brows were in a straight line and his body was tensed.

Bravely, I asked, "Jim, what did they say to you in Washington when you were there for the briefings in July?"

"They were ambivalent. It was the usual bureaucratic Pentagonese that boiled down to just keep an even keel and don't rock the boat. You know the cliches. You've heard them enough times."

I had and felt my own anger beginning to build.

"Every time I request something for Taiwan's defense, I'm told it's gone into the chain of command and will have to work its way up the ladder, which means nothing."

"Don't they know what the stakes are?"

"Of course they do, but there is no sense of urgency. My requests go to the Pentagon, then over to State, on to Commerce and who knows maybe the White House. By then, it's either too little or too late."

It was dark and I knew the staff at the Quarters would be uneasy, so I suggested we go back.

I asked, "Is there anything more you can do?"

"Not with the stonewalling that's going on in Washington."

"What's the attitude at the Embassy here?"

"The same. Keep a low profile and maybe it will go away. I don't understand any of it."

For the first time in months, the memory of the anonymous phone call from the State Department, telling me to unpack, slipped into my thoughts and like a jigsaw puzzle, I was watching it all fall into place.

I realized nothing had been solved as we pulled into the driveway, but at least he had said it aloud and maybe, because of that, he had a better perspective.

As we opened one of the red doors, we found Hogo with a broom in his hands, running around the living room. For a moment, I thought his problems had proved to be too stressful and he had lost it, but he was chasing bats. Three of them were swooping up and down, as frightened as I felt. We grabbed the fireplace tools and Jim began his chase with shovel in hand. I stood rooted with the poker and tried to keep them away from me. When it comes to bats, I am no hero. I realized that this must be where the dried bats in the pool dressing rooms came from.

At last, they swooped down the back hall and came to rest upside down on the tops of the guestroom draperies. Hogo and Jim, were now joined by the ambling 'Naldo who had secured The Girls in the kitchen and together, they gathered the bats in a large paper sack and dispatched them to the pool area, no doubt to be nailed to a board. I had learned that after drying, they were sold and used in some mysterious concoction that was either medicinal or aphrodisiac. I never found out which.

'Naldo's dinner was anticlimactic. I was still shaky from the bat encounter and Jim was still angry. Chasing the critters had somewhat calmed him down, and although we both saw the humor of the situation, his mind was firmly placed on the bigger picture. I wanted our discussion in the car to continue, but the fan hung like a listening vulture and it was too dark outside to sit by the pool. As it was, we both had a lot to think about.

Another birthday and more flowers and Chinese brandy. I registered each gift and placed the lovely ceramic and porcelain brandy containers in the storeroom off the kitchen. They sat on the bookshelves, end tables, any flat surface and I had simply run out of room for them. Hogo moved silently about the house, dusting and polishing. I wanted to ask him about his nephew David, but Jim, after hearing of the situation, advised me to stay out of it. So Hogo and I we were polite to each other, he knew I was sympathetic, but angry that I hadn't solved all of his problems.

A week later, he came to me with the news that one of his relatives had killed himself in Taipei. When the army came from the Mainland, Hogo and his brothers settled somewhere in the downtown suburbs. They lived together since their wives had been left in China. One of them had been terribly injured during the war and had come to Taiwan with only one leg. Hogo explained that he could no longer work because of his poor health and handicap, so he lay down on the railroad tracks and let the train run over him.

I was absolutely appalled and Hogo was beside himself with grief. I tried talking to him, but his growing anger made it almost impossible to reach him. Too much was happening to this man for him to know how to deal with it.

One Sunday in November, Jim had a breakfast and golf date with several Chinese officials. He dressed quietly and slipped out for the hour's drive to the golf course. When I finally started my day, I lingered in the sitting room, writing to the children.

Suddenly, there was a loud knock on the door and Hogo burst into the room. He was shouting as he came toward the desk and I was too astonished to do anything but hold onto the typewriter and stare at him.

We were alone in the Quarters.

Usually Sergeant Hsiu was here, but he had chauffeured Jim to the golf course in the Seville. I knew I was defenseless, except for the typewriter.

Hogo continued shouting and I was able to understand some of what he said.

"Robber come up hill. Look in window. See me. Try to come in room. My room."

He was shaking, his face getting darker by the minute.

"Hogo, please calm down. You must tell me what happened. I can't understand all you're saying."

He backed up two steps, repeated word for word what he had said, then added, "Me leave here. No stay here anymore."

Well, here's a new twist. After working in quarters A for twenty-two years, he's threatening to leave. But he wasn't the same man. The things that had happened to him in the past two months had simply overcome him.

I heard a door slam. Thank God. 'Naldo had come for the rest of the day.

"Hogo, 'Naldo's here and I want you to tell him what you have told me, then the three of us will talk about it. Will that be all right?"

He stood motionless, nothing on his face, eyes narrowed. Then he whirled around, hurried down the hall and five minutes later, reappeared with 'Naldo.

"Have you heard Hogo's story, 'Naldo?"

"A little of it, Mum. He told me on the way up here."

We waited for Hogo to calm down and his story unfolded. He had wakened as Jim left for golf and was sitting in his room, facing the small window that looked out on the pool area. It was positioned higher than the other windows in the house. As he looked up, a man's face appeared in the window and he looked at Hogo. He was a stranger, not one of the guards and Hogo panicked. So did the man. He hadn't expected to see anybody through the small window that looked like it belonged to the garage.

At this point, the guards entered the scene and caught the man. He had escaped from jail at the foot of the mountain, climbed up the face of it and unknowingly picked the only house with armed guards. How he slipped through them, I never found out, but there were new faces behind the bushes and trees the following week.

Hogo was beside himself. He continued to repeat that he wanted to leave. I told him to go on down to Taipei if he wished – that he could take the rest of the weekend off, but he stayed on.

Jim returned around two in the afternoon and by that time, I was more than a little nervous about the whole thing. Hogo's lack of stability, the awareness that he might very well leave for good and I would be dealing with a replacement who knew nothing about running a set of Quarters, gave me qualms I hadn't felt since arriving in Taipei.

Feeling a little resentful that he had spent a great day on the golf course while I was grappling with a frightening situation alone at home, I told Jim of the day's happenings. As we sat on the porch and discussed the possibilities, Hogo ran into the room with a can of Brasso in his hand, chattering in Chinese and shaking it at me. It was too much. I jumped to my feet and moved away from him. Jim stood, took Hogo by the arm and told him to stop.

Hogo twisted away and said,

"'Naldo say he buy too many cans Brasso. I use too many cans. He say I no polish so much. Too much polish."

I knew the man was near breaking and I called 'Naldo to come upstairs and help me with him while Jim called his Chinese liaison aide, Spencer, a Lieutenant Commander in the Chinese Navy. We seated Hogo on one of the chairs – something he never did in our presence, and 'Naldo cleared up the misunderstanding. It was a matter of translation but Hogo was too irrational to listen to reason.

When Spencer came to the Quarters, he spent quite a bit of time in the kitchen with Hogo, asking questions and trying to get coherent answers in Chinese. Then he came upstairs to speak with us. He told us Hogo would be leaving; he was simply too unstable to continue his job at the Quarters. In answer to his questions, I told him of my day and the things Hogo had shared with me during the past two months

Spencer's comment was, "Mrs. Linder, I don't know how you have stood it as long as you have. We've been aware of Hogo's problems, but we didn't know he was so close to breaking."

Well. All along I thought I was supposed to put up with it, without question. I began to feel sorry for myself.

"Spencer, what will we do for a replacement? It's nearing Christmas and there are parties coming up. There are also many things I will need help with. I'll have to have somebody."

Spencer understood my apprehension and said, "We'll do our best, Mrs. Linder. I don't know of anyone right now, but I'll call you as soon as we find someone."

My hands were shaking – delayed reaction to an otherwise awful day.

"Spencer, what will happen to Hogo? I'm fond of him and I care about him. He's been a good friend until the last few weeks and I know he's not responsible for what's happened."

"He won't be harmed. He just won't be in a position to harm anyone else."

Small comfort.

Spencer left with Hogo and I felt desolate that I couldn't even see him before he went down the mountain. The staff was subdued the next day when they heard the story first from 'Naldo and then from me and I felt confused and upset that I hadn't been stronger.

As I sat at my desk, reviewing the past events, I noticed a small card with Marie France's name on it. When she put Boom Boom into my arms the day of the tea, she also gave me her card with a name and phone number. Although they had moved to Hong Kong several weeks ago, I recalled it was the name of her maid and housekeeper, Julie. She had to leave both Julie and Boom Boom behind and told me if I ever needed a personal maid, this girl would be perfect. I did not need a personal maid, I could manage my own zippers and buttons thank you, but I hoped Julie could replace Hogo, at least through the holidays.

I called Spencer, gave him the information and two days later, Julie joined the staff. She was a gem. Everyone liked her and helped her learn Hogo's jobs. She was so happy to be gainfully employed once more that life resumed its usual pace at Quarters A.

Dr. Lin shook his head when he looked at my eyes. I knew they were bad. He knew they were bad. There was no trip to Clark soon, so I would live with it. When the doctor at Bethesda in Washington, D.C, read the typhoid fever suggestion, he was adamant I should not be subjected to that type of treatment. I had asked him, when he wrote it into my record, that he consider Dr. Lin's position and make his written comments such that the good doctor would not lose "face". He did just that. Dr.Lin glowed with the complimentary words, but showed sadness that he couldn't try his answer to my problem. He was genuinely worried at the speed the irises were sealing down to the lenses and so was I. We were coming into a very busy time and I needed my eyes, whatever shape they were in.

The Christmas gifts were wrapped and shipped back to the States and the rest were for our Chinese and American friends in Taipei. The house was decorated except for the two trees that hadn't arrived and our first party of the season was in the planning stage. Julie had been well trained for she knew what looked good and what didn't and I could leave more details to her than I could have with Hogo. Furthermore, she didn't test me. Boom Boom was in heaven with his old friend and Suzie, too.

The American wives operated a little boutique in the TDC compound and on Saturdays, I took my turn as a salesgirl. The boutique's profits went to various Chinese charities. Our inventory came from Taiwan and there were many examples of Taiwanese woodcarving, cloisonné, jewelry and porcelains. Sometimes, the women traveled to Hong Kong or Bangkok, taking some of the profits with them and returning with treasures from that part of the world. I enjoyed my Saturdays with the other wives and a careful perusal of the stock on the shelves and tables was a lesson in the unending cultural surprises of Taiwan.

It was the second Saturday in December and we were busy. There was hardly time to hunt for unusual decorations to take home. We knew the next Saturday would be the big one and we all worked to get the boxes unpacked and the merchandise on the shelves. Jimmy Chen, the tiny Taiwanese man who helped us, scurried around lifting cartons and crates that were bigger than he was. We worried Jimmy would sprout a hernia or something worse, but he giggled and chattered in Taiwanese and was indispensable. I gathered up my purchases at closing time and joined Sergeant Hsiu who waited by the car.

The next week was a killer with parties, gifts to be ready for delivery, menus and grocery lists to check. The Quarters needed to sparkle and Mama San was already busy with her washing and ironing of the linens. Julie had quickly learned where everything was and Hogo, in his anger and frustration had polished everything in and out of sight. We were ahead on that front.

I had no way of knowing how devastating the following Saturday would be. There was no premonition or warning.

The day of Thursday's big Chamber of Commerce dinner-dance arrived. Mama San and Julie made the decision of what I would wear, then disappeared downstairs for its final press. We were to share a table with the American Ambassador and his wife Ann, a pleasure I looked forward to. At seven, we rode down the mountain, resplendent in formal attire. Jim was in his Navy full dress (without the sword) and looked quite handsome. A professor friend of ours had once said that Jim looked like he was straight out of "central casting" and tonight he did.

CHAPTER NINETEEN
THE MESSAGE

December 15, 1978

The evening began well, but ended one step short of catastrophe. I had looked forward to seeing our Chinese and American friends at the annual Chamber of Commerce Christmas party. It was a good time to pass along holiday wishes and to enjoy what seems to happen to men when they put on tuxedos and to women when they wear long gowns. Couth sets in, not that these people were any other way, but on nights like this, they were more than usual. We greeted each other with genuine affection and because of our busy schedules, we were seeing some people for the first time in many weeks. There was a lot to catch up on; children's plans for college in the U.S., travel in this part of the world and holiday news.

First came the speeches, with reference to what had been accomplished during the past year, and dinner was served – or the other way around. We attended so many of these parties, I sometimes lost track of the sequence.

The men were busy, talking over whatever men talk over. Jim's face was serious. Sometimes I wondered if the man knew how to have fun. I could only remember him as serious. When we were dating in high school, my father called him The Thinker and I enjoyed teasing him about it.

The music began and couples moved onto the floor. I waved to a friend as the Ambassador asked me to dance and we found a spot that was not too crowded. As we chatted about totally inconsequential things, I noticed a man in a Marine uniform standing in the open archway, looking for someone. His eyes settled on my partner and he threaded his way across the floor, coming up behind Len. He tapped on the Ambassador's shoulder, waited a moment for his attention, then leaned forward and whispered into his ear.

Len immediately turned, looked for Jim, signaled him to come to us, spoke to him briefly, then followed the Marine out the door. We returned to the table with Ann and Jim said, "Ann, something's up. Len wants me to follow him, but I'll see that you ladies are taken home safely." His serious look had deepened.

Some of the guests attending the party were Chinese and although it didn't occur to me until later, they must have sensed what was happening. We were whisked out the door, bid each other a hurried goodnight and climbed into our respective official cars. Ann went down Chung San North to the Embassy and I went up Yangmingshan to the Quarters.

Twenty-four hours later, Jim came home. He had changed from his dress clothes into the work uniform he kept in his TDC office and after no sleep in those twenty-four hours, he looked drained – and older.

The U.S. President, Jimmy Carter, had refused to renew the Taiwan Treaty and the United States Government no longer had diplomatic relations with the Republic of China, Taiwan.

My first thought was of the people on this island. They were defenseless – and so were we, not only from an invasion but also from the people themselves. There was bound to be resentment and rage that this loyal ally of the United States was so unceremoniously booted out. For thirty years, they trained and kept their army ready to assist us in any theatre of war. And we, as part of the agreement, provided the shield that protected them and allowed them a normal way of life. Now it was gone and I knew they felt adrift and angry.

We shifted into the one- day -at -a -time mode and I realized that tomorrow, Saturday, was my day at the boutique in the Compound. Should I go? Jim said yes, keep things as normal for as long as possible. The announcement had not come yet and until it did, our routine would be status quo.

Saturday morning, Jim left for the office and Sergeant Hsiu drove me to the boutique. I hated this secret I harbored. I felt phony, chatting pleasantly with him as we journeyed down the mountain. He knew something was up because of the busier than usual traffic in official cars. But he said nothing and I said nothing. I felt like Benedict Arnold.

The girls at the boutique were busy setting out the jewelry in the glass cases and Jimmy scurried and chattered as always. The radio was on and in the middle of Bing Crosby's *White Christmas*, the station abruptly went off the air. A man's voice came on and announced first in Chinese, then in English that the Mutual Defense Treaty with the United States had been broken and all diplomatic relations had ceased.

The silence was palpable and every head turned to look at me.

"I'm afraid it's true. We were told, but I couldn't say anything until it was announced." Swallowing, I gathered myself together and finished with, "Jim and the Ambassador found out Thursday night, but until it became public, we were cautioned not to speak of it."

"What happens now?" It was Betty, who had found Suzie Wong in the ditch.

"Betty, I don't know, but if any of you feel uneasy and want to go home, we will simply close up." I tried to think ahead, but never having been in this kind of situation, my mind was blank.

"Are we in any danger?" This, from one of the younger wives who was new to the island.

"I can't even answer that. But as soon as TDC can, they will keep you informed, I promise you. In any event, call me. Just remember our phones are tapped and I may not be able to answer your questions, but I can pass them along to my husband."

I saw tears in their eyes and I knew I wasn't far away from them, myself. Jimmy stood rooted to the floor, confused and frightened. I walked over to him and asked,

"Jimmy, do you understand what has happened?"

"Linder Tai Tai, no."

I told him we must close up the shop – maybe not open again for a while. There was fear in his face and I knew part of that was because he saw the end of his job. I was to see many faces like this in the months to come. Taiwanese and Chinese alike held jobs with the U.S. military; the Commissary, Exchange, hospital, and the Compound. For twenty-five years, the U.S. had provided these people with a good living and overnight it was gone.

We did what was necessary and each of us left for our homes. There were children to think of and those with Chinese neighbors were concerned about their reaction. I walked slowly to the car but before I bent to get in, I asked Sergeant Hsiu to listen to me for a moment. His face was totally without expression as I told him what had happened. My tears were getting closer to the surface and he saw them. He bowed to me, opened the door, made sure I was safely in and we slowly moved out into traffic. It was a silent ride and when we stopped at the intersections along the way, I found I could no longer meet the eyes of the people waiting to cross.

For the first time in my life, I was ashamed of my country.

What they had done was wrong and regardless of their motives, these twenty-two million people mattered, they had lives and families that mattered and my country had tossed them aside.

At the Quarters, Sergeant Hsiu helped me out, then holding out his hand, shook mine. He knew we were not responsible and it was his way of telling me.

"Seay, seay, (thank you) Sergeant Hsiu. You are my best friend." I hurried into the house.

An hour later, I had gathered myself together enough to face the staff, but only Mama San was in the kitchen area. She sat in her little room next to the washer and dryer, television on and the eternal crocheting lying beside her on the little table with her tea. She had heard it on the television. I walked to her side, knelt down and she pulled my head into her lap.

"Oh Mama San, I am so sorry. I am so sorry."

We stayed like that for a while as she patted my shoulder Then she said, "Meyogwanchi" – never mind.

We went into quarantine. The families were told to stay inside their homes. The children were pulled out of school. Everything stopped. The parties on the calendar were canceled, Chinese and American alike. The men of TDC stayed longer hours, then took home food from the Commissary in the Compound. It was as if we didn't exist. One day Americans were on the streets and the next, they were gone. I saw only the Quarters Staff except for Sergeant Hsiu. He was on call to drive an official car when needed.

Each day, Jim came home just long enough to shower, change clothes, eat hurriedly and try to get a few hours of sleep. We couldn't talk, nor could he call because of the phone taps.

It was a solitary, lonely and fearful time.

I sat on the couch on the porch with The Girls on either side of me. Suzie knew something was different. She was watchful and stayed close against my leg. The mountains that so often gentled me down, only looked foreboding. Three guards passed below me on their way to their posts. They were new guards and as I watched them, they turned and looked up at me. Their faces were inscrutable and still, as always, but their eyes narrowed and glittered with hatred.

They walked to their posts and I realized their guns were trained on the house, not on the surrounding areas. Fear prickled at me. I was here alone with armed guards who were no longer friendly. Suzie growled low in her throat, then lowered her head onto her paws and watched them steadily.

When the telephone shrilled, I jumped to answer it.

"Mrs. Linder, we've taken our kids out of school and they're here with us, now. How long will this go on? Our son is a senior in high school and we've already sent in the money for his college tuition. He may lose his whole senior year of credits. We don't know what to do."

Dear God, I hadn't thought of that one. Because of this quarantine, the seniors would have to repeat their last year before going onto college. I sensed a note of panic. The woman had not given her name. I didn't ask for it.

"I'm so glad you called and told me about this. When Admiral Linder comes in tonight, I'll give him your message and as soon as they can work out a solution, you will all know what it is." She thanked me and hung up.

The calls continued to come in with questions I couldn't answer, at least with any authority. I logged them all in the days that followed and gave them to Jim whenever I saw him.

Someone in the government decided it was time to teach the bad guys a lesson and gave the college students time off from their classes to demonstrate against the Americans. We were about to have our first riot. Jim was at the Embassy for a Saturday morning meeting with the country team. For their own safety, I told the staff to go home and after answering the phone several times only to find no one on the other end of the line, I bolted the doors, checking the kitchen area for any lingering guards.

Climbing the kitchen stairs, I heard music that was loud and very familiar. I peeked through the sheer curtains on the library windows. A sound truck was parked on the other side of the stone wall and turned to its full volume. Aulde Lang Syne penetrated every corner of the house. This went on for twenty-four hours without pause.

Jim was under siege at the Embassy. The mob surrounded the Compound and cut the telephone wires. The Marine guards at the entrance held guns that had no bullets. A recent order from the Defense Department denied them loaded weapons and the Embassy was wide open to attack. What I did not know at the time was they could threaten, but they could not kill.

The guards at the gate had allowed the student rioters onto the grounds. They shouted and pounded on the front doors. I took The Girls to the sitting room, turned on the television to drown out the noise and held on. I knew that if I was going through this kind of harassment, the same thing was happening to Jim. He had told me of the Embassy meeting and I almost wished I didn't know.

At last the pounding on the doors stopped and the phone was quiet. I picked it up, called Skip who was, by this time, home with his family just a mile away and told him I couldn't hold out any longer. I was desperate for word of Jim.

"Hang on, Pat. I'm coming to get you."

The riots were no secret and the men of TDC returned to their homes to protect their families. Skip and Shannon lived only a block or two from the Cultural College and the rioting students knew where the Americans lived.

Jim's Master Chief, Mike Tatosian appeared, having come in through the kitchen and after hearing that Skip was on his way to take me to his house, Mike picked up a fireplace shovel and poker, intending to protect the inside of the house should any of the rioters break in.

"Mike, I'll never forget this."

He grinned. "Just part of the job. Now get going."

Holding Suzie and Boom Boom under my arms, I jumped into the car and we roared off. A few moments later, we were at Skip's house. On the street outside, the students shook their fists at us and I had a close look at real hatred. These same students had often waved and smiled when they saw the Seville, but today, they were intent on delivering a different kind of message and they succeeded.

Shannon was the calm in the storm. Their children, Chrissie and J.J. were enchanted with The Girls and I was glad I could provide some distraction for them.

"I have a walkie-talkie, Pat. Do you want to try to reach the Admiral?"

We worked at it for a while, static cutting out the connection. Suddenly, I heard Jim's voice.

"This is the Admiral. Is anyone where they can hear me? Over."

We told him of the riot at Quarters A and Mike Tatosian's determination to remain and protect the house. He told us he would make an attempt to escape the Embassy as soon as he could.

The warrior was in his element.

The children played with the dogs while Skip kept close to the walkie-talkie.

Mike called, saying it was safe to return to the Quarters, but I chose to remain with Skip and Shannon in case Jim called again. Two hours later, Jim's voice came through.

"I'm out and headed home. Over."

A shudder of relief went through me. "So am I. Mike called and it's safe at the Quarters now. See you there. Over." But I knew I wouldn't see him until the next day. Heavy message traffic to deal with was on his desk and home meant his office.

On Monday, classes resumed at the Universities and the students dutifully went back to school. It was as though someone had punched a button that said "Riot". They did, then the button was pushed again and it was over. The staff returned and life resumed its strange pace at Quarters A.

CHAPTER TWENTY
TEARS

Christmas was beside the point. The gifts for the Chinese were piled neatly on the guestroom bed, the decorations that were in place looked forlorn, as though out of season. No trees had arrived, so the French doors to the porch stood unadorned. There was an air of suspension, as though we were balanced for the next step, but just hadn't taken it yet.

No one knew what to expect. The House Staff went quietly about their chores with 'Naldo cooking more meals than he had since his arrival at the Quarters. Jim came home, but it was always late and his preoccupation was a tangible thing. He seemed oblivious to his surroundings. I could hardly imagine the monumental changes that he must address every day and my contribution was to be there to listen and see that Quarters A was a quiet and peaceful place in his otherwise cataclysmic day.

The guards no longer saluted him. For many years, his positions of command had come with this automatic courtesy and although he did not speak of it, I knew it was a new and different experience and one that only underlined his position on this uneasy island.

The calls still continued. Anxious wives with impossibly difficult questions kept my days busy. Some had already begun packing, yet were reluctant to take down their holiday decorations. We all tried to keep our lives as normal as possible. Their children had been told of the situation and what was ahead, but military children are incredibly flexible and learn early to take what comes without comment.

There had been no communication with any of my Chinese friends. Jim came home with his normally straight shoulders bowed. I hated to see him like this. He had never known defeat in his career and there were no ground rules to go by.

He wearily shed his uniform coat. "The State Department is sending out a team on the first of January."

"For what?" I took the coat and hung it in the closet.

He shrugged. "To formalize the ending of the treaty and talk about cultural and trade relations, I suppose."

"That should provide a lot of comfort to the Chinese."

Cynicism was beginning to creep into every conversation and we were no longer concerned about the bugs in the fan. " I wish I knew what to do about the gifts on the guestroom bed. Any suggestions?"

"Nope. Just wait, I guess." It was too small an item to worry about.

When we spoke of Christmas, I asked what he thought about having the single people on his Staff, Skip and his family here in the Quarters for Christmas dinner.

"Good idea. Skip mentioned today at the office that he won a turkey in a raffle. Find out from 'Naldo what's left in the kitchen. There's not much in the Commissary. Everyone panicked and stocked up. Maybe Mike can scrounge some things."

I smiled. Mike could find pheasant under glass if that's what we wanted.

"We'll make do. It might even provide a bright spot in this otherwise miserable time."

It was good to have a project. I made some calls, found out the turkey was available and dinner was planned. Christmas was only a few days away.

Early one morning, the phone rang. "Pat, it's Queenie Yao."

I couldn't believe it. This woman in such a high government position was on the other end of the line. Not only that, she was calling from her office.

"Queenie, you're the only one to call me. I don't know what to say." I could feel my throat beginning to tighten as I spoke.

Quietly, she said, "Pat, we love you."

That did it. I broke down. When I could speak again, I said, "I am so ashamed of what's happened and I can only pray you know how we feel."

"We know. Goodbye for now, Pat."

It was good to just let go.

That afternoon, the bell rang and when Julie answered the door, there were two huge trees, ready to be placed by the French doors to the porch. It was the only signal I needed. I called Skip and asked for Sergeant Hsiu and an official car to be sent up to the Quarters. When he arrived, I took him into the guestroom and said, "Help me load these gifts into the car, Sergeant. You and I are going visiting."

His smile was broad and once again, we shook hands.

As the Sergeant knocked on the doors and I presented the gifts, the faces of my Chinese friends reflected their affection for us and words were simply not necessary. The next morning began with a procession of flowers and gifts, each one bringing warm words of friendship. The house became

269

festive, lightness took the place of gloom as the Christmas spirit found its way back into Quarters A.

Christmas dinner was a tough old Tom turkey that barely served the people around the table, but 'Naldo found himself the star of the day with the dishes of whatever was left in the kitchen and there was laughter.

Time moved swiftly and the parties resumed on a limited basis. Throughout our time in Taipei, we were close friends with the man who was the Chief of the General Staff of the Republic of China. In short, he was the head of all the ROC military. Admiral Chris Soong and his wife Helen, never failed to make us feel like special friends. We knew them as talented people, almost courtly in their attitude towards us. We cherished all of our Chinese friends and each one gave us a special reason to like them. But during these uncertain times, Admiral Soong must have felt the tremendous burden that now rested solely on his shoulders – the protection of Taiwan without the help of the United States.

I had not seen Chris or Helen since the announcement of the U.S. normalization with communist China. It was just as well. There were no right words to say in a situation like this and I felt almost tongue-tied when I spoke with any Chinese.

One of the TDC officers, who lived in Tien Mou, had planned a party before everything was cancelled. During the week between Christmas and our New Year, he and his wife decided to go ahead with their plans. The invitation read six to eight. As usual, Jim was late and we hurried down the mountain, an hour past the suggested time.

I assumed the usual people would be there, but it did not occur to me the Chinese would attend. Our hostess opened the door, listened to our apologies for our lateness that was obviously understood, then ushered us into the living room area. Directly across the room was Admiral Chris Soong with Helen beside him. Our eyes made contact and Chris and I walked across the room to stand in the middle, facing each other.

He bowed his head and so did I. Together, we wept.

There wasn't a sound that I can remember; just the sight of this deeply affected man who loved and cared about his people and couldn't imagine what would happen to them now.

The incident triggered a release. People found they were sharing stories, fears and problems. Jim and Helen came to where we stood. It was not a time for words. Our nearness to each other said it all. They knew how hard it was on us to be representative of what they considered our country's betrayal of them.

In two days' time, it would be January first 1979. Jim spoke of meeting the delegation from Washington, D.C., at the airport. The Chinese Ministry of Foreign Affairs would supply the new black limousines to take them to the Grand Hotel for the conferences that would formally abrogate the Treaty and present the framework for trade and cultural relations between Taiwan and the United States. Warren Christopher from the State Department, Richard Holbrooke, Assistant Secretary of State for East Asian and Pacific Affairs and Admiral Maurice (Mickey) Weisner as the Commander-in-Chief-Pacific were flying in. They would be accompanied by their staffs and high ranking Chinese military and government officials. Lots of heavyweights.

I knew security was tight, but many times in the past two weeks, I wondered about the attitude of the people on Taiwan. The radio and television had continually fed the flames of unrest and in the back of my mind was the possibility of more serious unanticipated trouble. People had figured it out by now. What direction they would take, only they knew.

I was uncertain about the Quarters staff. I gathered them together, explained about the arrival of the Americans, told them I had no way of knowing if the students at the Cultural College would riot again and told them they could go if they wished.

They chose to stay.

I found it comforting, having them in the house, but I worried about their safety. The guards no longer hid behind trees or bushes. Armed, they stood in plain sight in their assigned places and the suggestion was one of house arrest. Jim left early the morning of the first. The once-a-week team meetings at the Embassy had become daily and there was a lot to do before the plane arrived late that afternoon.

The hours stretched endlessly. Boom Boom snoozed, but Suzie never left my side. I made lists of our household goods, carefully marking the things we had acquired while in Taiwan. They would be photographed and inventoried for insurance purposes. The phone was quiet. By now, the families knew what they must do and were making the same preparations I was.

When late afternoon came, Mama San and Papa San left for their homes as I watched them go safely through the gates. Julie and 'Naldo were in the kitchen area and at the assigned time, I switched on the television in the sitting room to watch the arrival of the plane. The limousines were in place, and as I feared, a large crowd of Chinese and Taiwanese had gathered outside the building. They were not friendly.

As the camera moved in closer, I could see what I thought were sticks in their hands. I realized those "sticks" were steel pipes, crowbars and long wooden poles. It was obvious they intended to use them either on the cars or on the occupants inside. Eggs, mud and tomatoes splattered against the shiny new limousines.

"This is going to be tough, Suzie. This is going to be very tough."

The steel pipes smashed through the windows of the black limousines snaking along the narrow road leading from the airport. As I had feared hundreds of angry Chinese and Taiwanese lined the way and surrounded the cars, bent on harassing the dignitaries inside. One of those cars carried my husband. Helpless, with the acid taste of fear on my tongue, I watched the riot unfold on television. Because of my eyesight, I sat on the floor, close to the set in the sitting room of our Quarters. If the worst happened, I would know it and have time to ready myself for the next crisis. The Girls, sensing my fear, huddled beside me. Gathering them close, I held on through the growing violence.

I knew Jim's life was in jeopardy. The crowd turned vicious as they pounded on the cars. The infuriated mob of Nationalist Chinese, Taiwanese people and students acted in odd concert, making their common statement. Hatred and anger twisted their faces and the occupants inside the limousines were completely vulnerable to their violence.

Jim was in the sixth car, now barely moving because of the screaming people surrounding them. I watched as the mob swiftly beat the cars to pieces. A long wooden pole shot through Jim's window and penetrated the glass on the driver's side. A young man swung a steel pipe into the rear window of Jim's limousine, smashing it into a mass of shattered glass.

The television camera focused on the battered sixth car and I knew its occupants; Jim as the official representative of the U.S. Government, the driver, the Commander-in-Chief, Pacific, Admiral Maurice Weisner and his aide. As I watched in desperation, a man separated himself from the crowd and plunged his hand into a brown sack he carried.

Remembering our bodyguard with his gun in a brown sack, I screamed, "Jim, get down. He has a gun." But when the man pulled his hand from the sack, his fist held peanuts and he threw them at the cars as a gesture of contempt for President Carter, the peanut farmer from Georgia. The camera moved and caught a woman on her hands and knees, crawling between the man's widespread legs to retrieve the symbols of scorn. It was food, and not to be wasted.

I felt remote, cut off and totally helpless. To watch my husband's life threatened, to touch the screen as though I could touch him, gave a surreal quality to the riot.

Barely moving, the cars reached the end of the airport road and turned onto the wide boulevard that led into the heart of Taipei. The crowd thinned. The limousines, because of the extensive damage they had sustained, crept at an uneven pace while an excited Chinese reporter talked into a microphone about the riot.

Long hours passed before there was any word of Jim. Waiting for his arrival, not knowing if he was alive or injured was our way of life and I summoned the control I had learned by living it. What he did not need was a hysterical wife, demanding a description of this nightmare day.

The official flight from Washington had arrived at dusk and not until four o'clock the next morning would his driver deliver him to the door of our Quarters.

He was uninjured but exhausted and his face looked drawn. "I'm due back at the Grand Hotel for conferences with the State Department team at nine. It's been one hell of a day."

"I know. I watched it on television. There was a moment when I thought you might be shot and I tried to warn you." I told him the story of the handful of peanuts.

Worn out with the surge of too much adrenaline, we both fell into bed. The next morning found us still tired and on edge. Jim left early and I spent the day alone in the Quarters, writing our children to assure them their father was safe. It was an endless day. That night, when Jim returned, he told me the story of the riot and what he saw from the front seat of the sixth car.

"I'm told an official signal was given for the mob to begin its destruction after we were in the cars, moving down the airport road. It was pretty hairy." He described how the people pressed their faces against the windows and spat at those inside. They threw eggs and tomatoes as they screamed and pounded with their fists on the outside of the cars.

Jim said, "Our driver was scared to death, but he kept us moving. It was slow going." Suzie and Boom Boom were at Jim's feet and absently, he rubbed Suzie's ears.

"Was anyone inside injured?"

"No, I turned around to tell Admiral Weisner to get down on the floor of the back seat and put his briefcase over his head just as a wooden pole came through my window. If I hadn't turned around and leaned over, I would have had it in the side of the head. As it was, it only missed our driver by an inch or two."

"I saw the back window go. Was anyone hurt from the glass?"

Jim shook his head. "It wasn't the glass we were afraid of, it was the steel pipe. The guy that had that in his hands was intent on something besides harassment."

As he talked, I learned the sixth car simply died from its beating in front of a small hotel in downtown Taipei. They ran into the building, out a side door and found taxis that took them to Jim's office, at the TDC Headquarters. Miraculously, there were only superficial injuries to the occupants of the other cars.

The Marines on the island of Okinawa were put on alert to be flown to Taiwan in case of further trouble. They were the nearest ready American defense forces available, but there was no guarantee the Chinese government would even let their planes land if they came.

After Jim left for the meeting at the Grand Hotel the following morning, I sat in the wing chair in the sitting room with Suzie Wong on my lap and Boom Boom at my feet. I remembered when we had come to Taiwan just a short year and a half before. I had no way of knowing then, it marked the beginning of a long, dark time.

CHAPTER TWENTY ONE
ENDINGS

It was a surrealistic bad dream. Seeing it on television in one dimension, watching my husband's life being threatened, looking at the destruction of the automobiles and the fierce determination of the rioters to destroy the people inside left me numb and punchy. Had I acknowledged my feelings, I would have lost control. That was not on the agenda.

The meetings were held at the Grand Hotel and the American and Chinese dignitaries arrived in taxis, leaving behind the destroyed limousines. The demonstrations by the Chinese and Taiwanese people continued but I put it out of my mind. I was helpless to do anything and to dwell on the unknown was pointless. The mechanics of moving took over. The past had taught me to keep busy, to use my mind in ways that would keep fear and frustration at bay.

When Jim returned to the Quarters at night for an exhausted sleep, we did not speak of the meetings. The listening monitors became more intimidating than ever before and many times during the days that followed, I shook my fist at the ceiling fans. I wanted to know. I needed to know. He did mention that one of the U.S. national television networks had sent a team to Taipei to cover the meetings. They were also there for the riots and I realized our family would see the pictures and would worry about our safety. I put in a call to my brother in Iowa.

"Hall, we're all right, so far."

His voice was as rich and deep as I remembered. "Well, Patti. It sounds like my little sister is homesick." They knew nothing about what was happening to us and I chose not to tell them. The report was suppressed and never made it to the American public. Much later, I learned that the Christopher entourage was angry because of the riots. They had not expected the reaction they received, to what was later labeled, "Carter's December Bombshell.".

Because the Chinese people had figured it out, the military dependents were more at risk than ever before. We obeyed orders and stayed inside our houses and out of sight. I grew accustomed to the obtrusive guards and with the students back in their classes, gave little thought to harassment at the Quarters. There just wasn't time. The order was given that all Taiwan Defense Command personnel and their families must leave the island by April first. We would be the last to go. But that honor eventually went to Skip and Shannon who waited until we were safely on the plane before they boarded the next one.

Besides the Defense Command were the Military Assistance Group (MAG), Kurt Sorenson's Naval Research Unit, the Embassy and countless installations scattered around the island with families attached. Everything had to be dismantled and all personnel had to leave. Accomplishing this in three months was a monumental job. There were only two moving companies available in Taipei at that time and turns were taken. China Airlines supplied the means to get off the island in what was essentially an evacuation.

We worked steadily. I knew nothing about the Chinese method of packing and could only hope the typewriter would not end up on top of the lampshades. I made endless lists of everything we owned. That was the sum of my day; move things and make lists.

The talks finally concluded and the beginning of the end began for Jim. Everything that belonged to the U.S. military was to be disposed of. The Marines on Guam and Okinawa wanted as much as he would give them; office supplies, chairs, desks, military equipment. It was a form of cannibalism and it shook him to know his own contemporaries were vying for the remnants of his command. Installations throughout the island would cease to exist. He had three months to remove and eradicate what had been a working military force for twenty-five years.

We sat in the little car on the country road and he told me what he could.

"The word is that Carter waited for the members of Congress to leave Washington for the Christmas holidays, then used that time to break the Treaty. That's why it's called the 'Carter bombshell'."

I knew how the people of Taiwan felt. It was betrayal.

He went on. "Obviously, Congress was shocked and Senator Goldwater said it was one of the most cowardly acts of any President in history. Pretty strong stuff going on back there." He was tired and his fighting instincts were dulled.

But what could we do? Follow orders and support the Commander-in-Chief, no matter how bitter the taste. The phrase, just another military benefit, crept into my thoughts and I realized how cynical I had become in the past few weeks.

"By the way, Mickey Weisner asked about you during the riot. He wondered if you get out much?"

It was a funny moment and we needed all we could get. "I hope you told him I've been held prisoner in the Quarters for so long, I'm mildewed."

I told Jim about the call to my brother.

"I'm not surprised. If what they say is true, I can understand the need to keep the news of it under wraps as long as possible. I saw the U.S. news team at the airport and the Grand Hotel. It must be frustrating for them to have a good, hot story and have it killed."

"What's on for tomorrow?"

"Well, let's see. Tomorrow, I give the order to close down the Commissary and Exchange in the Compound. And I begin pulling down American flags."

"Oh, Jim. Do you have to personally do that?" I couldn't imagine the effect it would have on him.

"There isn't time for me to cover the whole island's installations, but yes, I will have to do as many as I can." He sagged as he said it.

After a moment's silence, he continued, "I have to call the TDC personnel and their dependents together and give them instructions about leaving. I'll need your help."

"Tell me what to do. I'm in the dark about most of this, but maybe a woman's touch will soften the blows that just seem to keep coming." It was the way we had always worked and he knew I would help before he asked.

"I need you to tell them they must destroy their pets, or give them away. They cannot take them back to the U.S. It's an evacuation and there won't be room."

I was horrified and once again, close to tears. "Oh Jim, anything else. Don't ask me to do that."

"I'm sorry, but there's so much else to cover. I hope you'll do it."

Suzie and Boom Boom. I could feel cracks beginning in the vicinity of my heart.

"Can't they ship them back at their own expense?"

"Several have already tried and their pets never made it. The animal accommodations on a foreign aircraft are anything but healthy and it's probably better for them not to make the trip at all."

"Jim, the alternative is death. How can that be better?"

"Push for them to give their pets to friends."

For twenty- three years, I have kept the memory of that afternoon in the auditorium out of my thoughts. The big room was filled with military men and their families. Jim delivered blow upon blow and I remember the quiet. Some of these people had just arrived in Taiwan with orders reading, "report on or about 1 December 1978:" New orders would be cut in Washington and places had to be found to take them. It would negatively impact on their career patterns. Jim's orders were to accompany what was left of his command to Commander-in-Chief, Pacific, Honolulu.

The children in their last year of high school lost the entire semester and their parents were scrambling to get them accepted in summer schools in the United States to make up the credits necessary to enter colleges to which they had already sent their tuition payments. For many of these people, college was a big financial responsibility and this would only add to it.

The questions the women asked Jim were heart-rending and he addressed every one in the best way he could. I followed with instructions about their pets. Many knew I had two little dogs and would have to abide by the same rules.

It was an afternoon of penance for every wrong thing I had ever done.

When we arrived back at the Quarters, little Jimmy Chen from the boutique was crouched by the gate. He had no job and did not know what to do. When he saw the official car, he stood and beat against the metal of the gate with tears on his face. We tried to talk to him but he was past comprehending anything we said. The unsmiling guards merely stared at us. Jimmy Chen went in the official car back down the mountain to TDC and I hoped someone found a solution for him. Jim had been working with the Republic of China government to place the people who lost their jobs because of the closures, but little Jimmy Chen would so easily slip through the cracks in the transition. I felt totally helpless.

The flag lowering began down island and worked its way up. I knew each one was a physical blow to Jim, but there was simply nothing to say. The Kaohsiung and TDC flags would be the last to come down.

Our social life picked up speed and raged on with a frenzy of farewell parties. There was a ludicrous quality to it. Parties are for fun and nobody was having much of that. We gave one for some of our closest Chinese friends. During the evening, I noticed the women grouped in a far corner of the living room with their hands held up, chest-high, palms outward and the five fingers spread. I was completely mystified and later, I drew one of them aside.

"Margaret, what does this mean?" I imitated the gesture.

"It means we have five years to live before the communists invade and kill us."

My heart thumped and I felt slightly sick. "That sounds pretty dramatic. Surely it won't happen."

"It will. We're all on a list and we'll be the first to go. You would have to be Chinese to understand what they intend to do."

"My God, Margaret, I can't stand this."

"We all know how you and Jim feel. But there's nothing anyone can do."

I would have marched on the White House at that moment, Commander-in-Chief be damned.

At the next Officers' wives' luncheon, another one of farewells, I sat next to an older woman in dark clothes. She was an American Christian missionary who, after twenty years of captivity in a Chinese prison, escaped and came to Taiwan. She told me they forced her to sit on a three-legged stool for years and was not allowed to cough or sneeze or speak. I asked her about Maargaret's cryptic words.

"Believe it. My name is on the same list, as is every Christian missionary and minister on the island. They will do just what your friend said they would. I came to know them very well during those twenty years."

I touched her hand that rested on the table next to mine. She was an American. I was an American. We looked at each other and knew the sadness and shame that came along with that.

My friend and neighbor, Renee Praetorius called to say she had found someone willing to take our Boom Boom. The First Secretary to the South African Embassy, his wife and their little girl, lived at the Grand Hotel and the management had agreed to let them have the dog until their house was ready for their move-in. I was still waiting to hear about Suzie's destiny. I would keep them with me until we moved out of the Quarters into the Hilton Hotel. My determination to be with them as long as possible kept us at Quarters A several weeks after the furniture was packed and shipped to Honolulu where it would go into storage. We lived with little furniture, the bare essentials and no amenities.

The plum tree had blossomed. After I finished breakfast, I decided I would sit on the one remaining couch on the porch and look at the view that would soon go away forever. I was still in my robe and gown, Jim had left for TDC long before I wakened and I was indulging myself. The Girls were beside me as I sat down, and the three of us looked at the unfolding plum blossoms, the jagged mountains just beyond and the softer ones that held the Kuan Yin's peaceful profile. The Cultural College floated on the tip of its mountain. I would miss this sight and knew it would stay with me for the rest of my life.

I became aware of movement down to the left where the little shed stood. I focused on a group of men in coolie hats, sawing away at the shed door padlock. That was our emergency generator and the only source of electricity if the Chinese cut off the power to the Quarters. Without thinking, I flew out the door, raced down the stairs to the back lawn, robe and gown flapping, dogs at my heels and like an avenging angel pushed the men aside and spread my body against the door.

"Bu hau, bu hau. No. No." Bu hau means 'bad' and they understood that. Giggles replaced the shock on their faces as they backed off. I shook my fist at them and said again,

"No. No."

They turned and ran up the driveway, Suzie hot on their heels. Boom Boom sat on my left foot and muttered.

What I did not know was that Jim had promised them the generator after we left. There was a problem with translation. That was one thing I would not miss.

The Chinese military and government officials gave a final farewell party for us. It was a big one with everyone we ever knew; good food, fewer toasts than usual and an opera, written especially for us.

Jim came up the mountain early and as we dressed, he quietly said, "Pat, I'm going to retire after this tour of duty. Rather than a desk job in Washington, I want to do something different." He was sitting in the wing chair, elbows on his knees, studying his hands as he spoke.

We were both dealing with disillusionment and the motivation to continue just wasn't there anymore.

After a long pause, he said, "It's been thirty-six challenging years and it's time to move on."

I understood his intentions. When I could find my voice again, I asked, "Are you sure?"

"Yes."

"I'm delighted, Jim. I couldn't be happier."

We went to the opera.

It was quite a night. After dinner, we took our seats, dead center on the first row and surrounded by Chinese dignitaries and their wives, watched an opera that had been written just for us. The theme was the betrayal by the United States of its loyal ally the Republic of China with a translator, thoughtfully provided so we would not miss a word. To use an old cliché, we were a captive audience. The colorful costumes swirled and stocky, masked men jumped around the stage. The music defied comparison with lots of thumping and banging of cymbals to indicate invasion. The message was very clear.

I sat next to Jim, hands folded in my lap, both feet squarely on the floor, eyes fixed on the stage and thought about retirement. Out there was a whole world ready to be explored. The children were waiting for us and we would see them often instead of in increments. We could do anything we wanted and nobody would tell us not to. I could pick a place and live there. My mind hauled out possibilities long forgotten. The banging and clanging continued on the stage, but the smile on my face must have caused some wonderment among the members of the audience.

CHAPTER TWENTY TWO
CLOSING THE CHAPTER

The American flags came down the poles all over the island. The Kaohsiung installation in southern Taiwan was large enough that Jim felt he should be there when the flag was lowered for the last time. It was a tough decision but it was the right one. TDC personnel dwindled as the orders that came in were executed. Once the momentum began, it took on a life of its own and the two moving companies worked day and night. Jim's staff was pared down, so I was not too surprised when Admiral Chris Soong called, looking for him.

"Pat, I can't find Jim. The people at TDC were not anxious to tell me where he is."

"He's at the Kaohsiung installation, Chris, taking down the American Flag."

There was a long silence.

"That leaves us almost totally without protection. It leaves us defenseless."

"I know, Chris – and so does Jim – but he has no alternative but to follow the orders he's been given." My heart hurt.

There had been one hard moment after another since December fifteenth and I knew it would not end until we left the island. I also knew there was a good chance it would continue long after our departure as we worried about the safety of these people who had come to mean so much to us.

Julie was gone. She found another position so Mama San and I shared the care of the Quarters. Papa San would probably work in the garden, killing snakes for the rest of his life. The house would be occupied soon after we left by the head of the AIT – American Institute in Taiwan. As a result of the meetings held the first of January at the Grand Hotel, the Republic of China was left with a cultural and trade agreement and a representative who would reside in Quarters A.

I realized during the riots that no structural damage was done to the house because the Chinese government owned it. I was pleased to know it would be cared for and lived in. It had been my ivory tower and refuge during my stay there and I was grateful for that.

An order came from the Navy that we were to carry the Navy silver remaining in the Quarters on our persons when we left the island. This meant serving bowls, platters, plates, and flatware, anything necessary to give a large dinner party. We made a trip down the mountain to buy, at our own expense, another full set of luggage and the twelve suitcases were packed and ready to go to TDC for storage until we left on April first. We would be carrying sixteen pieces of luggage with us as we made our way to Honolulu. Only four held our own personal things.

Skip and Jim conferred about our coming trip and when he asked me if I would like to use some of his accumulated leave time to visit either Japan or the Micronesia Islands, I had no hesitation in opting for the latter choice. Japan meant laid-on official functions and thank you, I was finished with that. Skip took care of the arrangements and two weeks of snorkeling our way across the Pacific became more appealing every day.

But any hope of a leisurely trip through the Micronesian Islands, healing in body and spirit, dimmed. The logistics alone, of overseeing the safe arrival and departure of the silver as we island-hopped in planes small enough to land on the short runways of coral atolls, promised heart-stopping moments with each takeoff and landing. But it had to be, a phrase I was thoroughly sick of.

Sergeant Hsiu 's eyes met mine in the rear view mirror. His were full of concern and sadness. Mine were full of tears. Although his face wore the implacable look characteristic of the Chinese, I knew he was aware of my feelings and sympathized, but could do nothing to change the situation. It was a done deal. When I called for the car and explained to the sergeant to meet me in the lobby of the Hilton, I mentioned my destination.

"Sergeant, I want one more chance to see them before we leave."

The short moment of silence, followed by his answer told me he understood what I could not say. "Yes, Missy. I will be there."

My destination was the Grand Hotel at the foot of Yangmingshan Mountain where I would see my two little dogs for the last time. Of the heartaches we all went through during these past four months, this was one of the worst.

Our good neighbors Bill and Renee Praetorius knew of the many problems we faced. One morning, near the end of this bleak time and before our move to the Hilton Hotel, Renee had called to make arrangements for the transfer of Boom Boom to the family who wanted her.

291

Reluctantly, I agreed to a meeting and the little girl with her mother came calling. They were a handsome couple. The child reminded me of Alice in Wonderland with long, softly curling hair and single strap shoes. Her mother was tall and slim with a warmly regal air and we sat by the pool to talk over the pending adoption. Boom Boom would live at the Grand Hotel, arrangements had already been made. A garden was provided for her and she would share the little girl's Nanny. Throughout this conversation, Boom Boom snored contentedly in the girl's small lap.

Suzie the survivor sat watching the whole scene. She knew.

With one last, long look at me, Suzie daintily padded over to the mother and laid her head on the lady's knee. The mother and her little girl came for one dog and left with two.

I was left with a broken heart.

With The Girls in their new home at the Grand Hotel, there was no reason to stay in the empty Quarters. I had remained with the inconveniences to have as much time with them as possible. We moved to the Hilton and waited to leave Taiwan.

Sergeant Hsiu drove carefully, guiding the silver Seville through the insanity of Taipei traffic. I would miss this kind man. We had established rapport and shared many important moments together. Throughout the two years, he became my best friend, ready and willing to put his life on the line if that's what it took to keep me safe. Although it was his job, he knew this lady was going through what none of her predecessors had. The dangers were greater and the stakes were higher. But because I was born in the Chinese Year of the Tiger, both of us felt I had an edge on staying alive.

Sergeant Hsiu knew today would be the hardest task for me and I saw only compassion on his quiet face.

He drove the Seville smoothly into a small space at the foot of a grassy hill. To the right, the Grand Hotel rose like the great palace in Bejing. It sat alone at the foot of the mountain that served as its backdrop for all of Taipei to see. Second guessing me, the good Sergeant had scouted this out before and we were in a secluded area toward the back of the hotel.

Turning, he smiled, then said, "Missy, look. There they are."

Suzie and Boom Boom were chasing each other around a small piece of Chinese sculpture in the garden. I climbed out of the car and stood, watching them.

Suzie paused in her mad dash. Boom Boom ran into her and fell down. The almond eyes fastened on the silver car and the figure standing beside it. Like a white blur, she streaked down the hill and as I knelt, flew into my arms. Boom Boom made it a few seconds later and the three of us held on.

When at last I raised my head and looked at the implacable, inscrutable Sergeant Hsiu, there were tears on his cheeks as I told my Girls goodbye.

My last luncheon was with my Chinese friends and held in the hostess' home. I was physically and emotionally drained by now, but I looked forward to seeing them one more time. The apologies had been said so I hoped this would be a friendly afternoon of farewells. The unpleasant moment came after we finished our lunch. Then, in Chinese, bad jokes were told about my country. Granted, I was pretty disillusioned at that point, but this was the first time I listened to my native land being ridiculed and could in no way defend it. One of the ladies realized I knew what they were saying and I could see anger in her eyes. As we looked at each other, I shook my head to stop the words that were forming on her lips. Others noticed and the jokes finally stopped. Just another memory pushed into the far reaches of my mind.

I listlessly checked off our stops on the itinerary Skip had prepared for the Micronesian trip; Guam, Truk, Ponapei, Kwajalein – all familiar names of islands we fought for during World War II. I hoped their uniqueness would push the memories away. Something would have to. I didn't seem capable of doing it myself.

The radio station was to be shut down and the Europeans and remaining Americans on the island, those representing American businesses, were angry. They would be without any tie to the outside world and Jim waited as long as he could before giving the order. I could imagine their feeling of loss and isolation.

It was over. Jim brought the TDC flag down and our plane was waiting. The Embassy had closed during the month of March, the Seville was on its way to Honolulu, and April first was tomorrow. At the airport, friends gathered to tell us a bittersweet goodbye. Sergeant Hsiu tapped on the VIP lounge door and when I walked to where he stood, we simply looked at each other, shook hands and knew we would never forget the times we had shared. As a member of the Army, his future was secure and finally, he would have some time with his family.

As we headed out to the plane, a newspaper photographer hunkered down in front of us, shuffling backwards, snapping pictures.

Under his breath, Jim said quietly, " Don't smile."

It took some effort. I was ready to begin the next chapter of our lives, leaving the entire trauma behind us. I paused long enough to take one backward look at the slumbering mountains and the yellow-brown haze that hung over Taipei, then boarded the plane, wondering if I would every see it again as the free, democratic country of Taiwan, the Republic of China.

EPILOGUE

Taiwan, Republic of China has remained one of the economic miracles of the world. With its four hundred billion-dollar economy, it is a temptingly ripe plum, ready for picking. For the first time in the history of China, Taiwan's elections are free and democratic. In March 2004, the ROC held its first presidential referendum.

Political parties with other goals; nationalism, democracy, social well being and independence are steadily replacing Chiang Kai-shek's autocratic Kuomintang government. The current President, Chen-sui-bian, wants to turn the Republic of China into a human rights state.

The Vice President of Taiwan is a woman.

The five-year wait for the dreaded communist annihilation is past and the people are reclaiming their country as they continue their climb into democracy and the twenty-first century. There are more than forty colleges and universities on this tiny island that has a ninety-four percent literacy rate. As their children become more knowledgeable of the world around them through communications and education, they shape the future of Taiwan. And because the military has continued the build-up so proudly begun in 1979, any invasive war could be a bloody one.

This is a dynamic, diverse and ever-changing country. Its twenty-two million people number more than Bosnia, Croatia and Slovenia combined, and its population count is greater than the population of two-thirds of United Nations member countries, yet they are consistently denied entry into the UN.

Bejing has isolated Taiwan internationally. The predominant issue is sovereignty. Taiwan wants its independence from communism and it has continued this quest for fifty-five years. China considers the ROC a renegade province that belongs to China and will block any attempt toward a free democracy.

Although the Carter Administration wrote off Taiwan in January 1979 by refusing to renew the Mutual Defense Treaty, four months later, an angry Congress led by Senator Barry Goldwater, repudiated Carter's actions and drew up the Taiwan Relations Act. This action made it clear that the use of force (including passive aggression such as embargoes and boycotts) against Taiwan, would be of *grave concern* to the United States.

In March 1996, China made its move of aggression against Taiwan by test firing guided missiles in the Taiwan Straits. This brought a swift response from the United States. Two US aircraft carrier battle groups were sent to the Straits, thus convincing Bejing that the use of force or the threat of force would prompt similar, if not more serious consequences. As long as the United States supports the Taiwan Relations Act, Taiwan has a friend in court.

On June 30 1998, the President of the United States, Bill Clinton, visited communist China (PRC) and gave a speech in Shanghai that has become known as his *three no's* speech:

"Taiwan cannot be treated as a state." (therefore denying it membership in international organizations such as the United Nations, World Health Organization and the Word Trade Organization.)

" U.S. policy will not condone or support an independent future for it."

"The US will no longer give credence to a policy of two Chinas, or one China, one Taiwan."

President Clinton further stated, "We don't support independence for Taiwan."

Jiang Jemin, the Central Military Commission Chairman in Communist China has been quoted as saying, "Taiwan is the core and most sensitive issue in China-US relations". One of those relations refers to trade between the two nations.

Our current president, George W. Bush, has declared our country would do whatever is necessary to defend Taiwan from forcible seizure by Bejing. This is indicative of the delicate balance between the two countries on the two issues of trade and protection of Taiwan.

But due to the imminent threat and constant pressure from Bejing, reunification with China has for some Taiwanese, become a viable alternative to its independence. This push-pull between freedom and reunification is the subject of the presidential referendum.

China has warned the Taiwan government that referendums on sovereignty issues could bring disaster to its people.

Charles Freeman, a former State Department official, was told by Xiong Guangkai, the deputy chief of staff for the People's Liberation Army, that China was prepared to sacrifice millions of people in a nuclear exchange to defend its interest in preventing Taiwan's independence. He went on to say, "You, (the U.S.) will not sacrifice Los Angeles to protect Taiwan."*

At this writing, communist China claims the largest standing army in the world. With their nuclear capabilities, they are now able to launch short, medium and long range nuclear ballistic missiles.

Four hundred ninety-six of those missiles are aimed at Taiwan, ninety miles away.

*James Mann, "The Island in the Gulf Between the U.S. and China" Washington Post National Weekly Edition, January 18, 1999.

ABOUT THE AUTHOR

The Lady and the Tiger is author Patricia Linder's newest book, based on the life of a military wife caught in the middle of an international intrigue in the Far East.

During her husband's career as a Naval Officer, she spent many years, traveling through Europe and the Orient. Her memoir, Row, Row, Row Your Boat, chronicles the sometimes hilarious, sometimes tragic life as a Navy wife.

The author's latest book describes the frightening aspects of being in the right place at the wrong time, but by using her pragmatic Iowa background and having been born in the Year of the Tiger, she never doubted her ability to survive any situation.

If you wish to contact the author, please use the residence address: 37865 South Spoon Drive, Tucson, AZ. 85739 or e-mail: rowrowone@aol. com. Tel: 520-825-8335